"Daniel Flores' new book on I
vocative. It interweaves the eml
Methodist movement with th
Bangs' status as a major player in the drive towards greater Methodist respectability while never collapsing his motives into the purely economic. Flores gives us a well-rounded and nuanced picture of this pivotal second-generation Methodist leader, rooted in Bangs' own theological and cultural contexts and relevant to current debates."

—**JENNIFER WOODRUFF TAIT,**
editor, *Christian History Magazine*

"Daniel Flores has masterfully shown the outsize influence Bangs had on Methodism's shift to greater respectability. As a pastor, presiding elder, editor, and perennial General Conference delegate, he strongly supported clerical education, orderly worship, additional church construction, and an evolving approach to abolition consistent with the national mood. Flores has woven together little-known primary sources, helpful contextualizations, and insightful analyses in crafting a well-written, engaging, and fascinating study!"

—**PHILIP HARDT,**
author of *The Soul of Methodism*

"*Respectable Methodism* is a well-researched and well-documented exposition of the efforts of Nathan Bangs that shaped an early nineteenth-century frontier phenomenon into a respected American Methodist organization. Flores demonstrates convincingly that the desire for respectability by American people and Bangs' contributions 'intertwined to form a double-helix relationship' producing a 'new genetic code for the social structure' of American Methodist Christianity."

—**NORMAN A. BECK,**
Texas Lutheran University

"Daniel Flores has skillfully used the career of Nathaniel Bangs to produce a meticulously researched, eminently readable account of the transition of the Methodist Episcopal Church from a simple frontier religion into a denomination of 'respectability' in worship, preaching, hymnody, church order, and architecture. While covering antebellum America, its lasting impact challenges the MEC today."

—DONALD J. BRUGGINK,
Van Raalte Institute, emeritus

"Daniel Flores' impressive archival project offers a fresh and expanded view of Nathan Bangs, one of the most emblematic representatives of Methodist identity and aspirations in the early-to-mid nineteenth century. Bangs shaped Methodism's urban profile, charted its theological maturation, and set the Methodist Episcopal Church on a course of upward mobility and respectability that took it to the apex of religious, social, and political influence. Flores' sober analysis also counts the cost of that pursuit."

—DANIEL RAMIREZ,
Claremont Graduate University

Respectable Methodism

Wesleyan and Methodist Explorations

EDITORS

Daniel Castelo
Robert W. Wall

DESCRIPTION

The *Wesleyan and Methodist Explorations* series will offer some of the best Methodist Wesleyan scholarship for the church and academy by drawing from active participants in the international guilds of Methodist scholarship (Oxford Institute of Methodist Studies, Wesleyan Theological Society, American Academy of Religion—Methodist Studies Section, and others).

There is an urgent need within Wesleyan Methodist scholarship for constructive theological work that will advance the field into interdisciplinary and creative directions. The potential for the series is vast as it will seek to establish possible future directions for the field.

Another key concern of this series will be to tap the emerging field of theological interpretation of Scripture located in and for particular ecclesial traditions. Theological interpretation offers insight to historical study, especially the reception of Scripture and its effects within the Methodist church, as well as exploring the epistemic gains to particular biblical texts and themes. Theological interpretation offers insight into the holy ends of these gains for the life of the church in worship, instruction, mission, and personal devotions for a people called Methodist.

The series will seek out great monographs, while also considering superior and adapted doctoral dissertations and well-conceived and tightly focused edited volumes.

Respectable Methodism

Nathan Bangs and Respectability in Nineteenth-Century American Methodism

Daniel F. Flores

Foreword by Russell E. Richey

CASCADE *Books* · Eugene, Oregon

RESPECTABLE METHODISM
Nathan Bangs and Respectability in Nineteenth-Century American Methodism

Cascade Books
An Imprint of Wipf and Stock Publishers
199 W. 8th Ave., Suite 3
Eugene, OR 97401

www.wipfandstock.com

PAPERBACK ISBN: 978-1-6667-1396-1
HARDCOVER ISBN: 978-1-6667-1397-8
EBOOK ISBN: 978-1-6667-1398-5

Cataloguing-in-Publication data:

Names: Flores, Daniel F. | Richey, Russel E., foreword.

Title: Respectable methodism : Nathan Bangs and respectability in nineteenth-century American methodism / Daniel F. Flores ; foreword by Russell E. Richey.

Description: Eugene, OR: Cascade Books, 2023 | Series: Wesleyan and Methodist Explorations | Includes bibliographical references and index.

Identifiers: ISBN 978-1-6667-1396-1 (paperback) | ISBN 978-1-6667-1397-8 (hardcover) | ISBN 978-1-6667-1398-5 (ebook)

Subjects: LCSH: Bangs, Nathan, 1778–1862. | Methodism—History—19th century. | Methodist Episcopal Church.

Classification: BX8495.B28 .F56 2023 (print) | BX8495.B28 .F56 (ebook)

MARCH 7, 2023 11:12 AM

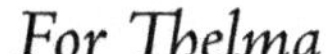

For Thelma

"Unlike most old men, he was, to the last, progressive in his views. He sympathized with all well-considered measures for the improvement of his Church. To him its history was all providential, and the very necessity of changes was the gracious summons of providence for it to arise and shine still brighter."

BISHOP EDMUND JANE[1]

1. Quoted in Stevens, *The Life and Times of Nathan Bangs*, 413.

CONTENTS

FOREWORD

Nathan Bangs—as Daniel Flores shows—led, supplied provisions for, and summoned American Methodism into systemic self-transformation. As creator, editor, model, and champion of the church's print revolution, Bangs served as the continent's John Wesley. Until his death in 1816, Francis Asbury had guided Wesley-like horseback itinerants with their Bibles and hymnbooks into conquering the landscape, bridging racial lines, finding frontier communities and gathering folk into the Methodist fold. Bangs urged increasingly settled Methodist communities to honor and sustain the field-preaching ministries that Wesley too had modeled and mandated *but also* to embrace his world of *Arminian Magazine*, books, tracts and Sunday school materials.

Bangs lived the transformation he then led. After frontier appointments in Upper Canada and Quebec, he served on the New York Conference's Albany District, in several appointments as presiding elder and as a preacher in New York. The New York Conference elected him secretary in 1811, sent him repeatedly to General Conference beginning with the first delegated General Conference, and would thereafter appoint him to almost every task that required study or statement.

From such conference leadership posts and comparably responsible ones on a national level, Bangs participated actively in building and promoting Methodism's socio-cultural-missional infrastructure. He was perhaps Methodism's most "visible" figure between the death of Bishop Francis Asbury and the Civil War Bishop, Matthew Simpson. Elected Book Agent in 1820, he assumed responsibility for the publishing enterprise of the church, undertook the editing of the newly established *Methodist Magazine*, exercised the leading role creating the weekly *Christian Advocate*, championed missions and education—indeed crafted their warranting, authorizing, and constituting documents—and assumed authority to interpret signal Methodist events and developments.

Like John Wesley and unlike other American Methodist leaders then and thereafter, his editor's posts gave Bangs a connection-wide and unequaled voice. Every week the entire church could read his words (and those writing for him) in the *Advocate* (the most widely circulated serial in the United States). Every month subscribing leaders had the magazine. As Flores shows:

> By his long and distinguished career, Bangs had the unique opportunity to exert his influence as a preacher, publisher, and educator to reshape American Methodism from the simple frontier religion of Asbury into a bureaucratic urbane denomination . . . [and to nurture] a widespread longing for respectability. . . . The two elements intertwined to form a relational double-helix which resulted in a new genetic code for the social structure of American Methodism. . . .
>
> Bangs [was] a symbol of "a movement's hunger for legitimation, intellectual respect, and cosmopolitan influence."

His effectiveness as official spokesperson earned Bangs teaching office responsibilities in successive general conferences, as head of Methodist missions, as president of Wesleyan University, as denominational apologist and historian, as presiding elder and as episcopal candidate.

As its "voice," Bangs fought prominent Presbyterian critics of Methodism with anti-Calvinist works, particularly *The Errors of Hopkinsianism Detected and Refuted* and *The Reformer Reformed* and defended hallmark Wesleyan doctrines of prevenient grace, human responsibility and freedom, holiness and moral agency. Among his books, what lives on? *The History of the Methodist Episcopal Church*, the four richly detailed volumes narrating the saga of the tribe he led.

Russell E. Richey
Dean Emeritus of Candler School of Theology and William R. Cannon Distinguished Professor of Church History Emeritus

ACKNOWLEDGMENTS

FIRST AND FOREMOST, I wish to thank my wife, Rev. Thelma Herrera Flores. She is my soulmate and my cherished partner in life. I am grateful for her selflessness, intellect, enthusiasm, humor, spirituality, and patience. We are blessed to share deep love for each other, God, the Wesleyan-Methodism, and the ecumenical church universal.

This study originated in my doctoral studies at Drew University under the guidance of Kenneth E. Rowe with readers Charles "Chuck" Yrigoyen Jr. and L. Dale Patterson. Professors Tom Oden and Charles Yrigoyen shared important insights on John Wesley while S T Kimbrough taught me to pay attention to the nuances of brother Charles. Philip F. Hardt, a frequent patron of the Methodist library, taught me all I needed to know about nineteenth century New York Methodism.

Three world-class scholars helped to shape my thinking about Nathan Bangs and the broader context of nineteenth century American Methodism. The late Donald Dayton urged me to develop my critique of Methodist respectability and the Wesleyan preferential option for the poor. The late Kenneth E. Rowe pushed me to explore how American Methodist hymnody, worship, and architecture supported my thesis. I met Russell Richey at the Oxford Institute for Methodist Theological Studies at Pembroke. He challenged me to think critically about Bangs' relationship with the denominational structure of the MEC, theological education, administrative leadership, and parish ministry. He suggested several critical revisions that greatly improved my argument and corrected my assumptions about this period. Many thanks to Dr. Richey for his encouragement to pursue publication.

Since 2015, I have made brief portions of my research on Bangs available to ministry students at Perkins School of Theology and the Methodist Theological School in Ohio. Feedback from these junior scholars and local pastors taught me to keep my studies relevant to the church. They also reminded me of the value of writing history with sensitivity to issues of diversity, equity, and inclusion. I am grateful to them all.

Many thanks to the librarians and archivists who granted access to their priceless collections of books and rare documents. Sources necessary for correcting bibliographic entries were generously supplied by librarians and archivists: Alex Gunter Parrish of Drew University, Pamela Greenlee and Sandy Harris of Olivet Nazarene University, Jennifer Miglus and Amanda Nelson of Wesleyan University, Ruth Sadlier of Master's College and Seminary, Amber Wessies of Union University, Elizabeth Walker-Papke of Spring Arbor University, Nathaniel "Nate" B. Aubin of Texas Lutheran University, and Frances Lyons of the General Commission on Archives and History of The United Methodist Church. The late Page Thomas, former director of the Center for Methodist Studies at the Bridwell Library at Perkins School of Theology, was particularly generous in providing access to rare Methodist hymnbooks and *Disciplines.* Wanda Smith at Perkins and Robert Drew Simpson at Drew provided several very helpful transcriptions of Nathan Bangs' otherwise undecipherable handwriting. Other curators granted me privileged access to prized resources at Dickinson College; Drew University; Duke University Divinity School; Garrett Evangelical Seminary; Gordon-Conwell Theological Seminary; Ohio Wesleyan University; Princeton Theological Seminary; Princeton University; Wesleyan University; and Yale University Divinity School. I also benefited from international resources at Canadian Methodist archives at Victoria University and the British Methodist archives at the John Rylands Library-Deansgate, University of Manchester, Oxford-Brookes University, and the former Wesley College, Bristol, England. Special thanks to Mr. Hoyt V. Bangs family for permission to publish the Bangs family portraits.

I am forever grateful to my family, colleagues, and students at Tarrant County College, Perkins School of Theology, Gordon-Conwell Theological Seminary, Indiana Wesleyan University, Western Theological Seminary, Methodist Theological School in Ohio, and Texas Lutheran University. Research and travel funds were received from the Hispanic Theological Initiative at Princeton Theological Seminary and the Edwards-Mercer Prize at Drew University. Funds for publication were provided by the generosity of Texas Lutheran University in Seguin, Texas.

It is humbling to have my book included in the Wesleyan and Methodist Explorations Series in Cascade Books. Thanks to Russell E. Richey for introducing my work to series editors Daniel Castelo and Robert W. Wall. I am thankful for their willingness to seriously consider its value and potential for future dialogue on American Methodism. I am grateful also to the members of the editorial board: Carla Works, Karen Winslow, Sangwoo Kim, Matt Sigler, Ashley Boggan Dreff, Hal Knight III, Priscilla Pope-Levison, Sharon Grant, Frederick L. Ware, and Dennis Dickerson. Many thanks to Wipf and Stock Publisher's skillful editorial team Charlie Collier, Emily Callihan, George Callihan, EJ Davila, Jonathan Hill, and Shannon Carter who helped me navigate the publication process from beginning to end. Their collective patience and professionalism were a much welcome gift. I sincerely apologize if I have missed thanking anyone. I am incredibly grateful for the privilege to publish this study on the development of the Wesleyan Methodist tradition in nineteenth-century America. In many ways, it has guided my personal philosophical and spiritual journey.

Soli Deo Gloria!

PREFACE

I WAS VERY FORTUNATE that my graduate years at Drew University afforded me the opportunity to serve as Graduate Assistant to Methodist Librarian Dr. Kenneth E. Rowe. My duties included answering genealogy research requests, locating rare books, and retrieving General Conference minutes from the Methodist Library and United Methodist Archives for visiting research scholars. Time after time I encountered references to the mysterious Rev. Dr. Nathan Bangs. It was then that I started my long quest to learn all I could about this nineteenth-century figure in American Methodist history. Bangs' presence seemed to be everywhere, except for my Methodist history textbooks. To be fair, some scholars located Bangs as an important theologian and organizer, but they stopped short of identifying him as a major change agent. Still, I could not comprehend how someone so prominent in the development of the MEC had been relegated to the occasional footnote.

Evidence led me to believe that Bangs was the key to understanding how the Wesleyan movement in America became the bureaucratic denomination of the nineteenth century. Deeper research confirmed this to be truer than expected. Moreover, it also answered a nagging question about his apparent obscurity. A lonely obelisk that marks his grave while a stained-glass window and framed portrait record his brief presidency at Wesleyan University. I have not found any other three-dimensional artifacts honoring his contributions or preserving his likeness. Nor have I discovered any institution or building bearing his name. Memorials are abundant for Asbury, Coke, Emory, McKendree, and numerous other bishops. Bangs is strangely absent though his fingerprints are clearly visible across nineteenth-century American Methodism. His efforts helped to shape nineteenth-century MEC and descendant denominations up to the twenty-first century. This study is about Bangs, respectability, and the in-house struggles that emerged.

Chapter I

THE REVIVAL OF AMERICAN METHODIST HISTORY

FROM THE BICENTENNIAL OF American Methodism to the tercentenary of John Wesley's birth, the latter quarter of the twentieth century witnessed a remarkable revival of studies in American Methodism. These celebrated events notwithstanding, there emerged a new trend in the wider discipline of American religious history that has continued to the twenty-first century. This reflects a sustained interest in the sociological aspects of American religious history. The strongest currents in American religious history have focused academic studies on questions of gender, race, and class. As a result, the academy produced a new interdisciplinary genre of historiographical literature analyzing the social effects of religious movements in discrete contexts of American history.[1] This is a radically different approach from the

1. Some important examples include: Avery-Quinn, *Cities of Zion*; Andrews, *Methodists and Revolutionary America*; Bonomi, *Under the Cope of Heaven*; Butler, *Awash in a Sea of Faith*; Case, *Faith and Fury*; Cole, *Lion of the Forest*; Donavan, *Henry Foxall*; Dreff, *Entangled*; Elder, *The Sacred Mirror*; Ford, *Bonds of Union*; George, *One Mississippi, Two Mississippi*; Greene, *No Depression in Heaven*; Haselby, *The Origins of American Religious Nationalism*; Hatch, *Democratization of American Christianity*; Hempton, *Methodism*; Heyrman, *Southern Cross*; Hildebrand, *The Times Were Strange and Stirring*; Holm, *A Kingdom Divided*; Lyerly, *Methodism and the Southern Mind*; Maddox, *Nathan Bangs*; Matthews, *The Renewal of United Methodism*; McLoughlin, *Revivals, Awakenings, and Reform*; Melton, *A Will to Choose*; Murray, *Methodists and the Crucible of Race*; Reiff, *Born of Conviction*; Richey, *Methodism in the American Forest*; Salter, *"God Cannot Do Without America"*; Schneider, *The Way of the Cross Leads Home*; Stein, *The Shaker Experience in America*; Watson, *Old or New School Methodism?*; Wigger, *Taking Heaven by Storm*; Wigger, *American Saint*; Williams, *Religion and Violence in Early American Methodism*; Wuthnow, *The Restructuring of American*

church historians of the nineteenth and the early twentieth centuries who concerned themselves with chronicling events primarily for expansionism and denominational self-aggrandizement. For example, William Warren Sweet began *The Story of Religion in America* by stating: "The greatest accomplishment of America is the conquest of the continent, and the greatest achievement of the American churches has been the extension of their work westward across the vast stretches of the continent, keeping abreast with the restless and ever-moving population."[2] Since the latter part of the twentieth to the twenty-first century, historians have applied social theory to interpret any social changes in American religion. Neither this method nor any other is guaranteed to be free of self-aggrandizement. However, it is a grand leap forward for interpreting the social landscape of religious history.

This study is an endeavor to interpret America's religious history in the early national period using the Methodist Episcopal Church as a case study and focusing on one of the emerging denomination's formative leaders, Nathan Bangs. Some of the major questions I will attempt to answer are: What was the relationship between the career of Nathan Bangs and the movement toward respectability? How did the shift from "outsider" to "insider" on the American religious scene manifest itself in the local and national church? What is this phenomenon's place in American Methodist history?

After the death of Bishop Francis Asbury in 1816, there were several notable Methodist leaders on the scene including Willbur Fisk, William McKendree, Joshua Soule, Matthew Simpson, and Nathan Bangs.[3] Each of them, in their way, made meaningful contributions to the development of the denomination. Yet, it is needful to limit the study to one key player, preferably someone of national significance and long-term influence on respectability. Bangs fits this profile like none other.

Among all the colorful or drab characters of early Methodism, no one else played as great a role in making American Methodism a

Religion.

2. Sweet, *The Story of Religion in America*, 3. Other examples of triumphal histories include Baird, *Religion in America*; Bangs, *A History of the Methodist Episcopal Church*; Latourette, *A History of the Expansion of Christianity*; Schaff et al., *The American Church History Series.*

3. My list differs slightly from that of Matthew Simpson's "creative minds" of 1816 to 1820: "Joshua Soule, Nathan Bangs, John Emory, Elijah Hedding, Willbur Fisk, and Martin Ruter." Simpson, *A Hundred Years of Methodism*, 104.

"respectable" denomination. By his long and distinguished career, Bangs had the unique opportunity to exert his influence as a preacher, publisher, and educator to reshape American Methodism from the simple frontier religion of Asbury into a bureaucratic urbane denomination. At the same time, the social climate in early national America nurtured a widespread longing for respectability. The career of Bangs and the movement toward respectability were complementary forces operating in an interdependent relationship. The two elements intertwined to form a double-helix relationship which resulted in a new genetic code for the social structure of American Methodism.

It is important to reiterate that this is a study of American Methodism—a distinction to remember. The rift between British and American Methodist movements was not wholly due to accidents of geographic location. The dearth of colonial Anglican bishops created an ecclesiastical crisis aggravated by the American Revolution. The result was John Wesley's unprecedented decision to pronounce himself a biblical bishop, or in his words a "scriptural Episcopus."[4] He exercised his self-imposed episcopal authority by ordaining Richard Whatcoat and Thomas Vasey as deacons and elders.[5] This anticipated the parting of the ways between the organized British Wesleyans and American Methodists which continued well into the nineteenth century. Both groups moved toward establishing their native forms of respectability resulting in increased political power in their respective contexts. The downside was that the working poor, Wesley's "plain people," were systematically marginalized often to the exclusion of their respective fellowships.

On the other hand, although they shared a common heritage, the British Wesleyans and American Methodists evolved into quite distinct organizations. This distinction, in a great measure, was due to the individual visions of their respective leaders. The British Wesleyans had Jabez Bunting as their leading institutional organizer.[6] At the same time, Bangs was one of the most influential church leaders in American Methodism. There is some evidence that Bangs influenced Bunting indirectly by way of his publications. In a letter to Bunting, Joseph Sutcliffe concluded a

4. John Wesley, Letter to the Rev.-, August 19, 1785, in *Works of John Wesley* (Jackson ed.), 13:253.

5. John Wesley, September 1, 1784, in Wesley, *Journal and Diaries VI*, *Works of John Wesley* (Bicentennial ed.), 23:329–30.

6. For an overview of British Methodism during this same period, see Logan, "After Wesley," 111–23.

review of the first edition of Bangs' *History of the Methodist Episcopal Church* by saying "we want reviving with these western lives."[7]

Social Historiography

Religious and secular historians alike have made cursory acknowledgments of the role of social history in the formation of religious institutions. In 1913, Elie Halevy published, *The Birth of Methodism in England.* He argued that the English "working class agitation of 1738" was sublimated into a religious movement. Thus, he credited Methodism with preventing the bloody conflict experienced in the French revolution.[8] The Halevy thesis spawned important scholarship investigating the relationship between Methodism and social history.[9] E. P. Thompson offered one of the more significant attempts at social analysis of British Methodist history in *Religion and the Working Class* (1963). Thompson was successful in capturing the imagination of scholars of European history with his analysis of the Methodist revival in Britain. He argued that the evangelical movement created a middling class that swallowed up the poor in the process. E. P. Thompson's charge of Wesley's "promiscuous opportunism" was not overlooked. Bernard Semmel fired back the accusation that Thompson misunderstood the distinctions between Methodism and Calvinism, especially regarding the importance of good works and faith in the former.[10] Despite Thompson's cynical interpretation of early Methodism, he alerted historians to the complicated interactions between religion and class. Thomas Walter Laqueur's study on respectability and the British Sunday School movement represents a continuation of the scholarly discussion started by Thompson and Semmel.[11]

Charles Ferguson's *Organizing to Beat the Devil* (1971) was an early effort to interpret the social dimension of American Methodism. Unfortunately, Ferguson's work fell short of the critical analysis needed for the interpretation of a social history of American Methodism. It was not

7. Joseph Sutcliffe to Jabez Bunting, Bayswater, August 3, 1848, in Ward, *Early Victorian Methodism*, 365. Sutcliffe refers to the same work again in a letter dated June 17, 1850, Ward, 397.

8. Halevy, *The Birth of Methodism in England*, 74.

9. Some early examples include Warner, *The Wesleyan Movement in the Industrial Revolution*; Wearmouth, *Methodism and the Working-Class*; Bready, *England.*

10. Semmel, *The Methodist Revolution*, 4.

11. Laqueur, *Religion and Respectability.*

until the publication of Nathan O. Hatch's *Democratization of American Christianity* (1989) that the discipline was taken to the next level. Hatch argued that "the theme of democratization is central to understanding the development of American Christianity, and that the years of the early republic are the most crucial in revealing that process."[12] Furthermore, the "cultural alienation" of Disciples, Methodists, Baptists, and Mormons "gave way to a pilgrimage toward respectability."[13] His book has since spawned a rich panoply of similar books on American religion, including some critical of his thesis. Jon Butler's *Awash in A Sea of Faith* (1990) challenged Hatch's assertions of the "republicanism" of antebellum evangelicals. Butler asserted that "the Christian contribution to a developing American democracy rested as fully on its pursuit of coercive authority and power as on its concern for individualism or its elusive antiauthoritarian rhetoric."[14] My analysis leans heavily in the direction of Butler's elliptical interpretation of authority issues but employs other elements of social theory as well.

Key Terms

Crucial for the analysis in this study are the key terms respectability and *embourgeoisement.* They are used interchangeably here to express the working-class preference to adopt the social status and values of the middle class. The term "*embourgeoisement* thesis" is derived from John H. Goldthorpe's classic study of the British working class, *The Affluent Worker in the Class Structure* (1969). Goldthorpe turned Karl Marx's class conflict theory on its head by arguing that working-class people will adopt middle-class values and reject collective goals.[15] Bangs used his national influence to enhance and promote the working class's tendency to embrace middle-class values. This amalgamated with the collective goal of American Methodists to strive for improved social standing and economic strength both individually and institutionally. Many Methodists succeeded in achieving a higher level of social respectability, but this was not without paying a dear price. Those who did not fit or adapt to the

12. Hatch, *Democratization*, 3.
13. Hatch, *Democratization*, 15–16.
14. Butler, *Awash in a Sea of Faith*, 286–87.
15. Goldthorpe et al., *The Affluent Worker*, 26.

respectable mold experienced disenfranchisement or exclusion from the benefits of social standing.

The subject of respectability in nineteenth-century America has for some time made its mark among secular historians. Kathryn Kish Sklar wrote one of the first serious works giving insight to the dynamics of respectability and gender in *Catherine Beecher: A Study in American Domesticity* (1976). Richard L. Bushman's work *The Refinement of America: Persons, Houses, Cities* (1992) offered an excellent study of material history and respectability from a secular historian's point of view. In 2001, Sven Beckert published a more focused study of the *embourgeoisement* phenomenon of the Gilded Age in *The Monied Metropolis.*

Although different terminologies may have been used, the application of the *embourgeoisement* thesis is familiar to scholars of American religious history. As mentioned above, Hatch is credited with leading this stream of interpretation for American religion. Other works of note following Hatch include Dee E. Andrew's *The Methodists and Revolutionary America, 1760–1800*; Cynthia Lyerly's *Methodism and the Southern Mind 1770–1810*; John H. Wigger's *Taking Heaven by Storm*; and A. Gregory Schneider's *The Way of the Cross Leads Home.*[16] These historians, both secular and religious, freely employ the related terms common to social theory: respectability; democratization; republicanism; and domesticity.

Nineteenth-Century American Studies

The context of this study is in the early national period of American history. A. Gregory Schneider's categories of periods of American religious history help interpret this time. The "Puritan Age" was typified by Jonathan Edwards and the other Reformed and Calvinist leaders of the Great Awakening. According to Schneider, the Second Great Awakening gave way to Methodists, thus inaugurating the "Methodist Age."[17] Francis Asbury and his army of "circuit riders" expanded the network seizing upon the economic successes of the young republic. Between 1773 and 1813, the number of preachers increased from ten to 678, and membership

16. A modest sampling of this genre includes Andrews, *Methodists and Revolutionary America*; Butler, *Awash in a Sea of Faith*; Lyerly, *Methodism and the Southern Mind*; Richey, *Early American Methodism*; Schneider, *The Way of the Cross Leads Home*; Sutton, *Journeyman for Jesus*; Wigger, *American Saint*; Wigger, *Taking Heaven by Storm.*

17. Schneider, *The Way of the Cross Leads Home*, xix–xx.

increased from 1,160 to 214,307.[18] Such exponential numerical growth continued in other Protestant denominations as well, but by mid-century, the Methodist Episcopal Church became the largest American Protestant denomination. The Methodist Age outstripped the Puritan Age by its popular piety which transcended national growth in population and economics. Those Methodist distinctions were eagerly adopted by United Brethren, Evangelical Association, the Free-Will Baptists, the Cumberland Presbyterians, and the celebrated Charles Grandison Finney. This was deemed the triumph of Methodism.[19] This challenged William Warren Sweet's interpretation that the growth of American Methodism was strictly owing to westward expansion.[20]

Hatch argues that "democratic upheavals" changed the way denominations functioned. The resulting social friction could be described in terms of seismic disturbances altering the religious landscape. The new trends toward respectability exerted an irresistible gravitational pull on the growing religious institutions. The Methodist Episcopal Church could not escape this irresistible force. Hatch identifies Bangs as a symbol of "a movement's hunger for legitimation, intellectual respect, and cosmopolitan influence. Religious populism thus enhanced social mobility even if it came as an unintended consequence realized by second generation adherents."[21] The intent was to cultivate the image and resources of the Methodist Episcopal Church for the upwardly mobile constituents. Bangs served as both mastermind and ramrod of the operation. His influence lingered in denominational and personal publications as well as in established institutions such as the Book Concern, the Missionary Society, and the Course of Study.

Since the 1784 separation from their British progenitors, American Methodists suffered an identity crisis that Bangs helped to cure. To grasp the severity of the crisis, it is important to consider the transition from the Wesleyan "catholic spirit" to an established Methodist theology during this phase. During the previous Methodist revival of the eighteenth century, in-house conflicts over issues of free grace and predestination ended in a virtual *detente* between the Wesleys and Whitefield. At the

18. "General Recapitulation," end page.

19. Hudson and Corrigan, *Religion in America*, 178–79.

20. Sweet, *The Story of Religion in America*, 218–21.

21. Hatch, *Democratization*, 195.

end of the day, for the sake of the unity of mission, the three preachers favored catholicity.

Unfortunately, theological conflicts between Calvinists and Arminians in nineteenth-century America sacrificed the irenic tone for strident doctrinal orthodoxy. The Methodist Episcopal Church distanced itself from the theological ideals associated with New England Calvinism, the intellectual representatives of the former "Puritan Age" of American religion. This is especially true regarding Hopkinsians, the theological heirs of Jonathan Edwards. Nathan Bangs was at the forefront of this argument with the publication of his anti-Calvinistic polemic and apologetic literature.[22]

This abandonment of Wesleyan catholicity helped American Methodists establish themselves as legitimate theological rivals for the American evangelical enterprise. It also boosted Bangs' national status as a defender of Methodist ideals. The formation of Methodist identity coincided with the social and economic changes of their new constituency.

American Methodists were under pressure to redefine themselves as partners in the capitalistic enterprise of early national America. Their characteristic of effervescent religious expressions was an important part of their emerging denominational identity. The Methodist Episcopal Church well earned its image as a popular evangelical sect typified by plain preaching and enthusiastic response. This identity was reinforced by the leadership of Francis Asbury, the so-called "prophet of the long road."[23] After he died in 1816, the denomination began a rapid transition that would transform its image to one of social respectability. William R. Sutton defined "respectable Methodists" as a combination of "the unpretentiousness of the rough with the enterprise of the ambitious while maintaining a strict sense of limits and decorum in both their work and amusements."[24] In the name of decorum, the expressive frontier religion was stifled, but not quenched. Rather, it was refitted into respectable attire. There was a demand for more educated preachers. Worship was formalized. Churches were built and old ones remodeled to accommodate the "respectable" constituency. This new reality was due to external and

22. Nathan Bangs' printed works of this genre include: *The Errors of Hopkinsianism Detected and Refuted*; *An Examination of the Doctrine of Predestination*; *The Reformer Reformed*; *Vindication of the Methodist Episcopacy*; *Methodist episcopacy*; and *Rights, Ceremonies, and usages*.

23. Tipple, *Francis Asbury*, 158.

24. Sutton, "To Extract Poison," 231.

internal pressures to conform to social respectability. Nathan Bangs did more than adjust the system to accommodate the erupting social flux. He reinvented it.

Rediscovery of Nathan Bangs

There is substantial evidence that Bangs was the most pivotal figure and agent in an age of transition in American Methodism. This is not to suggest that he was a Methodist Machiavelli.[25] Rather, acting in good faith, Bangs capitalized on his position to improve the social status of the Methodist Episcopal Church. The result was the transformation of the Methodist Episcopal Church from a frontier-style religion to an urbane denomination.

Bangs' importance has been recognized by several religious historians, despite their varied emphases. Aside from occasional mention in denominational histories, Nathan Bangs remains a sorely neglected subject in American Methodist history. But he is not entirely unknown. In 1863, Methodist Episcopal Church historian Abel Stevens wrote the first Bangs biography relying heavily on Bangs' journal and letters.[26] The timing was unfortunate as the book's publication followed President Lincoln's signing of the Emancipation Proclamation in January 1863. The optics of Bangs' failure to adequately support abolition could not be avoided by the book's critics.[27] In 1909, Alexander Harrison Tuttle also wrote a shorter biography of Bangs. Although it is slightly less hagiographic, it contributed nothing significant to the previous biography. Tuttle concluded that Bangs ranked "second only to Bishop Asbury among the makers of his Church."[28]

Denominational histories are sadly deficient in interpreting this period. The early offerings are now considered too general and hagiographic. Bangs' four-volume history is useful as a chronicle of the General Conference. However, Bangs could not offer an unbiased self-criticism,

25. Niccolo Machiavelli's *The Prince* (ca. 1513) is considered one of the classic handbooks on power politics. Bangs would have been familiar with John Wesley's distaste for this book: "If all the other doctrines of devils which have been committed to writing since letters were in the world were collected together in one volume, it would fall short of this." Wesley, *Works of John Wesley* (Jackson ed.), 1:44.

26. Stevens, *Life and Times of Nathan Bangs.*

27. Review of *The Life and Times of Nathan Bangs.*

28. Tuttle, *Nathan Bangs*, 7.

certainly not in terms of social history. George Peck's regional history (ca. 1860) reads more like a compendium of personal anecdotes than a critical history.[29]

Abel Stevens' history of the MEC (Methodist Episcopal Church), begun during the Civil War, is an early attempt at interpretive history but in the end, is another work of triumphalism.[30] No real interpretive histories of the period were written until 1912 when William Warren Sweet's history, based on his study at the University of Pennsylvania, was published as *The Methodist Episcopal Church and the Civil War.* Sweet's prolific pen continued for many years, finally co-writing *A Short History of Methodism* for The Methodist Church in 1956. Although Sweet's interpretations are no longer recognized as the last word on the Methodist history, his method represented a new phase in historiography.

Two decades later Frederick A. Norwood wrote the popular textbook *The Story of American Methodism.* This became a perennial favorite for Methodist history classes in seminaries. Norwood utilized a more critical method for interpreting denominational history.[31] The name "Nathan Bangs" appears no less than eleven times in *The Story of American Methodism.* Norwood's companion volume, *Sourcebook of American Methodism,* included a letter by Bangs along with a thumbnail sketch of his career. Norwood's assessment of Bangs was brief but grandiose. "Probably no one man, during the life of the [Methodist Episcopal] Church in America, has made a deeper or more lasting impression upon her history than Nathan Bangs."[32] The popular seminary textbook *United Methodism in America,* edited by John McEllhenney, has a separate chapter on the period 1816–43. Oddly enough, the book did not mention Bangs at all.[33] This was superseded by *The Methodist Experience in America, Volume I: A History* by Russell E. Richey, Kenneth E. Rowe, and Jean Miller Schmidt.[34] The 699-page tome was later condensed into 276-page book, a much more readable version for the populace appropriately entitled *American Methodism: A Compact History.* The former dedicated

29. Peck, *Early Methodism.*

30. Stevens, *History of the Methodist Episcopal Church.*

31. Norwood, *The Story of American Methodism.*

32. Norwood, *Sourcebook of American Methodism,* 287.

33. McEllhenney et al., *United Methodism in America.*

34. Interestingly, volume 1, *A History,* was published ten years after volume 2, *A Sourcebook.* Unfortunately, neither book includes documents directly related to Nathan Bangs.

the most pages to the career of Nathan Bangs of any contemporary denominational history, though many important details were unavoidably left out of the later compact version.

The above inconsistencies notwithstanding, Thomas A. Langford bequeathed upon Bangs the title "the first significant Wesleyan theologian in the United States." Langford supported his statement with a lavish discussion of Bangs' theology in Practical Divinity.[35] *Wesleyan Theology: A Sourcebook*, Langford's companion volume, even used a portrait of Bangs to grace the book jacket cover. The sourcebook included selections from *The Errors of Hopkinsianism* (1815) dealing with the doctrine of election and Christian perfection.[36] Excerpts from *The Errors of Hopkinsianism* (1815) and *The Reformer Reformed* (1818) were reproduced in *Sources of Christian Theology in America*, edited by Mark G. Toulouse and James O. Duke.[37] Notably, Nathan O. Hatch offered one of the most informed acknowledgments of Bangs' historical importance not only as a theologian but also as a church leader in *The Democratization of American Christianity*. The brief section summarizes Bangs' participation in the movement toward respectability. "If Asbury's career represented Methodism's triumph as a populist movement, with control at the cultural periphery, then Bangs' career illustrates the centripetal tug of respectable culture."[38] Bangs' theological contributions are celebrated in Mark A. Noll's *America's God: From Jonathan Edwards to Abraham Lincoln* (2002). In this groundbreaking theological history, Bangs is rated according to the degree of common-sense reasoning present in his theological writings. Using these criteria, Noll considered Bangs of secondary theological importance to his contemporary Willbur Fisk.[39] Another significant appreciation of Bangs as a theologian is offered in E. Brooks Holifield's *Theology in America* (2003).[40] Five years earlier, Holifield paid homage to the theological significance of Bangs by including a biographical article in *Makers of Christian Theology in America*.[41] Brief encyclopedic biographies on Bangs appear also in general works such as *The Blackwell*

35. Langford, *Theology in the Wesleyan Tradition*, 78–99.

36. Langford, *Wesleyan Theology*, 45–55. This book was reprinted as Langford, *Readings in Wesleyan Theology*.

37. Toulouse and Duke, *Sources of Christian Theology in America*, 165–73.

38. Hatch, *Democratization*, 202.

39. Noll, *America's God*, 352.

40. Holifield, *Theology in America*, 256–72.

41. Holified, "Nathan Bangs," 121–24.

Dictionary of Evangelical Biography: 1780–1860,[42] *The Methodists*,[43] and *Historical Dictionary of Methodism*.[44]

Few historical studies have included more than a footnote on the career of Nathan Bangs. In 1954, Leland Howard Scott included a summary of Bangs' theological treatises in his oft-quoted study on American Methodist theology in the nineteenth century.[45] In 1973, Richard Everett Herrmann wrote his study on the role of Bangs as an apologist for Methodism.[46] In 1998, Steven W. Lewis' study chronicled Bangs' involvement in the Arminian-Calvinist controversy in nineteenth-century America.[47] Herrmann and Lewis both focus on Bangs' theological disputations, especially with the Reformed tradition. These studies are exceptionally valuable for determining the theological pulse of the era. However, they leave a significant gap for understanding Bangs' interactions with the forces of the social milieu which demanded respectable religion. I am indebted to the foundational work of Nathan O. Hatch for initiating a conversation about Nathan Bangs as an agent toward respectability in the MEC. It provided much stimulus for pursuing this project.[48] In 2016, Jared Maddox made a case for Bangs as a promoter of scriptural holiness in the tradition of Francis Asbury.[49] Though his themes are arranged chronologically, they are strikingly similar to my earlier Bangs research.[50] More importantly his conclusions are distinctly different than mine. Maddox surmised that respectability was an unexpected by-product of Bangs' "mission to spread scriptural holiness."[51] Steven Rankin's sympathetic review of Maddox is on point calling his thesis "tantalizing" but failing on the organization of evidence.[52]

42. Lippy, "Nathan Bangs," 53–54.

43. Kirby et al., *The Methodists*, 263–65.

44. Charles I. Wallace Jr., "Nathan Bangs," in Yrigoyen and Warrick, *Historical Dictionary of Methodism*, 54.

45. Scott, "Methodist Theology in America."

46. Herrmann, "Nathan Bangs."

47. Lewis, "Nathan Bangs."

48. Note the extensive use of the term "respectability" in Hatch, *The Democratization of American Christianity*, 89, 93, 193, 195, 201–7.

49. Maddox, "Nathan Bangs."

50. Flores, "Respectable Methodists."

51. Maddox, *Nathan Bangs*.

52. Rankin, "Nathan Bangs," 230–33.

I will argue that Bangs' beliefs and career endeavors promoted his grand vision for a new form of Methodism that evoked respectability according to nineteenth-century American standards. He was uniquely positioned as an in-house change agent because of his high-profile leadership roles during the critical early years of development of the Methodist Episcopal Church. The following chapters will explore the relationship between the career of Bangs and respectability in the Methodist Episcopal Church in the early national period. Chapter 2 considers the career of Nathan Bangs as exemplary of the archetypical respectable Methodist. It discusses his influence as a preacher, publisher, and educator. Chapter 3 discusses the manifestation of respectability in worship specifically in preaching, hymnody, and church order. Chapter 4 focuses on the changes in worship spaces from simple preaching houses to elaborate buildings, addressing the preference for refined architecture and exquisite furnishings. Chapter 5 is an appraisal of the middling class and Methodism in nineteenth-century America. Chapter 6 explores how abolition of slavery impacted the push for respectability in the MEC. Chapter 7 concludes the study with a summation of the long-lasting effect of the phenomenon of respectability and the historic Wesleyan preferential option for the poor and marginalized peoples.

Chapter II

THE MODEL RESPECTABLE METHODIST

> When a stranger appears in these new countries the people are usually curious to know his name, whence he comes, whither he is bound, and what is his errand. I will try to satisfy you in brief. My name is Nathan Bangs. I was born in Connecticut May 2, 1778. I was born again in this province, May, 1800. I commenced itinerating as a preacher of the Gospel in the month of September, 1801. On the 18th of June, the present year, I left New York for the purpose of visiting you, of whom I heard about two years ago, and after a long and tedious journey I am here. I am bound for the heavenly city, and my errand among you is to persuade as many as I can to go with me. I am a Methodist preacher; and my manner of worship is, to stand while singing, kneel while praying, and then I stand while I preach, the people meanwhile sitting. As many of you as see fit to join me in this way can do so, and others may choose their own method.[1]

THE BRIEF SELF-INTRODUCTION ABOVE reveals that to no small extent Nathan Bangs was a person fit for his time. He entered the Methodist ministry when the mission was fresh and the organization was malleable. His labors positioned him to witness American intellectual expansionism from the vantage of the denominational apex. Earlier, the Methodist Episcopal Church enjoyed rapid numerical growth under

1. Stevens, *Life and Times of Nathan Bangs*, 136–37.

the iron-fisted guidance of Bishop Francis Asbury. His death in 1816, though somewhat expected for a man of his advanced age, accentuated the need for second-generation leaders in the MEC.

Nathan Bangs responded by blending a respect for the first generation with a vision for a more respectable organization. His own personal life of discipline was itself a model for a lifelong pursuit of improving the character of Methodism.[2] Bangs' fifty-year career path took him from the backwaters of society to the forefront of urbane respectability. He learned not only that respectability was desirable, but it was accessible to working-class Methodists. Thus, he made it his goal to improve the MEC which had been so long regarded as a coarse person's religion. Paradoxically, when Bangs' own career reached its capstone, his influence eroded until he retreated to a self-imposed exile and near obscurity. Nevertheless, the remnants of his contributions remained imbedded in the overall structure of the denomination for several decades following his departure from public life.

It is important to note that although this study contains biographical information pertaining to Nathan Bangs it is not intended as a biography. A project to write an exhaustive biography of Bangs is reserved for future consideration. Such would require a long-term focused evaluation of both his private and public life. A biographical project on Bangs would be difficult because primary source materials containing his more personal documents are scant.[3] Fortunately, for the purpose at hand, his published journal and archived letters provide a rich resource for understanding his career development. This chapter will examine Bangs' personal journey toward respectability limited to his roles as preacher, publisher, and educator. Furthermore, it will demonstrate that Bangs was

2. Stevens, *Life and Times of Nathan Bangs*, 191.

3. The two richest archival repositories for relevant original manuscripts are the Nathan Bangs Papers in the Methodist Archives at Drew University and the President Bangs Papers at Wesleyan University. Unfortunately, many of the extant letters are practically useless because of his illegible handwriting. Otherwise, it is quite fortunate that Bangs was such a prolific writer. There is a wide scattering of small caches of Bangs manuscripts housed in several research libraries including: the Waidner & Spahr Library Archives, Dickinson College; Ezekiel Cooper Papers, United Library, Garrett-Evangelical Seminary; United Church of Canada Papers; Boston University School of Theology Library Research Collections; Victoria University Archives; Martin Ruter Papers, Center for Methodist Studies at Bridwell Library, Southern Methodist University; Methodist Archives at John Rylands Library at the University of Manchester; James Bradley Finley Papers at Ohio Wesleyan University; and the James FinleyPapers at the Rutherford B. Hayes Library.

an active proponent of respectability in the organization of the Methodist Episcopal Church.

Formative Years

Nathan Bangs was born May 2, 1778, in Stratford, Connecticut. Lemuel Bangs, his father, and Rebecca Keeler, his mother, traced their religious roots to the Puritan variety of Anglicanism. The Bangs children were confirmed in the Protestant Episcopal Church. For Nathan Bangs, the pilgrimage from Anglicanism to Methodism was not easy road to tread. This is especially true considering his father's ardent resistance to Methodism. Lemuel's prejudices were well-known, especially his distaste for ignorant clergy.[4] An avid layman, he would often read the Anglican service to his neighbors. However, he "thought no man was duly qualified to preach, who had not a thorough Academic and Theological education."[5] Lemuel was a blacksmith and a surveyor. He apprenticed Nathan in the latter. Thus, he was able to leave home in search of his living as a surveyor.

In 1779, Nathan followed his sister and brother-in-law to Lower Canada in search of economic opportunity as a surveyor. Failing to find much survey work, he took a position as a schoolteacher. During his sojourn in Canada, Nathan enjoyed lively dialogues with Quakers, Calvinists, Methodists, and a "poor drunken card-playing" Anglican minister.[6] It was his discussions with Methodists that led him to a conversion experience. Upon hearing James Coleman preach, he was converted after meditating on the message. "Suddenly, I felt my burden removed. Filled with gratitude for God's long forbearance, I stood and silently adored."[7] At a later Quarterly Meeting, he received additional assurances of his salvation from Methodist preachers Christian Warner, Joseph Jewell, and Joseph Sawyer. Although Bangs recorded little or nothing about his sisters, Abel Stevens considered the relationship of one sister significant in Nathan's spiritual formation. Nathan did not name his "pious" sister, but she was either Sarah or the popular exhorter Elinor Bangs. "This

4. Stevens, *Life and Times of Nathan Bangs*, 17.

5. Bangs, *Autobiography and Journal*, 3.

6. Stevens, *Life and Times of Nathan Bangs*, 42.

7. Stevens, *Life and Times of Nathan Bangs*, 43.

sister was now in the wilderness of Canada, a guide and comforter of her brother Nathan, before whom the same career was about to open."[8]

Bangs' school teaching career was cut short as his new-found religious enthusiasm was not appreciated by the kindly Dutch folk who employed him.[9] His dismissal was perceived as persecution for his belief. In response, he imposed upon himself a rigor of dress by removing his fashionable ruffles and cutting his long hair.[10] Even more significantly, when he joined the MEC he praised them for their strictures, a sentiment that would guide his concept of respectable Methodism.

> When I became acquainted with the "General Rules," I was struck with their Scriptural character, and could not but remark the truth of Mr. Wesley's saying: "All these, we know, the Spirit of God writes on truly awakened hearts." Before I knew the Rules, as in the Methodist Discipline, or any of the rules of that Discipline, the Holy Spirit had written most of them on my heart.[11]

After reading Holy Scriptures, Wesley's *Plain Account of Christian Perfection*, and Fletcher's "writings" on perfection, Bangs became convinced that he needed to seek the deeper experience of sanctification. On February 6, 1801, he had such a religious experience. He described feeling "no extraordinary rapture," but a sense that "God's ineffable goodness" pervaded his soul.[12] This experience strengthened his conviction to take up the preaching task with "increased force."[13] In May 1801, he began itinerating as a licensed exhorter under the watchful eye of Joseph Sawyer who served as his mentor. His evident preaching gifts enabled him to be licensed three months later and appointed in a circuit.[14] In the year 1802, Nathan Bangs was ordained into the Methodist ministry by none other than Francis Asbury. Bangs' brothers John and Heman also became Methodist ministers.[15] As mentioned above, sister Elinor became well

8. Stevens, *Life and Times of Nathan Bangs*, 45.

9. Stevens, *Life and Times of Nathan Bangs*, 46.

10. Bangs adopted better fashion by the time he assumed the presidency of Wesleyan University. This is evident from his presidential portrait.

11. Stevens, *Life and Times of Nathan Bangs*, 47.

12. Stevens, *Life and Times of Nathan Bangs*, 57–59.

13. Stevens, *Life and Times of Nathan Bangs*, 59.

14. Stevens, *Life and Times of Nathan Bangs*, 61–65.

15. Bangs, *Autobiography of Rev. John Bangs*. His book features an appendix with a genealogy of the Bangs family. Heman Bangs also gives a very complete family history in *The Autobiography and Journal of Rev. Heman Bangs*.

known for her exhorting skills in Canada.[16] His brother, Elijah K. Bangs, took the secular option as an adventure seeking ship captain.[17] Many of Nathan Bangs' siblings became preachers and exhorters. Regardless, his father always remained a harsh critic of Methodist preaching. Heman Bangs noted their father's anti-Methodist resistance as equally weighed against them. "When the Methodists first came into his neighborhood he was bitterly opposed to them; and although most of his children joined them, he would not consent to hear them preach."[18] At long last, when the old patriarch attended Nathan's preaching, he did not hesitate to correct him publicly for misquoting an author.[19] Thus, began Nathan Bangs' long career as a preacher in the MEC.

The Preacher

> And oh *Asbury!* how do we blush when thy journals tell us of thy labours, of thy sufferings, of thy perils by sea and land, and among false brethren! What an example for our modem missionaries! The American Methodist preachers will long revere thy virtues; and while they read thy pages, will lift their hearts to God in devout thankfulness for having inspired thee with courage and perseverance in the cause of thy adorable Master.[20]

There was no formal procedure for becoming a Methodist preacher during the Asbury years of the MEC. Thus, Bangs merely presented himself as a volunteer to go to Canada as missionary. He served for seven years in the Canadian mission. Earlier, Methodism in Lower Canada had germinated under the lay missionary efforts of Barbara Heck, one of the charter members of New York's John Street Church.[21] Like many other Irish immigrants, her family fled to Lower Canada at the onset of the Revolutionary War.[22]

16. Carroll, *Case and His Contemporaries*, 224.
17. Stevens, *Life and Times of Nathan Bangs*, 310.
18. Stevens, *Life and Times of Nathan Bangs*, 17.
19. Stevens, *Life and Times of Nathan Bangs*, 17.
20. Bangs, *Letters to Young Ministers*, 74.
21. Sanderson, *First Century of Methodism in Canada*, 46.
22. Philip Embury died in 1773. His widow married John Lawrence, another Irishman. She emigrated to Canada with Philip's brother David Embury and Paul and Barbara Heck. Cook, *Ireland and the Centenary of American Methodism*, 191.

The Circuit Rider

Nathan Bangs' missionary itineracy in the Niagara circuit cut a long swath throughout the wilds of Lower Canada. The route encircled an area of 2,400 square miles from Lake Erie to Lake Ontario and Niagara to Oxford. This immense circuit required daily preaching over a six-week cycle.[23] Those early years of sacrificial mission on the Canadian frontier proved successful for Bangs, along with other notables, Joseph Sawyer, Hezekiah Calvin Wooster, Lorenzo Dow, Darius Dunham, and Elijah Woolsey. The harvest of converts was plentiful, and they developed a legendary reputation for their distinctive Methodist preaching.[24]

The War of 1812 forced Nathan Bangs to flee Canada and return to his homeland. Not willing to release Bangs from their service, the war-separated Canadian Methodists honored Bangs by electing him their bishop. However, he declined the episcopal office. Despite his decision to decline Canadian episcopacy, and his later failure to ascend to the episcopacy in the United States, this did not diminish his stature one whit. On the contrary, the Canadian nomination gained him international recognition. He became so prominent that even Perry Miller mistakenly referred to him as "Bishop Bangs."[25]

The Corresponding Missionary Secretary

Nathan Bangs ended his Canadian ministry and took a coveted place among the other stately and established preachers of New York. In 1819, he and a rather notable group of New Yorker preachers conceived and organized the Missionary Society of the MEC.

> At length, at a meeting of preachers stationed in New-York, and the book agents, the Rev. Laban Clark presented a resolution in favor of forming a Bible and missionary society of The Methodist Episcopal Church. At this time the following preachers were present, namely, Freeborn Garrettson, Joshua Soule, Samuel Merwin, Nathan Bangs, Laban Clark, Thomas Mason, Seth Crowell, Samuel Howe, and Thomas Thorp. After a free interchange of thoughts on the subject the resolution was adopted, and Freeborn Garrettson, Laban Clark, and Nathan Bangs were

23. Sutherland, *Methodism in Canada*, 69.
24. Sutherland, *Methodism in Canada*, 75.
25. Miller, *The Life of the Mind in America*, 88.

> appointed a committee to prepare a constitution to be submitted at a subsequent meeting of the above-mentioned preachers.[26]

The final draft of the constitution proposed to create the Missionary and Bible Society of the Methodist Episcopal Church in America. This was ratified by the General Conference of 1820.[27] In 1836, Bangs was appointed resident corresponding secretary for the Missionary Society.[28] He served faithfully in this post for twelve years without compensation. During that time, he directed the Mission Society.[29] The work of the Missionary Society was widely disseminated with the 1832 publication of Bangs' *Authentic History of the Missions under the care of the Missionary Society of The Methodist Episcopal Church.* The revivalist language suggested that a new Pentecost was arising from within camp meetings and conferences.[30]

His book was "greeted by the Church with no ordinary satisfaction.[31] This hearty reception of missions hagiography stirred the spirits of the readers and recalled their Wesleyan roots. It is interesting that the review alludes to the outpouring of the Holy Spirit on the indigenous people. Bangs' *Authentic History of the Missions* highlighted the efforts of missionaries among the American and Canadian "aboriginal" nations, particularly the Wyandotts, Creeks, Cherokees, Choctaws, Mohawks, and Onondagas. Bangs discovered early that publicizing Native American missions could raise support for other missions. He once invited missionary James B. Finley to bring Wyandott chieftains to New York for precisely that purpose.[32] The publication was an effective catalyst for new missions in Africa and Latin America.[33] That same year, the presiding elders were required to promote missions along with Sunday schools and religious books.[34]

In 1840, Bangs' successes as corresponding secretary in doubling the Society's funds were recognized by the General Conference. They

26. Bangs, *History of the Methodist Episcopal Church*, 3:82.
27. Sherman, *History of the Revisions*, 39.
28. Stevens, *Life and Times of Nathan Bangs*, 305.
29. Janes, *Sermon on the Death of Nathan Bangs*, 23.
30. Taves, *Fits, Trances, & Visions*, 112.
31. D., Review of *Authentic History*, 249.
32. Nathan Bangs to James B. Finley, "Wyandott Mission Letter of Invitation."
33. Sherman, *History of the Revisions*, 42.
34. Sherman, *History of the Revisions*, 43.

decided to install three coordinating secretaries: Nathan Bangs, resident secretary in New York; William Capers, in the South; and Edward R. Ames, in the West. Bangs only left the post May 19, 1841 to take the presidency of Wesleyan University.[35]

Publisher

> What a mighty engine is the press! What an event was that when this engine was first set in motion. Since then, what a revolution has been effected in the civilized world, in religion, in civil jurisprudence, in philosophy, and in every department of knowledge, human and divine! Mr. Wesley well knew the power of this instrument. He therefore availed himself of it to aid him in the great work of evangelizing the world. He made it speak, in clear and distinct tones, "the truth, the whole truth, and nothing but the truth." His sons in the gospel have had wisdom and perseverance enough to follow in his track, and make this speaking trumpet continue its "certain sound," and it has been, not a "tinkling cymbal," but a high-sounding instrument of peculiar force, warning the unruly, instructing the ignorant, and rejoicing the hearts, by its thrilling accents, of tens of thousands of immortal minds.[36]

Nathan Bangs understood the power of the press. His publishing career began as Steward of the Methodist Book Concern in 1820. From 1820 to 1828, Bangs cut his editorial teeth on the publication, *Methodist Magazine*. Not content with a monthly magazine the Book Committee and the New York Conference agreed to issue a weekly paper called the *Christian Advocate and Journal*. "Accordingly, on the 9th of September 1826, the first number of this advocate of Christian doctrines, morals, and the institutions of Methodism, made its first appearance, much to the gratification of all the members and friends of the Church."[37] Although Badger was the editor of the *Christian Advocate* from 1826 to 1828, Bangs provided much of the editorial material.[38] Thus, Bangs was the natural choice as the next editor of the *Christian Advocate*. He was appointed to

35. Barclay, *History of Methodist Missions*, 1:312.
36. Bangs, *History of the Methodist Episcopal Church*, 4:452–53.
37. Bangs, *History of the Methodist Episcopal Church*, 4:453.
38. Stevens, *Life and Times of Nathan Bangs*, 243.

that post in 1828 by vote of the General Conference.[39] By 1828, the *Christian Advocate* already boasted a circulation of 25,000 copies, the largest in the country.[40] This newspaper was quite a different publication from the heady *Methodist Magazine*. The *Christian Advocate* lent itself to popular religion and moralizing. Some people were wary of the increase in publications in the Methodist Episcopal Church. It threatened the comfortable old image of the circuit riding Methodist preachers who were much more concerned with spiritual devotion. George Peck noted the tensions which arose from a religious "free press."

> Then Methodist preachers within our bounds gave themselves to preaching and prayer. These duties, with their long rides and a little necessary reading, used up their time. Then we had no periodicals through which to communicate with the public, if the preachers had been disposed to write, and a new publication of any sort by a Methodist preacher was a strange thing. Still the press must be guarded. The whole thing now seems little less than ludicrous; but those were days of simplicity, of caution, and of timidity. If we have not now reached the opposite extreme we are but too near it. The old caution, like the old defenses, is gone, and what is exultingly called a *free press* is often a rampant invader of the old foundation and the old landmarks. We would not wish for the return of the old restrictions upon the press, but we would like to see the old feelings of brotherhood prevail, and the authorities and doctrines of the Church respected as of old. Precisely where the liberty of the press ends and its licentiousness begins is sometimes a delicate point, but one that needs to be studied at the present time.[41]

The earlier experience of Robert Williams' unauthorized publications of Wesley's sermons telegraphed a warning signal to the budding Methodist hierarchy. The control of publishing was a necessity to maintain order in the ranks. The 1773 Conference saw to it that no such thing would be allowed again.[42] The 1824 abolition of this prohibition in the *Discipline* was not the source of George Peck's lament. Rather, he was appalled at the content of the new "free press." The license to print spawned a plethora of new publications. One of the first of these papers was the

39. Stevens, *Life and Times of Nathan Bangs*, 270.

40. Smith, "How Methodism Became a National Church," 24.

41. Peck, *Early Methodism*, 497.

42. Cameron, "The New Church Takes Root," 279–80.

Wesleyan Repository and Religious Intelligencer, a newspaper for the cause of ecclesiastical reform on the issue of electing presiding elders. The only officially sanctioned publication was the *Methodist Magazine*, first issued in 1818 by Joshua Soule and Thomas Mason. It was later known as the *Quarterly Review*, then changed its name to *Methodist Magazine and Quarterly Review* in 1830. The original publication was issued monthly with a length of some forty pages. However, under the new quarterly format the "paper" swelled to one hundred twenty pages per issue.[43] When Nathan Bangs was appointed editor of the *Methodist Magazine* in 1820, he enacted "a new policy of repression."[44] The preface to the 1823 edition stated that "nothing would be admitted (in the *Magazine*) of a controversial character which go to disturb the peace and harmony of the Church." These publications may be classified according to their political categories. "The *Methodist Magazine* became the spokesman for the *status quo*; the *Wesleyan Repository*, and its successor, *Mutual Rights*, beat the drums of reform; the *Christian Advocate and Journal* (the New York *Christian Advocate*) from 1827 was the chief popular defender of established authority."[45]

The *Christian Advocate, Quarterly Review*, and a monthly called *Youth's Instructor* were the new official voices of the MEC. This fit Bangs' vision for an all around publication to different segments of the denomination. Meanwhile, the MEC's hierarchy was disturbed by unofficial publications which represented the opinions of reformers and activists. They feared that these renegade papers threatened the social order by disrupting the most delicate of religious and political issues. Uncensored social commentaries were now being distributed without regard to the Methodist Episcopal Church's editorial authority. Of all the issues they covered, the most bitter and divisive was slavery. More will be said about this below in chapter 6.

Educator

> By *study* is meant that application of the mind, in reading, meditation, reflection, and observation, which is necessary to enrich and adorn it with useful knowledge. In what may be said on this subject, it will be taken for granted that you have not now

43. Mudge, "The Centennial of the Methodist Review," 94.
44. Chandler, "Towards the Americanizing of Methodism," 13.
45. Norwood, *The Story of American Methodism*, 177–78.

> to learn the elementary principles of language. I will likewise be assumed that you are convinced satisfactorily of your call to the sacred work of the ministry, that you have experienced the renovating power of the Holy Ghost upon your heart, and consequently that you have not now to learn the first principles of religion. But if indeed, you be destitute of that knowledge of God through Jesus Christ which can be acquired only by experience, all the study in the universe, even were you master of the whole circle of the sciences, will never qualify you for the holy work of the ministry.[46]

Francis Asbury did not have the advantage of a classical Oxford education like that of his colleague Thomas Coke or the Wesleys. Indeed, Asbury had a rather humble educational background in Birmingham, England. He left school at age thirteen to become a blacksmith's apprentice. He converted to Methodism when he was eighteen and began the itinerant ministry. His journal entries indicate he was a voracious reader, teaching himself theology as he traveled. Asbury could no more demand formal theological training of his young ministers than he could of himself. This was evidently a matter of some irritation for those who were formally educated. At Asbury's eulogy, Ezekiel Cooper felt it necessary to defend him on this point.

> Perhaps, it may not be necessary to speak of his literary attainments; though probably some will expect it. It is understood, and admitted, that he was not distinguished as a scientific, or literary Scholar. He was not considered a critical Linguist; nor as being eminent in the arts and sciences. He made little pretention to either; and never sought to rank with the *Literati.* Though languages, arts and sciences, ought to be encouraged, and, no doubt have their various excellent uses; yet, nevertheless, they are not the essential, nor pre-eminent qualifications, of an apostolic, primitive, or modem, christian minister, or bishop. The scriptures are clear on this point. The apostles were not learned men.[47]

Nathan Bangs was also self-educated. However, he did not share that romantic idea of a self-made clergy. As mentioned above, he inherited his prejudices about education from his father, Lemuel Bangs. The early Methodist disdain for educated clergy was exacerbated by the frequent

46. Bangs, *Letters to Young Ministers*, 9–10.

47. Cooper, *The Substance of a Funeral Discourse*, 117.

conflicts between the Methodist "Circuit Riders" and Presbyterian clergy. Bitter arguments fostered resentment against the more educated Presbyterians.[48] There was a certain pride in being a self-educated minister dependent on the power of the Spirit rather than intellect. Asbury and his itinerants modeled this type of minister by ferrying their meager libraries in their saddlebags, reading as they went the Bible, the *Discipline*, Wesley's *Sermons*, and Fletcher's *Appeals*.[49]

American Presbyterians had access to advanced theological education in the early nineteenth century, but they did not share with American Methodists in the rapid growth of evangelical religion. Ironically, this was due partially to the heavy educational requirements placed on clergy candidates.[50] The expense and time required for a classical education discouraged many of the "young gifts." Because of a shortage of available ministers, Presbyterians missed their opportunity to expand south and west.[51] On the other hand, the genius of the Methodist Episcopal Church was their ability to get their itinerant clergy into the field quickly. Methodists were not burdened by the impediments of a "settled ministry" or educational requirements. Rather, they trusted in the "inner claims" of gifts and calling as the ruling prerequisite for candidacy. The candidate would then enter a period of apprenticeship under a seasoned mentor. Successful completion of the probation period would lead to ordination and membership in a regional conference of Methodist preachers.

> The Methodists cultivated an eager recruit by licensing him to exhort or appointing him to serve as class leader and then urging him to accompany an itinerant on his rounds for a few months. If a young man showed the makings of a minister, he was assigned a circuit and received "on trial" into the "traveling connection" of itinerant preachers. After two years, if he proved his worth, he was admitted to their itinerancy in "full connection."[52]

Despite the apparent success of the apprentice system the MEC was not satisfied to garner the occasional uneducated convert. They were

48. Sweet, *The Rise of Methodism*, 49.

49. Sweet, *The Rise of Methodism*, 54.

50. The General Assembly of the Presbyterian Church established The Theological Seminary at Princeton in 1812. This action confirmed a tradition of formal education as a prerequisite for Presbyterian clergy candidates in America.

51. Heyrman, *Southern Cross*, 82–83.

52. Heyrman, *Southern Cross*, 83.

becoming increasingly more anxious to compete in the intellectual arena with New England Calvinists. In his private study, Bangs read the works of Jonathan Edwards and other Calvinists. Though he was not especially religious in his youth, his intellect was challenged by the spiritual writings of both Reformed and Wesleyan traditions. Like John Wesley, Bangs found much to commend in the piety and theology of Richard Baxter, David Brainerd, and Jonathan Edwards, though he could not easily accept Calvinism's doctrines of predestination and limited atonement. His suspicion of Calvinism was later transformed into a personal anti-Calvinist crusade which resulted in a flurry of polemic writings.[53] Bangs first gained national attention by virtue of his reputation as a bold polemicist against Calvinism and an unabashed apologist for Methodism. His notoriety eased his eventual placement in the proto-bureaucratic structure of the Methodist Episcopal Church. Bangs was sufficiently impressed by the Presbyterian form of government to propose aspects of it later in life to his own Methodist Episcopal Church. Furthermore, their high standards for clergy education had the greatest and most lasting influence on Bangs. The more respectable Methodists soon mimicked their competitors by demanding theologically educated ministers. It is notable that the first Methodist seminaries were in New England, the hotbed of Calvinism.[54] Nathan Bangs used his strategic influence to work toward changing the denomination's attitude toward theological education. There were at least four major actions in which Bangs engaged to establish a more respectable intellect in the Methodist clergy. First, he lobbied the General Conference to adopt educational requirements for clergy candidates. He believed in the importance of a "classical" education broadly defined as engaging history, literature, philosophy, the classical languages, and rhetoric. This led to his second major action. He wrote a series of articles for *Methodist Magazine* which were later edited and bound under the title, *Letters to Young Ministers of the Gospel, on the Importance and Method of Study* (1826). Third, Nathan Bangs founded the Wesleyan Seminary in New York City. Although the school did not

53. The best overview of Bangs' role in the Arminian–Calvinist debates is Richard Everett Herrmann's dissertation, "Nathan Bangs: Apologist for American Methodism." For a discussion of his placement in Methodist theology, see Lewis, "Nathan Bangs."

54. Baptists and Methodists in New England demonstrated their new attitudes toward theological education with the establishment of Andover Newton Theological Seminary (1824) and the precursor to Boston University School of Theology (1839), respectively. Sweet, *Religion in the Development of American Culture*, 183.

thrive, its brief existence planted the germ of theological education firmly in the psyche of American Methodism. Fourth, despite his personal intellectual achievements as an author and editor, Bangs was always self-conscious of his lack of a college education. He attempted to correct this poor self-image by upgrading the image of Methodist institutional education. As a president of Wesleyan University, Bangs revised the course offerings in an attempt to raise the overall level of respectability of the institution. The sections following will discuss the four major actions listed above in chronological order.

Educator

Course of Study (1817)

> The same committee reported the rule, which was this year incorporated into the Discipline, requiring a course of study for candidates for the ministry. I [Nathan Bangs] was the author of this rule. These measures encountered great opposition from many delegates and were debated through three or four days. They were amended in such various ways that we could make nothing of them. I finally proposed to a brother delegate, Stephen G. Roszel, that if he would second my motion I would move to lay all the amendments on the table, and take up the original report of the committee and adopt it. To this he assented, and the resolutions, as seen in the Discipline, were adopted. That these regulations have had a salutary influence on the Church I have no doubt, and therefore I reflect with much pleasure on the agency I had in drafting the report in its adoption.[55]

In the General Conference of 1816, a resolution was passed "to point out the course of study" for the young preachers as preparation for holy orders.[56] In the early years, college educated Methodist preachers were few and far between.[57] The alternate and time-honored method of ministerial training was a mentor–protege system. The success of this depended on the good graces of an elder minister nurturing and guiding along a young candidate until he could get along on his own. This did not excuse young ministers from devoting themselves to a life of study. On the contrary, the

55. Stevens, *Life and Times of Nathan Bangs*, 214–15.

56. Sherman, *History of the Revisions*, 37.

57. Frederick V. Mills errs by listing Nathan Bangs as "college trained." See Mills, "Mentors of Methodism," 51.

1784 *Discipline* required ministers to devote five hours of daily study and to preach periodic sermons on education.[58] This led to a variety of *ad hoc* courses of study created by the ministers themselves. There is evidence of this in the journals of James Sewell, William Colbert, Thomas Mann, and Elijah Steele.[59] Asbury and Bangs at least shared the experience of learning under this method of self-education. Bangs began his extensive reading prior to receiving a call to ministry. He went straight to the sources of the Wesleyan tradition. Bangs noted his theological odyssey in his journal: "Before I became acquainted with the Methodist . . . my theological reading had been confined mostly to Calvinistic authors; but now I began to read the writings of John Wesley and John Fletcher."[60]

The role of Bangs in the debate leading to the Course of Study has been scarcely recognized by Methodist historians.[61] Even studies focusing on Bangs mention little or nothing about his role in shaping theological education. For example, Richard Everett Herrmann's study does not mention it at all.[62] On the other hand, Steven W. Lewis observed that Bangs "pushed for higher educational standards" which led eventually to the mandated Course of Study.[63] Louis Dale Patterson provided a superbly thorough analysis of the Course of Study content from 1880 to 1920.[64] Russell E. Richey's *Formation for Ministry in American Methodism* mention's Nathan Bangs in his chapter on the course of study, but he does not credit him as the champion of the course of study.[65] Jared Maddox takes the position that Bangs "never meant for the Course of Study to be the first step toward requiring formal education for ordination."[66] However, there is strong evidence to suggest the contrary is true.

In 1816, the same year of Asbury's demise, the General Conference approved of Bangs' proposal for the Course of Study. This was truly a watershed event for the Methodist Episcopal Church. The Discipline was

58. Mills, "Mentors of Methodism," 52.

59. Mills, "Mentors of Methodism," 52.

60. Stevens, *Life and Times of Nathan Bangs*, 51.

61. Kenneth E. Rowe cites the example of Howard, "Controversies in Methodism." See Rowe, "New Light," 59.

62. Herrmann, "Nathan Bangs."

63. Lewis, "Nathan Bangs," 97.

64. Patterson, "Ministerial Mind."

65. Richey, *Formation for Ministry*, 34.

66. Maddox, *Nathan Bangs*, 29.

amended to reflect the change so that all future candidates would need to meet this requirement.[67]

> The Committee [on Ways and Means], chaired by Nathan Bangs of New York, specifically recommended that the Bishops, or annual conference committees appointed by them, "point out a course of reading and study proper to be pursued by candidates for the ministry" and that the Presiding Elders "shall direct" candidates to those studies. Henceforth no candidate was to be "received in full connexion" in an annual conference unless he could give satisfactory evidence to an examining committee of his attention to this requirement. The recommendation, which Bangs himself claimed to have authored, "encountered great opposition," but was finally approved after several days of debate.[68]

The list of required books in the first Course of Study was not officially recorded. However, there is an early list of important books recorded in the papers of Freeborn Garrettson (1752–1827).[69] The reading list is an impressive array of general works on theology, philosophy, and secular and sacred history. It is heavily dependent on Wesley's works and the Bible.[70] It is similar to a list compiled by the Illinois Conference of 1827. The list includes: "Wesley's *Notes* and *Sermons*, Benson's, Coke's and Clarke's commentaries, Fletcher's *Checks to Antinomianism*, Watson's *Institutes of Theology*, Locke's *On the Understanding*, Paley's *Philosophy*, Watt's *Logic*, *The Methodist Discipline*, and the *Methodist Magazine*."[71] The Philadelphia Conference of 1833 list is similar: "Watson, *Biblical and Theological Dictionary*, Porteus, *Evidences of Christianity*, Watson, *Theological Institutes*, and Wesley, *Sermons*; also included, but not required, were Fletcher, *Works*, Baxter, *Reformed Pastor*, and Paley, *View of the Evidences of Christianity* and *Natural Theology and Moral Philosophy*."[72]

There is a simple reason for the variations in the book lists. Although the requirement to complete the Course of Study was universal, the book

67. Rowe, "New Light," 61–62.

68. Rowe, "New Light," 59–60.

69. Nathan Bangs listed Freeborn Garrettson's earliest books as Russel's *Seven Sermons*, unspecified writings of Mr. Hervey, *The Travels of True Godliness*, Alleine's *Alarm to the Unconverted*, and unspecified publications by John Wesley. Bangs, *Life of Freeborn Garrettson*, 22–23.

70. Rowe, "New Light," 61–62.

71. Sweet, *The Methodists*, 303–4.

72. Barclay, *History of Methodist Missions*, 2:406n.

list was determined by the presiding elder or mentor. Not all presiding elders agreed on a standardized list. The Course of Study book list was first made uniform in 1848 when it was published in the *Discipline*.[73] The widespread use of this mode of theological education reveals a short list of Methodist "teachers" including: Adam Clarke, Richard Watson, and Daniel Whedon.[74]

The Wesleyan theologian who dominated during Bangs' time was British Methodist Richard Watson. His *Theological Institutes* was the only true standard work of systematic theology available to American Methodists. "The first part of this opus became a standard text in 1825 (before the last part was completed); the finished work continued on the Course of Study through 1876."[75] It is significant that Nathan Bangs edited and published Watson's *A Biblical and Theological Dictionary* (1833). Apparently his editorial work changed very little for the American edition: "Only that part of the work from the eight hundred and forty second page has been printed under the superintendence of the present editor."[76]

Nathan Bangs and his contemporary Willbur Fisk both made theological contributions to nineteenth-century American Methodism. However, they were largely limited to controversies with the Calvinists.[77] Steven W. Lewis considers Bangs as a significant theologian based on the Course of Study list provided in the *Christian Spectator* (ca. 1829). "The only American works on the course list were Nathan Bangs' treatises, *The Errors of Hopkinsianism* and *Examination of the Doctrine of Predestination*. This suggests the importance of Bangs' theological writings on early nineteenth-century American Methodism."[78]

Lewis is correct in his identification of Bangs as a significant theological thinker of the nineteenth century. However, he overstates the case by focusing only on his controversial works. The book list cited in the New Haven Congregationalist magazine *Christian Spectator* referred to a regional list, not a national list as Lewis erroneously concluded.

The design for the Course of Study passed, but not without later criticism. Rev. La Roy Sunderland wrote an article critiquing the Course

73. Chiles, *Theological Transition*, 32.

74. Chiles, *Theological Transition*, 32–33.

75. Chiles, *Theological Transition*, 33–34.

76. Nathan Bangs, "Advertisement to the American Edition," in Watson, *A Biblical and Theological Dictionary*.

77. Chiles, *Theological Transition*, 34.

78. Lewis, "Nathan Bangs," 97–99.

of Study at the request of the Junior Preachers' Society of the New England Conference. Originally the article was intended to be published in 1834 in the *Christian Advocate and Journal.* The senior editor refused to publish it because he "thought it unadvisable to insert it, as the subject had not been discussed in that paper." The following week it began as a series in the editorial section of the same paper but was soon discontinued. The full article was finally published in the *Methodist Magazine and Quarterly Review.* In brief, Sunderland considered the Course of Study inadequate in scope for the training of ministers.

> The course of study alluded to above, which the conferences require candidates for deacon's and eider's orders to pursue, embraces, on the subject of Christian theology, seven different works! Watson's Dictionary, Preacher's Manual, Wesley's Sermons, Fletcher's Portraiture of St. Paul, Porteus' Evidences, Watson's Apology for the Bible, and Watson's Theological Institutes—in all seven different works! And are these thought sufficient to give a student a competent knowledge of the science of interpreting the Bible? A sufficient knowledge of Christian theology for a public teacher of religion, to be derived from some half a dozen books![79]

The article notes that at the time of publication there were six colleges and fourteen seminaries under the direction of the Methodist Episcopal Church. Sunderland argued that increased requirements in theological education should be mandated in the *Discipline.* The motivation for advancing theological education was primarily evangelical, but with a definite sense of the prophetic.

> It is as clear as the light of noon day, that, for The Methodist Episcopal Church to do her part toward evangelizing the world, she must advance in the education of her ministers. Nay, if we mean to do our part of the work, which is due from the Church of God to the people of these United States, we must advance in the education of our ministers. This is a new country; the moral and intellectual habits of the people are yet, in no small degree, to be formed. This must be done by education, by sanctified education. Matter is moved by mind. And who will furnish the reading and the influence which is to mould and fashion the general character of this great and growing people? Those ministers who take the lead in promoting the means and blessings of

79. Sunderland, "Essay on a Theological Education," 431.

> sanctified learning will wield the future destinies of this powerful nation.[80]

The following issue featured a response to Sunderland's "doctrines dangerous to Methodism." Nathan Bangs, in his role as editor, included an extensive disclaimer defending Sunderland's essay. On several points the respondent "misapprehended" the sense of the argument. Furthermore, the editor noted his pleasure in that the essay resulted in the New England Conference adopting the measure to require theological education of their ministerial candidates prior to admission on trial.[81] Interesting to note that John Wesley's "Address to the Clergy" was considered authoritative enough to be quoted in Sunderland's defense.[82]

The criticism of Sunderland was leveled by David Meredith Reese, MD. His distaste for calling for increased theological requirements was filled with passion. Of his many examples of the folly of seminaries, his example of John Wesley's calling by the Holy Ghost calling is the most ironic for conveniently disregarding his Oxford education.

> Here we see what kind of minister Mr. Wesley was made by his "literary and theological training." . . . The truth is, he was made a minister by the Holy Ghost, either simultaneously with his conversion, or immediately after it; for he was not a minister of Christ until then, in his own opinion, notwithstanding his "training," and his ordinations superadded.[83]

Reese argued that it was never the case in early Methodism to require literary or theological education as an "indispensable" qualification for ministry. As further proofs, he alluded to the writings of British Methodists such as Wesley, Fletcher, Clarke, Watson, and American Methodists Asbury, Cooper, Bangs, and Emory. Most importantly, he offered the successful examples of such untrained ministers as John Newton, Francis Asbury, William Bramwell, Benjamin Abbott, and Freeborn Garrettson.[84] He cursed the MEC for following the way of theological seminaries.

> The name of "theological seminary" carries with its associations utterly repugnant to the feelings of our people, from the fact,

80. Sunderland, "Essay on a Theological Education," 437.

81. "Theological Education," editorial, 85.

82. John Wesley, "An Address to the Clergy," delivered in London, February 6, 1756, in *Works of John Wesley* (Jackson ed.), 10:480–500.

83. Reese, "Brief Strictures," 110.

84. Reese, "Brief Strictures," 112.

> that it is inseparable from the idea of "men-made ministers," by which we mean, those who have no "other qualification than the appointment of men, and human erudition," a class with which we have no fellowship, and with whom we love to have none. And if in the Methodist Church a distinct organization should ever be formed, in which young men are to be placed for a "theological training" to make them ministers, before the Church shall have acknowledged their call of God to this work, the glory will have departed from us as a people, and the purity of the sacred office, that high and holy calling, will be degenerated into a mere secular profession.[85]

In the end, Bangs and Sunderland won the battle for formalized theological education. These early theological schools were so successful that by 1855 Randolph S. Foster challenged the usefulness of the Course of Study for the training of MEC ministers.[86] James H. Perry's defense of the value of the Course of Study helped to keep it as a basic requirement for ministerial training.[87] The Course of Study enjoyed the greatest popularity from the mid-nineteenth to the early twentieth century when candidates for ministry gained access to divinity schools and seminaries.[88] Although seminaries have eclipsed the role of the Course of Study, it remains as an alternative method of theological education in the *Book of Discipline of The United Methodist Church.*[89]

Wesleyan Seminary (1822)

The late eighteenth-century experiments with Cokesbury College in Maryland (ca. 1787), Ebenezer Academy in Virginia (ca. 1784), Union School in Pennsylvania (1792), Bethel Academy in South Carolina (ca. 1793), and several smaller schools focused on the needs of young children, much in the tradition of Wesley's Kingswood School.[90] However,

85. Reese, "Brief Strictures," 115.

86. Foster, *A Treatise.*

87. Perry, *A Defense of the Present Mode.*

88. Louis Dale Patterson's 1984 dissertation, "The Ministerial Mind," remains the most thorough work on the role of the Course of Study in nineteenth-century American Methodism.

89. United Methodist Church, *Book of Discipline*, 1421.3d.

90. Cameron, "The New Church Takes Root," 266–71. For a detailed description of the educational philosophy of Kingswood School, see Body, *John Wesley and Education.*

most of these schools did not endure. Very little has been written concerning Wesleyan Seminary. This is odd since it was the real first attempt by Methodists to bring theological education out of the backwaters and into the city. The previous schemes to build denominational schools were unsuccessful, partly because of their primitive settings. In this sense, Wesleyan Seminary was ahead of its time. It is more curious as to why it failed.

As one might expect, Nathan Bangs was the most visible supporter of Wesleyan Seminary. He lost few opportunities to promote its usefulness. Bangs heaped praise upon Nathaniel Porter of the Philadelphia Conference and a particularly successful student of Wesleyan Seminary.

> The Wesleyan Seminary had just been established in the city of New York, and as one object of it was to give an education to pious young men whom we had reason to believe God had called to preach, brother Porter, soon after his conversion, entered as a student in this seminary, where he made rapid advancement in the knowledge of the Latin and Greek languages, and in mathematics, giving evidence, in the meantime, of his deep piety, and exercising his gifts occasionally in the pulpit, after having received license as a local preacher. In the spring of 1823, he was received on trial in the New York conference, and he soon gave satisfactory evidence of his call to the work of the ministry, and of his qualification for the faithful and successful discharge of its duties.[91]

Wesleyan Seminary was moved to a leased lot on Crosby Street in New York City. There they built a 2600-square-foot building for their classrooms and worship. Endeavoring to garner greater support, Nathan Bangs published a letter from William T. Alvis, a Wesleyan Seminary student and a member of the Tuscarora Native American Tribe. The emphasis was clearly the importance of theological education for missionary expansion. The language contains as much ingratiation as any contemporary alumni support letter.

> Rev. Sir,
>
> I address you, as you are the President of the Trustees, for the Wesleyan Seminary. By this means, I want you and the Trustees of the Wesleyan Seminary to understand my feelings toward you. I cannot, however, express all my feelings to you. I rejoice particularly, my good friends and patrons, that the Lord

91. Bangs, *A History of the Methodist Episcopal Church*, 4:135.

> has so disposed your hearts with His love, that you have been moved by compassion to aid and assist so unworthy a being as I am. My dear friends; I am now expressing the real sentiments of my heart—I feel as though I was not worthy of the least of God's notice, or of his people. I have been the greater part of my life brought up in ignorance, heathenish darkness and sin. And I do rejoice, and have rejoiced, and hope that I shall rejoice through all eternity, in the condescending mercy and goodness of God, and his people, in that he has invited me to come and partake of the blessings which He offers and gives to all who will accept of them, and that He has made his people subservient to my further progress and advancement in his holy way. My worthy and beloved patrons; I feel that I am under a thousand obligations to you, in that you have obeyed the Lord, and have administered so many comforts and blessings, in supplying my wants and necessities. Be pleased therefore to accept of my most humble thanks for all your kindnesses and favours, which you have bestowed upon me.
>
> I am now going by your permission to visit my beloved nation. I intend to start next Monday, and I sincerely wish and beg the prayers of your board. I do not know what my fate will be yet; but I put my trust in Him who is able to direct me in all his ways. Please to accept these my humble thanks and gratitude.
>
> I am your humble servant, William T. Alvis.[92]

Unfortunately, Alvis' appeals for Wesleyan Seminary were insufficient to generate the financial support needed to keep the school afloat. The school was moved to White Plains, New York in 1824. Meanwhile, the Book Concern purchased and occupied the Crosby Street building. The assets of Wesleyan Seminary were liquidated shortly thereafter and given to the White Plains academy for boys and girls.[93]

The ephemeral existence of Wesleyan Seminary was just another of several poor starts for Methodist higher education. The first was Cokesbury College in Abingdon, Maryland. Named in honor of Thomas Coke and Francis Asbury, Cokesbury College opened in 1787. Unfortunately, it burned down December 7, 1795, and again December 4, 1796. Some critics rejoiced at its closure. Devereux Jarratt, an Episcopalian, quipped, "I see not how any considerate man could expect any great things from a seminary of learning, while under the supreme direction and control of

92. Alvis, "Letter From William T. Alvis," 357–58.

93. Bangs, *A History of the Methodist Episcopal Church*, 3:216.

tinkers and taylors, weavers, shoemakers and country mechanics of all kinds."[94] Francis Asbury counted it as Divine judgment saying, "The Lord called not Mr. Whitefield nor the Methodists to build colleges. I wished only for schools—Doctor Coke wanted a college."[95]

Bangs' remarks about the closing of Wesleyan Seminary were much more positive. True, he conceded that the time was not quite right for Wesleyan Seminary. In his *History of the Methodist Episcopal Church*, Bangs concludes that the Wesleyan Seminary experiment was not a total failure, but the beginnings of something much better. "Though the Wesleyan seminary did not fully answer the benevolent designs of its original founders, it is believed that its establishment gave an impulse to the cause of education which has gone on increasing in power and influence to the present day."[96]

Bangs regularly published ministerial advice in the *Methodist Magazine*. The series was recognized for its usefulness and published into a book by vote of the New York Conference of 1825.[97] In light of the failure of Wesleyan Seminary, it was considered a reasonable supplement to the Course of Study. The Canadian Conference also passed a similar resolution to publish the series.

> Resolved, That the Conference respectfully request the Agents to republish, in a convenient volume, the excellent course of study published in the late volumes of the Magazine; at the same time wishing the author to make such amendments in the work as may to him appear most proper. Sept. 20, 1825
>
> Signed, William Case, Secretary[98]

The finished product included fifteen "letters" bound together as a 198-page pocket-sized book. The *Letters* covered a wide range of topics including: the importance of study and piety, biblical exegesis, apologetics, history, prophecy, miracles, theology, devotional literature, philosophy, rhetoric, poetry, biblical languages, polemics, ecclesiology, bibliographies, and practical theology. The sage advice was presented from the elder statesman Nathan Bangs himself. The originality of the series is somewhat in question. John Wesley's *Address to the Clergy* (1756)

94. Wigger, *Taking Heaven by Storm*, 176.
95. Asbury, *Journal of Rev. Francis Asbury*, 2:287.
96. Bangs, *History of The Methodist Episcopal Church*, 3:216.
97. Bangs, *Letters to Young Ministers*, iv.
98. Quoted in footnote in Bangs, *Letters to Young Ministers*, iv.

demonstrated the importance of theological education.[99] Bangs' book may also have been inspired by Adam Clarke's, *To the Junior Preachers (both Local and Traveling) in the Methodist Connexion* (1800).[100] It is undeniable that Bangs knew of Clarke's book since he reprinted parts of it along with his own in 1834.[101] The two books bear an uncanny resemblance to each other. Both advocate vital piety and broad reading in secular and sacred literature. A key passage in Clarke referred to preachers opposed to learning. "A treasury he has none; his coffers are all empty."[102]

Another related book was published containing Thomas Coke's *Four Discourses on the Duties of a Minister of the Gospel.*[103] This version of *The Preacher's Manual* went through several reprints in 1842, 1860, 1868, and 1880. The reprints are proof of the long-term commitment of the Methodist Episcopal Church to improve the quality of ministerial training. It also demonstrates the difficulty of the task begun by Nathan Bangs to alter popular attitudes resistant to an educated clergy.

Wesleyan University (1841)

> Surely an Institution of Learning consecrated to God by the prayers of a Fisk, and having inscribed upon its portals the name of a Wesley, who ever considered the Bible as the one book of his choice--an Institution founded, patronized, and supported by a Church which makes this Book of Books the rule of its faith and practice, should not be backward in adopting such a book as the guide of its youth, and the prime director of all its literary, as well as religious movements.[104]

A vigorous education campaign was begun following Asbury's death. It is estimated that over two hundred schools and colleges were founded by the Methodists between 1830 and 1860.[105] The flagship school was Wesleyan University, founded 1831 in Middletown, Connecticut.

99. John Wesley, "An Address to the Clergy,"" delivered in London, February 6, 1756, in *Works of John Wesley* (Jackson ed.), 10:480–500.

100. Macquiban, "Practical Piety or Lettered Learning," 92.

101. Bangs, *The Preacher's Manual*; Bangs, *Letters to Young Ministers.*

102. Adam Clarke, quoted in Macquiban "Practical Piety or Lettered Learning," 92.

103. Clarke and Coke, *The Preacher's Manual.*

104. Bangs, "Inaugural Address," 2.

105. Wigger, *Taking Heaven by Storm*, 176.

Willbur Fisk, a college educated Methodist minister, was appointed the first president of Wesleyan University. As Bangs would later proclaim, Fisk held a high view of both the Bible and Wesley.[106] Speaking at the 1835 anniversary celebration of the American Bible Society, Fisk gave the Bible the highest commendation. "The Bible—the Bible must direct and control the wheels of government, the principles of education, the character of the rising generation: this is our spiritual palladium, the glory of the churches, the honour of our nation, the salvation of the world."[107] He was also a great promoter of the doctrine of Christian perfection which he found in the writings of the exemplars of the faith including: the Fathers, Reformers, Thomas à Kempis, François Fénelon, the Marquis Gaston de Renty, Richard Hooker, George Herbert, Robert Leighton, John Bunyan, Henry Scougal, Philip Doddridge, Dr. and Mrs. Jonathan Edwards, David Brainerd, and Edward Payson.[108]

After Fisk's untimely death, Stephen Olin was installed as president of Wesleyan University. Olin was too ill to assume the duties necessary to run a university. It began to suffer the loss of funding and student enrollment. Nathan Bangs' brother Heman, a respected Methodist minister in Middletown, recommended brother Nathan as a replacement while Fisk prepared to visit England. Miles Martindale had objected to Fisk in a long letter.

> I am fully convinced that Dr. Bangs should come into the University as Professor of Moral and Intellectual Philosophy; and nothing more except that his character in the Faculty might assist in the Government of the Institution, but not that he should fill the place of the Presidency with many wishes Sir that this business may be settled to your satisfaction and to the satisfaction of Dr. Bangs.[109]

Now that Olin was unable to perform his duties, the Trustees seriously considered Heman's earlier recommendation. Nathan Bangs was asked to assume the presidency in Olin's absence. Acknowledging his lack of education and other inadequacies, Nathan Bangs finally accepted the presidency after repeated requests from the Trustees. Unfortunately, Bangs could not foresee the high cost which that would be exacted on his

106. Bangs, "Inaugural Address," 2.

107. Quoted in Holdich, *Life of Willbur Fisk*, 333.

108. Holdich, *Life of Willbur Fisk*, 69–70.

109. Miles Martindale to Willbur Fisk, 22 December 1834.

person. It was later said that his noble gift of two and a half years was the most sacrificial of all in Wesleyan's history.

> And yet probably there has been no man in the whole history of the college who for his faith in, and his affection for, Wesleyan University made greater sacrifices than did Nathan Bangs. He practically surrendered his career as an outstanding leader in his denomination to come to the rescue of the struggling college in her desperate plight, and he never again regained that leadership.[110]

The initial meeting of the student's association at Wesleyan University was very warm toward accepting Bangs as president. They acknowledged that it was not the best of circumstances. Yet, they were willing to give the Trustees due respect for their selection of Bangs.

> Resolved, That we highly appreciate the services rendered by Professor A. W. Smith, while our acting president, and that we present to him our grateful acknowledgments of his constant exertions to promote our literary advancement and personal happiness.
>
> Resolved, That we affectionately sympathize with Dr. Olin in his afflictions, occasioned by the prostration of his health, and sincerely lament his resignation as president of Wesleyan University.
>
> Resolved, That we heartily commend the wisdom of the joint board of trustees and visitors in their judicious selection of Dr. Bangs to the presidential chair, and cordially welcome him to our confidence and respect.
>
> Resolved, That these resolutions be signed by the president and secretary, and published in the "Constitution" and "Sentinel and Witness" of this city, the "Christian Advocate and Journal," and "Zion's Herald."[111]

The presence of Nathan Bangs immediately restored faith in the school. He already had a long history with Wesleyan University due to his chairing a joint board from 1833 to 1841.[112] Benefactors, confidence restored by a residential president, gave generously to relieve the mounting debts of the university. The initial reaction of the student body was very positive. E. Otis Haven, a Wesleyan student, reported this good favor

110. Price, "Nathan Bangs," 129.

111. "Wesleyan University," *Christian Advocate and Journal*, 127.

112. Potts, *Wesleyan University*, 24.

to an alumnus, Nathaniel C. Lewis. There is only a hint of reluctance to approve of his appointment.

> The University, your *Alma Mater*, is in good health, faithfully, under the guidance of Dr. Bangs, nursing and preparing us, your young brethren, to meet the world's demands, and buffet her storms. You are doubtless anxious to learn how we are pleased with the superintendence of Dr. Bangs. Though from long indulged expectation, & his extensive reputation, as a scholar, divine & gentleman, we should have much preferred Dr. Olin, yet Dr. Bangs, being, like Tippecanoe, "the most available candidate," & perhaps the best man in the Methodist connection to supply his place, is far from being unpropitious. The profs appear to be satisfied, & anxious as ever for the University's prosperity; & the students, aware of the exigencies of the case, are pleased from *necessity.* Moreover, Dr. Bangs is far from being such a man as you may have imagined. He is not reserved, haughty, nor over-bearing, but communicative & pleasant. You may have seen the resolutions, passed by the students a few weeks since, published in the "Advocate", etc.--they express no more than the sentiments of a majority of the students. The Dr. intends to establish a Theological class next term. From this enterprise, & eminent practical talents, we anticipate much prosperity, if N. England & N. York will pour in a sufficient quantum of Freshmen.[113]

The irenic tone of the letter gave no warning of the gathering storm. Nathan Bangs embarked on a dubious quest to make Wesleyan University "what its name implies—a university."[114] He introduced the study of medicine, law, theology, and teacher education. Confidence in his judgment was diminished even further when he stressed the Bible as the main document for study.

An unfortunate incident occurred when some students began circulating a petition for the removal of President Bangs. The idea had occurred to a group of students that Bangs was not sufficiently educated for the university presidency. This petition would lead to the ultimate destruction of Bangs' role as an educator and public figure. The petition in the form of a personal letter by Charles F. Stockwell, a Wesleyan student, sounded the discontentment of the student body.

113. Haven, "1842 to Nathaniel C. Lewis," Nathaniel C. Lewis.

114. Potts, *Wesleyan University*, 25.

> To president N. Bangs, D.D.
>
> Reverend Sir, we the undersigned members of the Wes. University, with all proper deference to yourself, as a worthy citizen & experienced clergyman, respectfully beg leave to say,
>
> We are & have been for a long time convinced that the sentiments of community & the interests of the University demand a change in the presidency of the college and we therefore hope, you will find it convenient to resign your office—please accept considerations of esteem.[115]

Bangs, his heart rent in two by the students' petition, promptly offered his resignation. The students celebrated upon hearing the news. The Trustees, on the other hand, were furious at the affair and tried to prevent his resigning. They gathered the students together and demanded an apology. Those who refused were threatened with expulsion. Stockwell's handwritten apology was sent to Wesleyan University.

> Whereas it is the opinion of the Faculty of the Wesleyan University that the Communication made by us on the 19th of May to the President, in regards to his official relation to this Institution, is a personal indignity to the President, an offense against the Government of the Institution, and an improper interference with the rights and duties of its official Guardians:
>
> Therefore, We the undersigned, while we disavow all wrong intention in the course which we adopted, do hereby express our acquiescence in the above opinion & our regret at having made the communication, and request that our names may be withdrawn from it.[116]

The Trustees were desperate to save the school from this crisis. However, not all the student petitioners agreed to sign the apology. After seventeen days of coercion and intimidation, more students were coaxed into signing a second apology.

> The undersigned hereby subscribe to the foregoing Documents and also acknowledge our fault in refusing to do so when the paper was previously presented by the Faculty.[117]

There was one holdout. John D. Pettee would not be permitted to graduate without an apology to the faculty. Realizing that his potential

115. Quoted in letter from Charles F. Stockwell to R. B. Hoyt, July 12, 1842.

116. "Acknowledgment of Students," June 13, 1842.

117. "Addendum to Acknowledgment," July 30, 1842.

for personal loss, he condescended with the greatest humility and economy of words. He was careful to address the president with his honorary title of "Dr."

> To the Faculty of the Wesleyan University
>
> Messrs. I acknowledge my contumacy in refusing to obey your commands and am willing to abide by your decision respecting the communication sent to Dr. Bangs.[118]

Though the apologies were received, Nathan Bangs refused to retract his resignation. Stephen Olin returned to the post in 1842. Bangs had the additional misfortune of being a New York Conference minister in a gerrymandered area of New England. There was already a great deal of resentment toward the New York Conference for control of southern New England. Bangs' brief tenure was as damaging to the reputation of Wesleyan University as to his own. Wesleyan's image became "too parochial in its patronage and mission, lacking in educational prestige, and overly expansionist in its curricular development."[119]

The profound sadness which Bangs felt is revealed in his personal letter to his friend, Dr. Stephen Olin, as he handed back the reins of Wesleyan to him. "I most earnestly pray that you may never be subjected to the same severity of trial as I have been—for it nigh well killed me."[120] Despite his few successes as a supporter of higher education, Bangs was ill equipped to fulfill the role of university president. His first and last efforts at developing educational institutions ended in failure. Abel Stevens offered this observation concerning Nathan Bangs' lifelong commitment to education.

> Nathan Bangs was not only one of the earliest, but one of the most active and persistent promoters of education in the denomination. Down to the last year of his life, his zeal for this great interest never abated. His early New England training had left an indelible impression of the importance of sound learning upon his liberal mind. He believed that the success of Methodism rendered it more responsible than any other American Christian body for the education of the common people, immense masses of whom had been gathered under his guardianship. Nor did he fear the influence of learning on its more intimately religious or ecclesiastical interests. As far as these

118. Pettee, "Apology to the Faculty."

119. Potts, *Wesleyan University*, 25.

120. Nathan Bangs to Stephen Olin, 20 August 1842.

> might be risked by education he was willing to risk them, assured that the result could not fail to be favorable to genuine religion.[121]

Summary

It has been argued that Nathan Bangs was not just the "representative" Methodist depicted by Abel Stevens but something more significant. According to E. Brooks Holifield: "He represented not the typical Methodist circuit rider but the relatively small number of clerical theologians who formulated an indigenous American theological tradition."[122] In other words, Bangs represented the minority ruling class of Methodist leaders. Clearly, Nathan Bangs devoted his career to improving Methodist respectability through his actions as a preacher, a publisher, and an educator. Although his motivation was likely pietistic, his devices were unquestionably political. His involvement in acts of annual conference legislation offers ample proof of his political prowess.[123] As a preacher, he entered the primal structure of the Methodist Episcopal Church and implemented organizational changes needed during a time of massive growth. The MEC's expansion into denominational publishing gave him the perfect "bully pulpit" for disseminating his ideas and censoring dissonant voices. As an educator, he designed a system for indoctrinating new recruits to ministry. Furthermore, he helped establish educational guidelines for intellectual and spiritual formation for the new generation of Methodists. The reorganization of church bureaucracy, publishing, and education created a new way of being a Methodist. It was no

121. Stevens, *Life and Times of Nathan Bangs*, 233.

122. Holifield, "Nathan Bangs," 121.

123. Journals of the General Conference indicate Bangs' high profile, although he made no motions in 1808. In all the other General Conferences attended he had a higher-than-average presence in the presentation of resolutions, motions, co-sponsoring the same, and taking appointment on committees to consider important items such as: Episcopacy, Revisal and Publishing of the Discipline, Ways and Means, British and Canadian Affairs, Missions and Bible Society, Book Concern, Education, American Colonization Society, Temporal Economy, History, and hearings of appeals for expelled clergy. He was conspicuously absent from the 1848 General Conference. See MEC, *Journals of the General Conference*, 1:1796–836. Bangs claimed that he was left off as a delegate because of his open opposition to the editor of *The Christian Advocate* regarding his own antislavery position and his vote to repeal the 1840 Act of the Session to disregard the testimony of "colored people" in Church trials. Stevens, *Life and Times of Nathan Bangs*, 338–41.

longer merely a rudimentary system of organized circuits, chapels, Bibles and Discipline. The second generation of the MEC fully evolved into a political machine complete with bureaucratic controls and limiting institutional structures.

Bangs' career successes raised the social status of the MEC resulting in several immediate gains. The denomination's expansions via organized missions helped extend the territory of the United States. Besides the increased membership by evangelism, the MEC also gained political clout by virtue of its size, widespread influence, and increased wealth. Literacy and communications improved with the expansion of denominational publications. So, also did the shaping of public thought work to raise social expectations to new levels of respectability. Educational standards were almost certainly improved with the establishment of educational institutions for the rising middle class. Theological education of Methodist clergy improved in quality and consistency because of the Course of Study and the establishment of theological seminaries. As the next chapter will demonstrate, these significant gains contributed to a new class consciousness for the MEC which in turn contributed to making Methodist worship "respectable."

Chapter III

DECOROUS WORSHIP

> "Methodist," said I; "what's that? What sort of people are they?" "Ah," said he, "they are the strangest people you ever saw; they shout and halloo so loud you may hear them for miles; they hold that all will be saved, and a man can live without sin in this life and yet that a Christian can fall from grace."[1]

MIDDLE-CLASS METHODISTS MAY HAVE grimaced on the unhappy occasion when one of their country preachers wandered into town dressed in his black Quaker-style outfit. No less embarrassing was the corybantic worship style of rural Methodists. The infamous circuit rider Peter Cartwright was not ashamed to admit he was a "shouting Methodist." In the early years, the MEC was largely identified as a revivalist movement. As such, Methodists and their constituent members prized enthusiastic worship, vital piety, and perfectionist doctrine. Their informal mode of worship extended beyond the local circuits to broader fields of missions. Camp meetings were the populist arena for religious expression and the seed bed for popular piety. There the "practical and experimental divinity" of the Wesleys found unlikely bedfellows with the rustic maxims of the brush arbor revivalists. The result was an odd blending of sacred hymns and nostalgic choruses. As a byproduct, Methodist meetings were also known as venues for public displays of emotion and religious fanaticism.

1. Cartwright, *Autobiography*, 148.

Earlier, Bishop Francis Asbury's army of circuit riders disseminated the Wesleyan message of holiness wherever they preached. The popularity of exciting missionary anecdotes lured Methodist preachers to the far reaches of the frontier. Rural Methodist chapels depended on traveling preachers to nurture and feed them according to their place on the circuit. Circuit riders had the additional burden of organizing stations into new chapels. These points were often used to hold evangelistic worship services in the mode of camp meetings. From Long Island to the Western Reserve, Methodist preachers used camp meetings to evangelize *en masse.* New churches that formed out of these campaigns were able to "sustain and routinize the socializing power of the camp meeting."[2] By the mid-nineteenth century, the evangelistic successes of the MEC reached deep into the fast-moving socialite scenes of city life. Backwoods Methodist preachers, legendary for their plain form of preaching and singing, became an oddity in urban America.

The movement toward respectability exerted tectonic pressure on the social structure of the local church often resulting in white-hot friction between the generations. Changes in class in turn effected the preferred oratory worship styles of the local congregation. By 1832, it was plain that the MEC's in New York City were becoming more "church-like." They demanded educated clergy to lead more formalized Sunday services. Churches were being pulled away from the idea of circuit preachers and implemented the concept of a "settled pastorate."[3] Nathan Bangs, one of the first settled pastors and a strong champion of settled pastorates, experienced the change firsthand. The occasional incursions of ecstatic behavior into churches grated hard on the up and coming Methodists. As Bangs demonstrated at New York's John Street Church, the spirits of these prophets were subject to the order of the *Discipline.* This chapter will examine how rising respectability altered sacred speech in Methodist worship especially in preaching, hymnody, discipline and prayer.

Preaching

> His [Bangs'] ability in the pulpit attracted the people in crowds at his numerous appointments, for his word was in "demonstration of the Spirit and of power." . . . If not intellectually polished,

2. Mcloughlin, *Revivals, Awakenings, and Reform*, 133.

3. Hardt, *The Soul of Methodism*, 65.

> he was intellectually powerful; a certain mightiness of thought and feeling bore down at times all before him, especially when he preached to large assemblies at quarterly and camp-meetings. At one of the latter it was estimated that two hundred hearers were awakened under a single sermon; they fell, like wounded men, on the right and on the left; he preached on for two hours; and it is said that an earthquake, shaking the camp throughout those awful hours, could hardly have produced a more irresistible excitement.[4]

Preaching has always been the central element in Protestant worship. Methodism is no exception. John Wesley suggested that preaching Gospel and Law should be in this order. "At our first beginning to preach at any place, after a general declaration of the love of God to sinners, and his willingness that they should be saved, to preach the law, in the strongest, the closest, the most searching manner possible; only intermixing the gospel here and there, and showing if, as it were, afar off."[5] After Wesley, early Methodist preachers disregarded exegetical accuracy in favor of inflaming "stone-cold hearts" and rekindling "the lukewarm by the power of the gospel, through the agency of the Holy Spirit."[6] Nathan Bangs method of evangelistic preaching relied on the power of the Spirit and human reason. His presentation style marked him as "a master of theology and logic, and better known among the sects than almost any Methodist preacher, except Asbury."[7]

Mass Evangelism

The Methodist emphasis on evangelistic preaching was by no means confined to the venue of the local chapel. Rather, it became the preferred mode for communicating to the masses at public gatherings such as camp meetings and quarterly meetings. The techniques of calling sinners to repentance were refined in the emotional smelting pots of camp meetings. This informal mode of religious gathering was especially popular in rural areas, although it was not an exclusively rural phenomenon. It flourished so widely that it is difficult to separate camp meetings from

4. Stevens, *Life and Times of Nathan Bangs*, 207.

5. John Wesley, "Letter on Preaching Christ," London, December 20, 1751, in *Works of John Wesley* (Jackson ed.), 11:486–87.

6. Tucker, *American Methodist Worship*, 36.

7. Stevens, *Life and Times of Nathan Bangs*, 207.

American Methodist piety. They became most popular during the liminal period between the Great Awakening and the Second Great Awakening.[8] Such gatherings produced an environment where evangelistic preaching was highly effective. Therefore, they became the preferred and well-worn tool by which Methodists extended and sustained the effects of the Second Great Awakening.[9] The camp meeting was already an institution by the time Nathan Bangs entered national prominence. Samuel Kennerly reported to Bangs of the visible effectiveness of camp meetings for mass evangelism.

> On the last morning of the meeting, we called up the penitents to pray with them for the last time at that place, and there were about thirty who came forward; five and twenty of them were males, and some of the first families in that country. The second camp-meeting also appeared to commence, progress and end, under the superintendence of the Most High. It is thought that a least one hundred souls were raised from a death of sin to a life of righteousness, at this meeting, the most of whom were young men of respectability. It was observed that in general their struggle for redemption was much more severe than usual, and the evidence of their acceptance much clearer than common.[10]

Methodist camp meetings originated from three separate traditions: Methodist, Scottish Reformed, and Quaker. The Methodist roots can be traced to the open-air preaching of George Whitefield, John Wesley, and Charles Wesley. Methodist preachers were often not welcome in Church of England pulpits, even though the Wesleys and Whitefield were ordained Anglican ministers.[11] John Wesley first preached outdoors when he was put out of his father's church at Epworth. The familiar engraving by George Washington Brownlow illustrates Wesley preaching from atop his father's tombstone outside St. Andrew's Church.[12] This exercise was distinct from his later experiences of field preaching because graves were considered the property of the family of the deceased. George Whitefield encouraged Wesley to emulate his own successes by field preaching to the poor colliers at Hanham Mount near Kingswood. A well-rehearsed description of this first open-air preaching is quite dramatic. "The first

8. Richey, *Early American Methodism*, 21.

9. Ruth, *A Little Heaven Below*, 189.

10. Kennerly, "Work of God," 348.

11. Edwards, "John Wesley," 53.

12. Pudney, *John Wesley and His World*, 82.

discovery of their being affected was to see the white gutters made by their tears, which plentifully fell down their black cheeks as they came out of their coal pits."[13] Wesley, convinced of the efficacy of field preaching, thereafter "submitted to be more vile" by following Whitefield's example.

Charles Wesley also had firsthand experience with preaching in the open air at Thaxted, or Thackstead, at the invitation of some Quakers.[14] Charles Wesley recorded this outdoor evangelism event in his journal. "Many Quakers, and near seven hundred others, attended, while I declared in the highways, 'the Scripture hath concluded all under sin.'"[15] Shortly afterward Charles preached from a tomb stone when put out of his Islington parish.[16] The three evangelists regularly preached at Hanham Mount and the "brickyards" and the "bowling green" in Bristol. Thus, they established open air preaching as a normative aspect of Methodist ministry.[17] Whitefield later carried his method of open-air preaching to America. His powerful voice and masterful oratory even drew the attention of the Philadelphia statesman Benjamin Franklin.[18]

American Methodists were influenced by another important outdoor worship tradition of "sacramental seasons" imported and practiced openly by Scottish Protestant immigrants. This tradition was also called "communion seasons" or "holy fairs."[19] During the Scottish Reformation, the Ulster-Scots, or Scotch-Irish, developed an open-air service, a formal ancestor of the informal camp meeting. These religious gatherings were held in outlying areas to meet the sacramental needs of rural folk. They were marked by periods of fasting and reflection. This annual or biannual event would continue for a matter of days before culminating in celebration of the Lord's Supper in the outdoors.[20]

George Whitefield reportedly preached to over thirty-thousand people at the famed "Cambuslang Wark" in 1742.[21] Furthermore, he

13. Eayrs, *Wesley and Kingswood*, 46.
14. Jackson, *Life of Charles Wesley*, 156.
15. Wesley, *Journal of Charles Wesley*, 1:151.
16. Jackson, *Life of Charles Wesley*, 156.
17. Wakefield, *The Spiritual Life*, 80–81.
18. Stout, *The Divine Dramatist*, 220.
19. Schmidt, *Holy Fairs*, 3.
20. Noll, *A History of Christianity*, 69.
21. Burleigh, *A Church History of Scotland*, 292–93.

made at least fourteen trips to Scotland during his career, often participating in the sacramental seasons.[22]

> Last Lord's day, I preached in the morning, in the park at Edinburgh, to a great multitude. Afterwards, I attended, and partook of the holy sacrament, and served four tables. In the afternoon, I preached in the churchyard, to a far greater number. Such a passover, I never saw before.[23]

Although John Wesley made as many as twenty-two visits to Scotland, he was not impressed by the Scottish form of communion. "How much more simple, as well as more solemn, is the service of the Church of England."[24] Wesley's preference for the Anglican sacramental ritual prevented him from adopting the Scottish service for his Wesleyan preachers. The Scottish tradition entered America by way of the Scottish and Ulster-Scot Presbyterian immigrants. Enclaves of Presbyterian immigrants almost immediately staged sacramental occasions fully reminiscent of Scotland and Ulster.[25] The most famous of these immigrants was James McGready. He successfully celebrated the sacramental season eighteen times from 1797 to 1800.[26] Shortly thereafter, he joined Barton W. Stone, another Presbyterian, in organizing teams of Presbyterian, Methodist, and Baptist preachers for a meeting at Cane Ridge. Elements reminiscent of the sacramental season such as the action sermon, table service, and plurality of ministers were evident at Cane Ridge.[27] Presbyterians, Baptists, and Methodists participated in the event together creating a nonsectarian atmosphere. Consider the utopian account offered by Levi Purviance.

> This was not a sectarian meeting, although it was held at a Presbyterian meeting house. Baptist, Methodist, and Presbyterians were simultaneously engaged.
>
> Perfect friendship, unanimity, and brotherly kindness prevailed. They had come together, to the help of the Lord against the mighty, and "Zion was terrible as an army with banners." The meeting lasted six days; the last sermon that was delivered

22. Burleigh, *A Church History of Scotland*, 293.
23. Whitefield to Mr. John Cennick, 16 June 1742, in Whitefield, *Letters*, 513.
24. Burleigh, *A Church History of Scotland*, 294.
25. Schmidt, *Holy Fairs*, 53.
26. Schmidt, *Holy Fairs*, 63.
27. Schmidt, *Holy Fairs*, 64.

> on the occasion was by a Methodist preacher, by the name of Samuel Hitt. It is known only to God how many were converted at this meeting. There were no means by which even to ascertain how many professed religion. The object of the meeting was not to build up any sect or party, but to bring sinners to the Savior.[28]

From the enterprising evangelist's perspective, the camp meeting was the perfect method for mass evangelism. It created an atmosphere where worship appealed to the heart, Christian virtues were profound, and resistance to conversion was diminished. Barton Stone was so affected by the catholicity of Cane Ridge that he defected from Presbyterianism. He later joined Alexander Campbell in founding the restorationist group known as the Christian Church or Disciples of Christ. Fifty years afterward, Stone recollected Cane Ridge as a fruitful revival, though mixed with fanaticism.

> Having heard of a remarkable religious excitement in the south of Kentucky, and in Tennessee, under the labors of James McGready and other Presbyterian ministers, I was very anxious to be among them; and, early in the spring of 1801, went there to attend a camp-meeting. . . . The scene to me was new, and passing strange. It baffled description. Many, very many fell down, as men slain in battle, and continued for hours together in an apparently breathless and motionless state—sometimes for a few moments reviving, and exhibiting symptoms of life by a deep groan, or piercing shriek, or by a prayer for mercy most fervently uttered. After lying thus for hours, they obtained deliverance. The gloomy cloud, which had covered their faces, seemed gradually and visibly to disappear, and hope in smiles brightened into joy—they would rise shouting deliverance, and then would address the surrounding multitude in language truly eloquent and impressive.[29]

Nathan Bangs appreciated the spirit of catholicity prevalent in camp meetings. He was also well aware of its historical connection to the Reformed tradition. As mentioned above, Bangs was rarely known to put aside his strong prejudices against Calvinists. Yet, he was willing to overlook the Reformed connection to camp meetings for the promise of spiritual blessings. In this instance, he was a true Wesleyan pragmatist.

28. Purviance, *Biography of Elder David Purviance*, 301.

29. Stone, *Biography of Elder Barton Warren Stone*, 35.

On the other hand, Bangs had no qualms about writing camp meetings into Methodist history and tradition.

> It will be seen by the preceding remarks that these camp meetings were not the result of a previously digested plan, but like every other peculiarity of Methodism, were introduced by providential occurrences, and were embraced and followed up by God's servants because they found them subservient to the grand design they had in view, namely, the salvation of the world by Jesus Christ. Indeed, they did not originate with the Methodists, but upon a sacramental occasion among the Presbyterians, at which time there was such a remarkable outpouring of the Divine Spirit in the people as inclined them to protract their exercises to an unusual period; and then this being noised abroad brought others to the place, and finally so many that no house could hold them; this induced them to go into the field, and erect temporary shelters for themselves, and to bring provision for their sustenance; and finding God so abundantly blessed them in these meetings, they were led to continue them, until they at length became very general among the Methodists throughout the country.[30]

Initially, the Presbyterians, like other groups, received numerous converts from camp meetings. However, Presbyterians were less at ease with the disorderly conduct associated with these gatherings. Furthermore, they were not reticent to express publicly their disenchantment. In 1805, the General Assembly denounced camp meetings on the grounds that "God is a God of order and not of confusion, and whatever tends to destroy the comely order of his worship is not from him."[31] The earlier form of Scottish Reform communion festivals peaked in significance for American religious life by 1815.[32] A similar fate befell camp meetings in England. Lay preachers Hugh Bourne and William Clowes invited the eccentric American lay evangelist Lorenzo Dow to organize an American style camp meeting. The first English camp meeting was held at a hill called Mow Cop on May 31, 1807. The Wesleyan Conference feared the camp meetings were havens for violent emotionalism, sexual promiscuity,

30. Bangs, *History of the Methodist Episcopal Church*, 2:111–12.

31. Hudson and Corrigan, *Religion in America*, 149.

32. Schmidt, *Holy Fairs*, 60.

and seditious activity.[33] Later that year, they officially condemned camp meetings.

> It is our judgment, that even supposing such meetings to be allowable in America, they are highly improper in England, and likely to be productive of considerable mischief. And we disclaim all connexion with them.[34]

The peripatetic lay preacher Hugh Bourne was expelled from the British Wesleyans in 1808 on the flimsy grounds that he missed a class meeting. This was a serious offense according to the class rules. However, Bourne and Clowes continued to promote camp meetings under the aegis of their newly formed Society of Primitive Methodists, 1810.[35] American Methodists had no trouble accommodating the Spirit-filled religion of the camp meeting. It engendered a receptive mood for evangelism and renewal. It was so well received that it practically became a means of grace among American Methodists.

In 1748, the British itinerant John Bennet scheduled quarterly meetings for two circuits. The success of this experiment caught John Wesley's attention. He decided to adopt this Quaker tradition rather than the Scottish Reform tradition. At the 1749 Annual Conference, Wesley appointed Bennet to instruct his preachers in mandatory quarterly meetings.[36] Bishop Asbury adopted the camp meeting as an expansion of the quarterly meeting.[37] The quarterly meeting insured a certain regularity for camp meetings. The importance of quarterly meetings as a venue for Methodist worship began to fade in 1802, so that camp meetings dominated the scene by 1812.[38] Quarterly meetings were still important for administrative purposes, but camp meetings took over the "liturgical and evangelistic aspects" of American Methodism.[39] The early Methodist camp meetings were considered liturgical because they included communion as part of the service.[40]

33. Davies, *Methodism*, 115–16.
34. Wesleyan Methodist Conference, *Minutes*, 2:403.
35. Davies, *Methodism*, 116–17.
36. Ruth, *A Little Heaven Below*, 18–19.
37. Richey, *Early American Methodism*, 31.
38. Ruth, *A Little Heaven Below*, 187.
39. Ruth, *A Little Heaven Below*, 188–89.
40. Schmidt, *Holy Fairs*, 214.

In 1805, Henry Ryan and William Case introduced camp meetings to Canada while Nathan Bangs was still a missionary there.[41] As an added benefit, the extended worship services brought spiritual refreshment for weary Canadian itinerants. Bangs reported an instance of personal renewal as a result of these services. "Great was the good that followed. . . . I returned to Augusta Circuit and renewed my labors, somewhat worn, but full of faith and the Holy Ghost."[42] Bangs was very successful in utilizing camp meetings and quarterly meetings to plant new congregations in his circuit. At his eulogy, Bishop Edmund Storer Janes would remark on this aspect of Bangs' ministry in the Rhinebeck District (ca. 1813).

> Dr. Bangs was then at the maturity of his manhood. His preaching was powerful; his quarterly meetings and camp-meetings were jubilatic occasions, crowded by multitudes from many miles around. He traversed his vast district a son of thunder, and before he left it was begun that zealous provision of chapels and parsonages which has dotted the whole region with Methodist edifices—a chapel and a preacher's house in almost every village.[43]

A century later, Joseph Edward Sanderson judged Canadian camp meetings as having "harmonized with the earnest, evangelizing spirit of Methodism and proved mightily effective in awakening and arousing whole communities."[44] Francis Asbury was solidly convinced of the camp meeting's usefulness in evangelism. This is evident from his journal entry dated 24 September 1808. "I rejoice to think there will be perhaps four or five hundred camp-meetings this year; may this year outdo all former years in the conversion of precious souls to God! Work, Lord, for this own honour and glory!"[45]

Nathan Bangs credited the massive growth of the MEC to camp meetings. "If the Methodist Church in America has increased beyond any parallel during one fourth of a century past, we must ascribe much of her spiritual prosperity, under God, to the blessed influence of such meetings."[46]

41. Sanderson, *First Century of Methodism in Canada*, 44–45.

42. Stevens, *Life and Times of Nathan Bangs*, 154–55.

43. Janes, *Sermon on the Death of Nathan Bangs*, 20.

44. Sanderson, *First Century of Methodism in Canada*, 45.

45. Asbury, *Journal of Rev. Francis Asbury*, 3:287.

46. Nathan Bangs, editorial in *Christian Advocate*, September 9, 1826, quoted in McNaim, "Mission to Canada," 58.

The main criticism of American Presbyterians and British Wesleyans against camp meetings was that they elicited emotional and unruly behavior. Unquestionably, there were ample reports of emotionalism and motor phenomena. Excitement was manifested vocally as "a sudden burst of the groans, shrieks, and cries of sinners, and acclamations of joy and shouts of Christians."[47] Nathan Bangs reported having personally experienced physical evidence of affective religion when he was preaching at a camp meeting in Canada.

> At midnight, on the last night, while an indescribable sense of the divine presence prevailed throughout the encampment, he stood on a log and exhorted the people with overwhelming effect, his powerful voice reverberating over the ground and through the woods. While stretching out his arms, as if to bless the weeping multitude, they stiffened and remained extended, and for some time he stood thus addressing the hearers, weeping with them that wept. He was at last led to a tent, but with still extended arms. The strange effect continued there, but did not disturb his religious joy.
>
> "I was continually uttering praise; the tent was soon crowded, and at a single utterance the whole group fell to the ground.
>
> 'O'erwhelmed with His stupendous grace
> They did not in His presence move:
> But breathed unutterable praise
> in rapturous awe and silent love.'
>
> [I felt] a prickling sensation over the whole body, like that felt when a limb is said to be asleep; but this was followed by a soft, soothing feeling, as if I were anointed with oil, and such a consciousness of the presence and peace of God pervaded me as I cannot describe."[48]

Despite numerous critiques against religious fanaticism, camp meetings thrived as the preferred venue for evangelistic preaching for many years. Their popularity was their simple and effective means of generating new recruits.[49] On the other hand, evangelistic preaching styles most associated with emotional outbursts did not easily cross over into congregational settings. A "widening gulf" formed between expressions

47. Wright, *Sketches*, 181.

48. Stevens, *Life and Times of Nathan Bangs*, 155, 156.

49. Hatch, *Democratization*, 55.

of camp meeting religion and structure of church religion.[50] Consequently, evangelistic preaching, associated with camp meetings, became less prominent in the local church.

Class Meetings

> The revival for the first fortnight was rapid in its spread—glorious in its progress. . . . To forcible and energetic exhortations our pastors added the precepts and doctrines of practical and experimental religion—while polemical divinity and disputes concerning non-essentials (those bulwarks on which bigotry erects her throne, and from which she hurls her anathemas) were as much as possible avoided.[51]

Converts of revivals were usually funneled into classes where they would be taught doctrine in the Methodist tradition. Preaching didactic sermons bypassed the process. As local congregations became more important, evangelistic preaching lost prominence.[52] The camp meeting demanded evangelistic fervor. Settled congregations demanded education in the pulpits and in the pews. Abel Stevens noted that the former preachers "came out from the people, and knew how to address the people; and the popular effects of their preaching, the great massive in-gatherings of the people into their communion, are a demonstration of their power nothing short of magnificent."[53] The induction of ministerial candidates into seminaries received criticism for removing students from real life situations and isolating them in cloisters of theological education.[54] The importance of teaching, rather than converting, was instilled into the young preachers. This emphasis may be traced to the practice of using class meetings as a follow-up to mass evangelism.

> Have just returned from Camp-meeting held at Compo. It was a time of God's power; many were converted, many reclaimed, many sanctified. Glory be to God—to His name be praise forever and ever! We had a trial of our faith, being detained by

50. Taves, *Fits, Trances, & Visions*, 235.

51. Bangs, "Revival of the Work of God," 350, 351.

52. Hatch, *Democratization*, 49.

53. Stevens, *Essays on the Preaching Required*, 125. This book is a compilation of articles originally published in the *National Magazine* (1854) and *Methodist Quarterly Review* (1852).

54. Holland, *The Preaching Tradition*, 68.

> a terrible storm from Friday until Monday noon. We continued our meetings, and about thirty were converted during the storm. I took sixteen from this place into Class.[55]

In the quote above, Heman Bangs confirmed that converts were usually channeled into the Methodist system by way of class meetings. Their simple, but organized structure created a new subgroup apart from the normal social order. The genius of the class meeting was its inner and outer experience of living discipleship and grace.[56] However, it could not keep pace with the momentum of the social upheaval at this time. Lack of accountability and dry formalism were blamed for low attendance and defunct classes.[57] The class leader functioned as a lay pastor who was expected to exhort class members in the absence of a preacher. The availability of "stationed ministers" not only eliminated circuits, but it also diminished the role of the class leader.[58] The class meeting faded as the MEC was divided between camp meeting religion and the liturgically based church religion. Consequently, the more formal churches directed resources into mission societies and service groups.[59] The teaching emphasis naturally carried over into preaching by the settled ministers.

> Let us not think, then, that we require in our large cities only educated and polished preachers and restricted modes of labor; these we must have, but we get need these, as much as if not more than in the first days of Methodism, voices "crying in the wilderness, Prepare ye the way of the Lord"—men who will "circuit" these cities as did our fathers, and, like them, preach continually and powerfully the primary truths of religion among the neglected populace.[60]

Upwardly mobile Methodists demanded educated preachers with a mastery of elocution. But they still wanted substance in the message. The senior Methodists, represented by figures such as James Quinn, a pioneer preacher from Ohio, reluctantly acknowledged the demand. However, they regarded it with suspicion in the work of the preaching ministry.

55. Bangs, *Autobiography and Journal*, 139.
56. Watson, *The Early Methodist Class Meeting*, 145.
57. Watson, *The Early Methodist Class Meeting*, 146–47.
58. Hardt, *The Soul of Methodism*, 69.
59. Taves, *Fits, Trances, & Visions*, 235.
60. Stevens, *Essays on the Preaching Required*, 151.

> Well, now, I think that this plain, Scriptural, common-sense kind of preaching, goes very well; and with intelligent, well-informed men, I know many that greatly prefer it; and as to those who only *think* themselves intelligent, or wise, perhaps there is as little hope of them now as there was in the days of Solomon; and, may be, St. Paul would tell them that they must become fools, that they may become wise.[61]

Those preachers who graduated from the so-called "Brush College" of mentored ministry did not have the advantages belonging to Course of Study trained ministers. Between 1830 and 1858, the list included as preaching instruction *Preacher's Manual*, by Adam Clarke, and *Rhetoric*, by Alexander Jamieson. These were replaced in 1858 by Nicholas Snethen's *Identifier*.[62]

Ministerial candidates outside the bounds of Course of Study could make use of short articles on preaching reprinted and serialized in MEC publications. The availability of these resources facilitated continuing education for active ministers in the field, regardless of age or experience. In 1828, John Wesley's "Thoughts on Preaching the Gospel" was reprinted in the Methodist Review as an aid to young preachers. In the article, Wesley stated that the three emphases of preaching were doctrine, salvation, and experience.[63] Nathan Bangs focused more on the attitude and carriage of the preaching task. In his serialized *Letters to Young Ministers of the Gospel*, Bangs offered seven keys to oratory success.

> Well, then, first study yourself. 2. Understand your subject. 3. Feel its importance. 4. Keep master of yourself- that is, be not depressed by timidity, nor swoln [*sic*] with self-confidence and vanity. 5. While you derive all the knowledge you can from every source, and especially from all you hear and read, make no efforts to imitate any man, neither in his gestures, the intonations of his voice, nor the peculiar enunciation of his words. 6. Set God always before you; and as if standing upon the threshold of eternity, labour as though this might be your last effort to save those who now hear you. And if you must have artificial helps, study Blair, Campbell, Maury, Knox, and Wesley. But, above all, if you would succeed in accomplishing the all-important end of your mission, be most solicitous for the holy anointing.[64]

61. James Quinn, quoted in Wright, *Sketches*, 260.

62. Patterson, "Ministerial Mind," 56.

63. Wesley, "Thoughts on Preaching the Gospel," 346–48.

64. Bangs, *Letters to Young Ministers*, 99.

Bangs' suggestions were very much in Wesley's tradition of pairing together knowledge and vital piety. His published advice to a "Junior Preacher" to be of a "serious and solemn" deportment meant that preaching was not a craft to be taken lightly. Rather, it was a "labour for God."[65] This was a way of teaching the congregation, by example, that preaching was sacred speech, not merely human oratory to be mimicked.

William Jay's lectures taught that didactic preaching offered the potential to lift a congregation beyond their own level on knowledge. Such preaching was not only admonished, but it was also considered a duty to the uneducated.

> Now a preacher need not grovel down to the lowest level of the vulgar; yea, he should always take his aim a little above them, in order to raise and improve their taste: but he must not soar out of their sight and reach. He yet may be tempted to this by the presence of others. But let him remember, that those who are more educated and refined, ought not only to endure but to commend his accommodation;—yea, and they will commend instead of censuring him, if they are really concerned for the welfare of their brethren less privileged than themselves.[66]

Thomas Maddin was not as happy with the developments of Methodist preaching in the 1850s. He lamented that some preachers left behind the fiery form of piety of "Young Methodism" for a "form without the power of godliness."[67] In his exposé of an unidentified "Mr. R," he cited several unfavorable characteristics of the gentlemanly, though apostate, Methodist preacher.

> His congregations were of the *elite*. His discourses were of the popular character. His position might be regarded as by the would-be-great, for though there were but too evidently the marks of deterioration of his piety, there were none of his popularity. His sermons were fine specimens of cultivated intellect, finely arranged, naturally connected, logically argued, rhetorically polished, and sonorously delivered.[68]

Mr. R stood in quite a contrast to the earlier descriptions of Cartwright and Bangs. Cartwright possessed none of Bangs' polish but

65. Bangs, "Letter to a Junior Preacher," 114.

66. Jay, "Remarks on Preaching," 208.

67. Maddin, *The Apostate Methodist Preacher*, 67.

68. Maddin, *The Apostate Methodist Preacher*, 67.

depended on his spiritual fervor. Bangs achieved eloquence, but maintained his appreciation of religious fervor, though in controlled measures. A. Vinet, the nineteenth-century French homiletics professor, taught preachers that instructing doctrine was the goal of pulpit eloquence. "The preacher's chief business is instruction; this is the basis of his work; exhortation, reproof, sharpens his teaching, but it is always teaching."[69] In fact, didactic preaching created a tendency to be more uniform in emphasis by keeping Methodist doctrine central. Polemical preaching, more popular in Bangs' early ministry, was de-emphasized where Methodism became more respectable.[70] On the other hand, after 1858 the General Conference added polemical doctrinal works defending Methodist history and ecclesiology to the Course of Study reading list.[71]

Pulpit Princes

> I have heard sermons in which the essentials of the gospel were scarcely touched. Should the preacher have a propensity to display his oratory, and be anxious to turn his periods handsomely, at least his application should be pungent, pointed, and to the purpose. The designs of preaching is to awaken sinners, and to bring them to Christ;—to urge believers to the attainment of holiness of heart and life;—to show sinners the turpitude of their hearts and sinfulness of their practice, and to bring them to the foot of the cross, stripped of self and of all self dependence;—to press the old Methodistical doctrines by faith; the direct evidence from God, through faith in the merits of Christ, of the forgiveness of sin; and the adoption into his family. Nor are we to be ashamed of that unfashionable doctrine, Christian perfection:—but we should point out clearly a travail of soul, not only for justification, but for sanctification, and the evidence of it.[72]

As early as 1827, Freeborn Garrettson could already detect another shift in the emphasis of many preachers. He described a style of preaching that was "entertaining and useful" devoid of "a dry detail of uninteresting

69. Vinet, *Homiletics*, 80.

70. Webber, *History of Preaching*, 329.

71. Patterson, "Ministerial Mind," 55, 56.

72. Garrettson, *American Methodist Pioneer*, 399–400.

matter, or with speculations which did not profit the hearer."[73] Such interesting discourses were very welcome to audiences bored by the daily routines of middle-class industrial or rural life. Preaching narrative sermons was not as much a theological decision as it was a market decision. In other words, preachers were tempted to entertain or provide sensational experiences in worship. This gave rise to the "pulpit princes" who enjoyed cross-denominational popularity.

Perhaps the most famous "pulpit prince" of the nineteenth century was Charles Grandison Finney. Finney was strongly influenced by the Methodist tradition of revivalism and camp meeting preaching. By the same token, he influenced Methodists with his promotion of protracted meetings, social reform, encouragement of female participation, and use of the "anxious bench."[74] Finney experimented with his "new measures revivalism" in major cities, targeting poor and middle-class subjects. His revival methods, serialized in his publication, the *New York Evangelist*, were compiled as *Lectures on Revivals of Religion* (1848).[75] Finney was criticized for assuming "doubtful positions without proof" and dogmatizing "without the least diffidence."[76] Nevertheless, it was widely read by Methodists.

Essentially, his preaching style was a type of popular drama complete with extravagant set, exaggerated gestures, and commonplace illustrations. It fed on a culture seeking pulpit princes who tantalized and excited the crowd besieged with the routine of industrialized living. Finney preached using the vocabulary of the people. Thus, his messages were accessible to his audience whether they were simple farmers or sophisticated lawyers. He avoided doctrinal disputes and focused on conversion.[77] The content of his sermons was based on the Calvinistic idea of total depravity, or innate moral degradation. However, his co-opting the Methodist idea of Christian perfection led his followers to move upward toward "refined respectability."[78]

Horace Bushnell was another well-known "pulpit prince." As a Calvinist, he agreed with the notion of total depravity, but tended to

73. Bangs, *Life of Freeborn Garrettson*, 333.

74. Yrigoyen, Review of *Charles* G. *Finney*, 200.

75. Review of *Lectures on Revivals*, 477.

76. Review of *Lectures on Revivals*, 477.

77. Sweet, "The View of Man," 213.

78. Sweet, "The View of Man," 221.

de-emphasize the inability of humankind to respond to God's grace. "Take any scheme of depravity you please, there is yet nothing in it to forbid the possibility that a child should be led, in his first moral act, to cleave unto what is good and right, any more than in the first of his twentieth year."[79] Furthermore, he disagreed with the tactics of revivals. He felt that conversion is not an event restricted to the individualism of revivalism. Rather, it is a process in which the Christian is nurtured in the organic connections of community.

> Any scheme of nurture that brings up children thus for revivals of religion is a virtual abuse and cruelty. And it is none the less cruel that some pious-looking pretexts are cunningly blended with it. Instead of that steady, formative, new creating power that ought to be exerted by holiness in the house, it looks to campaigns of force that really dispense with holiness, and it results that all the best ends of Christian nurture are practically lost.[80]

Bushnell's *Christian Nurture* was criticized for "imply[ing] that a man became a Christian by education rather than by the direct change of his heart by a sovereign act of God."[81] Despite the initial controversy surrounding the book, it gained acceptance as a guide for religious education of children.[82] Bushnell's rejection of revivalism in favor of Christian nurture was clearly reflected in the type of sermons he preached. In his sermon "The Gospel of the face," he decried the misguided desire for "high preaching, sturdier arguments on points of theology, better command of logical resources, more science, more fine rhetoric, more I know not what." Rather, he insisted on seeking "the divine light of souls" manifest in "genuine good living."[83]

Methodist "pulpit princes" were to be found in the many anecdotes and memoirs published by the church press. The periodical the *Methodist Preacher*, featured sermons from popular preachers. Though it appeared in only four volumes from 1830 to 1831, it elevated the status of preachers to property of the public domain. A book followed by the same title and featured sermons on "doctrinal and practical subjects" written by

79. Bushnell, *Christian Nurture*, 9.

80. Bushnell, *Christian Nurture*, 64.

81. Thompson, *Changing Emphasis*, 21.

82. Thompson, *Changing Emphasis*, 21.

83. Bushnell, *Sermons on Living Subjects*, 94, 95.

such notables as Bishop Elijah Hedding, Dr. Willbur Fisk, Dr. Nathan Bangs, and Dr. John Durbin. Fisk, preaching in Broadway Tabernacle, New York, on the occasion of the American Bible Society meeting, gave his famous sermon on the "transition age" with utopian vision. "The Bible—the Bible must direct and control the wheels of government, the principles of education, the character of the rising generation: this is our spiritual palladium, the glory of the churches, the honour of the nation, the salvation of the world."[84] Fisk's qualifications as a true "pulpit prince" are doubtful. In a memorial service for Fisk, Bangs lauded his oratory style as "near to perfection," but his homiletical ability was definitely too dependent on logic. "His sermons were generally of a didactic character, and on this account might have appeared to those who did not fully enter into his views, and follow his chain of reasoning, somewhat dry and dull."[85]

D. Holmes, the editor of the book, *Methodist Preacher*, lauded Bangs more for his overall actions in the church than his preaching. "Then the venerable Dr. Nathan Bangs, eminently worthy to be classed with the Apostles of American Methodism; he has by his pen, his pulpit labors, and personal influence, done more to promote the growth and prosperity of the church of his choice, than any other living man."[86] Bangs elicited his own imitators, especially students of the ministry.[87] John Durbin, lesser known of the four, was much later described as "one of the most magnetic advocates and preachers, both on the platform and in the pulpit, that the Church in America ever produced."[88]

Arguably the most famous of American Methodist preachers was Matthew Simpson. He known as "the peerless orator of the American pulpit."[89] Besides rising to the rank of bishop, Simpson was celebrated

84. Holdich, *Life of Willbur Fisk*, 332–33.

85. Bangs, *Discourse*, 19.

86. Holmes, *The Methodist Preacher*, vi.

87. During Bangs' brief tenure at Wesleyan University, students were known to imitate his unique style of elocution. They "unconsciously" mimicked his trademark crook neck and tilted head, due to a physical disability known as "torticollis." He also had damaged vocal cords which gave a "double voice" effect to his speech. Price, *Wesleyan's First Century*, 70. The position of Bangs' head was tilted in the presidential stained glass windows of the Memorial Chapel at Wesleyan University to match the other three presidents' postures.

88. Daniels, *Illustrated History of Methodism*, 727.

89. Daniels, *Illustrated History of Methodism*, 705.

nationally as a confidant of President Lincoln. He offered prayers at Lincoln's wake and presided over the stately burial service.

> While minute guns sounded, and a choir of 250 voices sang hymns on the State House steps. With General Hooker at its head, the long procession started towards Oak Ridge. The cemetery reached, the choir sang again while the body was placed in the tomb. A minister offered a prayer, another read scripture, a third read the second inaugural. The choir sang a dirge, and Bishop Simpson pronounced the funeral oration. There was a closing prayer, the Doxology, a benediction. Slowly, silently, the vast crowd dispersed.[90]

Late in life, Bishop Simpson was elected to deliver Yale College's prestigious Lyman Beecher Lectures on Preaching. His remarks reveal that Methodism was influenced in part by Bushnell's emphasis on Christian nurture rather than immediate conversion. Furthermore, Simpson suggested that preaching extemporaneously, so coveted by Methodists at the beginning of the century, was no longer a desirable or necessary skill.[91] On the other hand, preachers of the emerging Gilded Age were warned of making their sermons into heartless essays.[92]

The eventual decline of extemporaneous preaching among the less famous preachers may be attributed to the decrease in oratory skills, emphasis on academics, and intellectual demands of the congregation.[93] Methodist "pulpit princes" certainly excelled in all three areas. Each developed their own unique style of oratory which helped distinguish themselves as outstanding preachers. The downside was the popular messengers risked becoming more interesting than the message.[94] The "princes" influenced many imitators and devoted hearers who fashioned preaching palaces around the pulpit. The strength of these preachers may have influenced the revisions of the service. By the 1860s, the *Disciplines* of both the Methodist Episcopal Church and the Methodist Episcopal Church, South dropped the requirement to read a chapter each of the New and Old Testaments. Rather, preachers focused on a text or word often as a pretext for a topical sermon. The resulting message likely

90. Angle, "Here I Have Lived," 292.
91. Simpson, *Lectures on Preaching*, 98.
92. Simpson, *Lectures on Preaching*, 304.
93. Tucker, *American Methodist Worship*, 38.
94. Tucker, *American Methodist Worship*, 39.

reflected the preacher's fancy more than the full sense of the scripture in context.[95] It is interesting to note that except for occasional services, topical sermons before the Civil War seldom addressed the slavery issue. Rather, such preaching was relegated to the abolition, antislavery, and pro-slavery contingents.[96] Such departures from the general order were dealt with accordingly.

Hymnody

> Sinners through the camp are falling,
> Deep distress their souls pervades,
> Wondering why they are not rolling
> In the dark infernal shades.[97]

Accounts of worship at early Methodist meetings reveal an atmosphere resplendent with emotional fervor and vigorous singing. It has been suggested that singing may have been more prominent in camp meetings and revival meetings than in Wesley's congregations.[98] However, quantity did not guarantee quality in the songs and hymns. The cherished hymns of Wesley and Watts were more frequently reduced to warm up exercises for revivalist songs. J. Ernest Rattenbury famously quipped, "The greatest of all the specific religious values of Methodism is to be found in its hymnody."[99] At least sixteen Methodist songbooks were printed in the United States between 1805 and 1840, and one more in 1843. These songbooks were principally compilations of songs made popular at camp meetings and revivalistic worship services. Three popular songbooks were *Hymns and Spiritual Songs* edited by Stith Mead (1805); *Spiritual Song Book* edited by David B. Mintz (1805); and *The Pilgrim Songster* edited by Thomas S. Hinde (1810).[100]

The Wesleys dignified hymn singing by making it an alternative medium for their evangelical message. Revivalist preachers who disregarded the rich theological content of hymnody were accused of reducing the

95. Hickman, *Worshiping with United Methodists*, 55.

96. Taylor, "Preaching on Slavery," 170–71.

97. This song stanza describing the scene of a camp meetings was typical of those sung in the camps. Luccock, *The Story of Methodism*, 267.

98. Luccock, *The Story of Methodism*, 267.

99. Rattenbury, *Vital Elements of Public Worship*, 86.

100. Johnson, *The Frontier Camp Meeting*, 193.

hymn to "doggerel."[101] Camp meeting songs tended toward repetition and textual simplification. "Verses were shortened, refrains added, and expressions and ejaculations interpolated."[102] An excellent example of the popular revival songs of the period is "Stop, poor sinner!"

> Stop, poor sinner! Stop and think.
> Before you farther go!
> Can you sport upon the brink
> Of everlasting wo [*sic*]?
> Hell beneath is gaping wide,
> Vengeance waits the dread command
> Soon he'll stop your sport and pride,
> And sink you with the damn'd.[103]

Theology in Lyrics

The four major themes of camp meeting songs were: pilgrimage; centrality of Jesus; gathered church; and personal faith assurance.[104] Although these themes resonated well with Methodism's evangelical message, they were still too shallow in terms of theological content. Nathan Bangs disliked the weak theology of the lyrics of camp meeting songs and judged them as inferior. It must be remembered that he was a strong advocate of Christian perfection, a prevalent theme within Wesley hymns. He testified to a personal experience of sanctification that was not dramatic, but significant in scope of meaning.

> My supplications were importunate, so that I know not how long I continued to pray. When I ceased, I sank down into an inexpressible calmness, as lying passive at the feet of God. I felt relieved and comforted, as though I had been "cleansed from all filthiness of the flesh and spirit." I had no extraordinary rapture, no more than I had often experienced before, but such a sense of my own littleness that I thought, "What a wonder is it that God condescends to notice me at all!" All my inward distress was gone. I could look up with a childlike composure and trust, and behold God as my heavenly Father. We staid all night, and the next morning in family prayer I seemed surrounded with

101. Luccock, *The Story of Methodism*, 267.
102. Johnson, *The Frontier Camp Meeting*, 201.
103. Hymn I, in Mason, *Zion's Songster*, 1.
104. Warren, *O For a Thousand Tongues*, 104–12.

> the divine glory. I certainly was filled at that time with the "perfect love which casteth out fear," for I had no fear of death or judgement.[105]

Charles Wesley considered "perfection" and "sanctification" as interchangeable terms. His use of words related to "perfection" appears almost five times more frequently than "sanctification" words, especially in his later hymns. Wesley's preference for the term "perfection" was due to poetic rather than theological considerations.[106] Bangs also used the terms "perfection" and "sanctification" interchangeably.

> I care not by what name this great blessing be designated, whether holiness, sanctification, perfect love, Christian perfection, so long as is meant by it an entire consecration of soul and body to God, accompanied with faith that he accepts the sacrifice through the merits of Christ alone.[107]

Curiously, there is no exact definition of "perfection" to be found in the *corpus* of Charles Wesley's hymns. However, a journal entry dated Monday 26 September 1740 gives a revealing glimpse of his understanding of the doctrine of perfection. According to Charles Wesley, perfection is "utter dominion over sin, constant peace, and love and joy in the Holy Ghost; the full assurance of faith, righteousness, and true holiness."[108] He interpreted perfection as the sanctifying work of the Holy Spirit. There are both inward and outward elements of perfection in Wesley hymns.[109] A prime example of a Charles Wesley hymn on personal holiness is "Forth in Thy Name." It is probably the most descriptive Wesley hymn on the topic of perfection. The tone is contrition leading to a state of repentance to "sanctify the whole."

> Give me to bear thy easy yoke,
> And every moment watch and pray,
> And still to things eternal look,
> And hasten to thy glorious day.[110]

105. Stevens, *Life and Times of Nathan Bangs*, 58–59.

106. Tyson, *Charles Wesley on Sanctification*, 176.

107. Stevens, *Life and Times of Nathan Bangs*, 351.

108. Tyson, *Charles Wesley on Sanctification*, 177.

109. Jeffrey, *English Spirituality in the Age of Wesley*, 31.

110. "Forth in thy name, O Lord," in Wesley, *A Collection of Hymns*, *Works of John Wesley* (Bicentennial ed.), 7:470.

John Wesley considered Christian perfection as more as teleological, not a static condition. Christians are made free by grace "not to commit sin" so they could live in active holiness. However, "perfection" does not equivocate justification and sanctification. Albert C. Outler explained that John Wesley considered "perfection" as "correlated with the whole process of Christian maturation and hope."[111] Bangs thoroughly supported John Wesley's idea that Christian perfection was attainable prior to death. However, like Charles Wesley, he did not distinguish between "sanctification" and "perfection."

> In addition to reading the sacred Scriptures with diligence and prayer, and conversing with God's people in reference to it, I read Mr. Wesley's "Plain Account of Christian Perfection," some portions of Mr. Fletcher's writings on the subject, and was fully convinced of its necessity, nature, and fruits, so that I sought it understandingly, and found it, to the joy of my heart.[112]

Bangs commended sanctification as a transformative and punctiliar experience to be sought after for holy living. He published his definitive treatise on sanctification in 1851.[113] More importantly, in exercising his role as hymnal editor he was able to promote Wesleyan hymnody, including the twin themes of sanctification and perfection long after his personal influence dwindled. Individually, a person moving on to perfection became more respectable in the process.[114] Furthermore, the concept of self-improvement in perfectionist spirituality contributed greatly to the collective goal of respectability in the MEC.

Hymnbook Revisions

> Singing forms such an interesting and important branch of divine service, that every effort to improve the science of sacred music should meet with corresponding encouragement. Nothing tends more, when rightly performed, to elevate the mind, and tune it to the strains of pure devotion. . . . Indeed, every considerable revival of true godliness has been attended, not only

111. Outler, *John Wesley*, 253.

112. Stevens, *Life and Times of Nathan Bangs*, 396.

113. Bangs, *Necessity, Nature, and Fruits.*

114. The popularity of Phoebe Palmer's books and teachings indicate that perfectionist doctrine was actually in demand among upwardly mobile and urbane Methodists. See Long, "Consecrated Respectability," 284–85.

> with the cultivation and enlargement of knowledge in general, but of sacred poetry and music in particular.[115]

In 1820 Nathan Bangs, acting as the new editor of the Book Concern, took on the task of editing a new hymn book. He hoped that reintroducing the "practical and experimental divinity" of the Wesleys would quell any unruly religious enthusiasm. Thus, the revision committee placed control on the inferior revivalist songs by returning to the sound standards of Wesley and Watts. "Watts you need not despise; but the Wesleys you will hold in the highest estimation; for, if they may not be ranked among the sublimest of poets, they are certainly among the most pious and spiritual."[116] The new edition was considered necessary to correct the problems associated with an unauthorized *Pocket Hymn-Book* by Robert Spence of York. His unsolicited publications and distributions were not appreciated by John Wesley. At the end of the day, grace prevailed in the matter so that Wesley and Spence reconciled their relationship.

> [Spence] had published a Pocket Hymnbook in which he had included many of Mr. Wesley's most popular hymns. As this occurred just at the time Mr. Wesley was contemplating a similar volume, the latter in his preface reflected upon the action of the York bookseller in vigorous terms. The sharp passage was soon forgiven and forgotten, and when they next met it was in a friendly spirit.[117]

Spence's hymn book, though unauthorized, became very popular in Britain and America. It was so sought after that Wesley grudgingly incorporated some of it into his own hymn book, referring to the additions as "grievous doggerel."[118] Wesley was cautious not to allow this situation to overtake him again.

> Many gentlemen have done my brother and me (though without naming us) the honour to reprint many of our hymns. Now they are perfectly welcome so to do, provided they print them just as they are. But I desire they would not attempt to mend them—for really they are not able. None of them is able to mend either the

115. Excerpted from the preface of the *Methodist Hymnbook* (1836) in Bangs, *A History of the Methodist Episcopal Church*, 3:135.

116. Bangs, *Letters to Young Ministers*, 116.

117. Lyth, *Glimpses of Early Methodism*, 165.

118. John Wesley, "Introduction," in Wesley, *A Collection of Hymns*, *Works of John Wesley* (Bicentennial ed.), 7:29.

> sense or the verse. Therefore I must beg of them one of these two favours: either to let them stand just as they are, to take them for better or worse; or to add the true reading in the margin, or at the bottom of the page, that we may no longer be accountable either for the nonsense or for the doggerel of other men.[119]

Even with the availability of Wesley's 1780 hymn book, Spence's *Pocket Hymn Book* was published and distributed in America as early as 1786.[120] Bangs was concerned that the *Pocket Hymn-Book* was too small and lacked the necessary content for private devotion or public worship. Therefore, an enlarged edition was published in 1808, but it still contained very few Wesley hymns with corrupted and incomplete lyrics.[121] Interest in producing an authorized tune book resulted in the publication of *David's Companion* in 1808. It clearly reflected the worship music that was popular at historic John Street Church. Although it was approved in principle by the General Conference of 1808, revised in 1810 and again in 1817, it never gained official approval.[122]

The New York Annual Conference commissioned a revision of the hymnbook in 1819 with the intent of presenting it to the following General Conference. The preface included a note of explanation for the revision which restored the glory of Wesleyan hymnody to the song book.

> The greater part of the hymns contained in the former edition are retained in this, and several from Wesley and Coke's collections, not before published in this country, as added. The principal improvements which have been made consist in restoring those which had been altered, as is believed, for the worse, to their original state, as they came from the poetical pen of the Wesleys; for the following hymns were, except a few which have been taken from other authors, composed by the Rev. John and Charles Wesley—names that will ever be held dear and in high estimation by every lover of sacred poetry.[123]

The success of the 1821 hymn book seemed guaranteed by the tremendous growth of the market. This fact did not escape the notice of certain opponents to the Methodist movement. The *Quarterly Christian*

119. John Wesley, "Introduction," in Wesley, *A Collection of Hymns*, 75, *Works of John Wesley* (Bicentennial ed.), 7:75.

120. Ruth, *A Little Heaven Below*, 140.

121. Bangs, *A History of the Methodist Episcopal Church*, 3:133.

122. Young, "American Methodist Hymnbooks," 56.

123. Bangs, *History of the Methodist Episcopal Church*, 3:134.

Spectator severely criticized the Book Concern for placing such a high centrality on the Methodist hymn book. Worse yet, they accused them of taking financial advantage of their constituents.

> Every Methodist, rich or poor, must have a hymn book: and multitudes who attend on the worship of that denomination without adding themselves to the 420,000, must have hymn books also. All these books are published at one office from stereotype plates, and are sold at nearly or quite double the price at which a bookseller might publish them and realize a profit, besides paying for the use of copy-right.[124]

The charge that only one set of plates was used in the printing is entirely false. A second set of plates was made to lower the production cost of the new hymnal. Evidence for this is in a letter (1821) sent to Martin Ruter at the Book Concern's Cincinnati publishing house.

> We have commenced stereotyping the New Hymn Book, and shall have a set of plates made also for your use, as by having two sets made at the same time they come much lower. But we shall not use them until the present Edition is out.[125]

Bangs answered his critics in a series of articles published in the *Christian Advocate and Journal* and *Zion's Herald.* By unanimous vote of the New York Conference, the articles were compiled into a pamphlet and distributed as the *Reviewer Answered.* The articles defended the publishing practices of the Methodist Book Concern against the criticisms of Congregationalist "officers in Yale College" who "vented their spleen" against them.[126] Thus, amid external criticism, Bangs was able to retain control over controversies surrounding the production of hymn books. Furthermore, a defense of the publication rights suggests a struggle to maintain order in publishing and distribution. The preface of the 1836 hymnbook included a disclaimer and a solemn warning against purchasing unauthorized versions not bearing the MEC's episcopal *imprimatur.*

> We are the more delighted with this design, as no personal advantage is concerned, but the public good alone. For after the necessary expenses of publications are discharged, we shall make it a noble charity, by applying the profits arising therefrom to religious and charitable purposes.

124. "Editorial," 521.
125. Nathan Bangs and Thomas Mason to Martin Ruter.
126. Bangs, *The Reviewer Answered*, 5.

> No motive of a sinister nature has therefore influenced us in any degree to publish this excellent compilation. As the profits of the former editions have been scrupulously applied as above, so the same appropriation of the profits of the present shall be conscientiously observed. We must therefore earnestly entreat you, if you have any respect for the authority of the conference, or of us, or any regard for the prosperity of the Church of which you are members and friends, to purchase no Hymnbooks but what are published by our own agents, and signed with the names of your bishops. And as we intend to keep a constant supply, the complaint of our congregations, "that they cannot procure our Hymnbooks," will be stopped.[127]

Sandwiched between the preface and the first hymn is an intriguing repetition of the warning against purchasing unauthorized hymnbooks. This double warning was perhaps the most brazen exercise of bureaucratic authority ever witnessed in the MEC.

> CAUTION
>
> All persons desirous of possessing the true revised and improved official edition of the Methodist Hymnbook, with the Supplement, are advised to be careful to examine the *imprint*, and to purchase those only published by our General Book Agents, for the Methodist Episcopal Church, or by the Agents at Cincinnati.[128]

An unfortunate fired destroyed the Book Concern in New York and the printing plates for the 1821 hymnbook, 1832 revision. Bangs issued the 1836 *Hymnal* along with a supplement of ninety hymns.[129]

> As the plates for the Hymn-book were destroyed by that disastrous event, by which it has become necessary to prepare a new set, we have availed ourselves of this opportunity to add the following Supplement, consisting chiefly of hymns adapted to special occasions, such as dedications, anniversaries, &c. Some of these are original, having been prepared expressly for this purpose, but the most of them are selected from the festival and other Hymns of the late Rev. Charles Wesley, than whom no man ever united the spirit of poetry, fervent piety, and evangelical sentiment more firmly and delightfully together.[130]

127. "Editor's Preface," in MEC, *A Collection of Hymns*, 4.

128. "Editor's Preface," in MEC, *A Collection of Hymns*, 6.

129. McCutchan, *Our Hymnody*, 10.

130. Nathan Bangs, advertisement to "A Supplement to the Collection of Hymns

Bangs was keen to recover the theological richness of Wesley hymns for Methodist worship. It is significant in that, even with the supplement, it did not contain works by American composers nor did it acknowledge camp meeting songs.[131] By issuing the 1836 edition, Bangs re-emphasized the importance of understanding the Methodist hymn book as Wesley's "little body of experimental and practical divinity."[132] The re-introduction of Wesley hymns revived an important source of theological documents.[133]

An intriguing restatement of the role of hymnody in worship appeared in the preface of the 1836 and 1843 hymn books. It defined and limited the sphere of private and public worship. Thus, the controls were extended to dimensions previously unspecified.

> In presenting this revised Hymnbook to you for your use, we humbly trust that we are putting into your hands one of the choicest selections of evangelical hymns, suitable for private devotion, as well as for family, social, and public worship, by which you will be much aided in the performance of these important parts of divine service.[134]

The 1836 revised hymn book provided American Methodists a more faithful and complete text of Wesley hymns. This was improved by the 1849 revision which was touted as "the fullest and most correct presentation of Wesleyan poetry" with works by American composers.[135] The value of the hymn books for personal spirituality was well recognized. Nathan Bangs noted that he used the hymn book to share devotions with his spiritual father, Joseph Sawyer. "At the breakfast table on Sunday morning each of the company repeated a passage from the Holy Scriptures, after which, at Dr. Bangs' instance, they cited each a stanza from the Church Hymn Book."[136] After reciting a stanza from John Wesley's

---

for the use of The Methodist Episcopal Church," in MEC, *A Collection of Hymns*, 527–28.

131. Foote, *Three Centuries of American Hymnody*.

132. Wesley, *Collection of Hymns*, *Works of John Wesley* (Bicentennial ed.), 7:74.

133. Langford, "Charles Wesley as Theologian," 99.

134. "Editor's Preface," in MEC, *A Collection of Hymns*, 4.

135. Foote, *Three Centuries of American Hymnody*, 231.

136. Stevens, *Life and Times of Nathan Bangs*, 347–48.

translation of Paul Gerhardt's "Jesu, Thy boundless love to me," Bangs was so overwhelmed with emotion that he "could utter but a word or two."[137]

The editing and distribution of authorized hymn books guaranteed the promotion of the enlarged authority of the MEC, but did not guarantee obedience to it. Thus, resistance against denominational control and formalism continued in the face of efforts to maintain Methodist respectability.

Congregational Singing

> Improvements doubtless may be made: yet, as a whole, for our congregational singing, we question whether a better guide can be found that the "Methodist Harmonist." . . . We beg leave, in closing, to express our gratification that the compilers of our Tunebook concur with us in deprecating the frequent introduction into ordinary congregational singing of fugue tunes, and a complicated artificial harmony. We have often felt and mourned over this as a lamentable destroyer of the glory of *Methodist* congregational singing; and as the chief, if not the sole cause, in fact, of that deplorable evil so extensively, we fear, creeping in among us, by which this heavenly part of worship is confined, as in the orchestras of public shows or theatres, to a few individuals, technically styled *the singers.*[138]

Bishop John Emory was a great supporter of the hymns of the Wesleys and Watts. Thus, he supported Bangs' revision of the hymn book. The revised hymn book brought a welcome sense of order to singing. At the same time congregational singing was de-emphasized in favor of choirs. William Nash Wade notes that professional choir music flourished among New England Congregationalists, however, Methodists in the latter eighteenth century were still trying to avoid the "involved and intricate music more suitable to performance by professional choirs or at least musically advanced singers." This is evident in the language of the 1792 *Discipline* which disapproved fugue tunes.[139] The General Conference of 1832 authorized a reprinting of the 1822 *Methodist Harmonist* improved by the inclusion of anthems, sentences, and pieces. Karen B. Westerfield Tucker suggests that this may indicate acceptance of the new

137. Stevens, *Life and Times of Nathan Bangs*, 348.

138. Emory, *Life of John Emory*, 347.

139. Wade, "A History of Public Worship," 239.

forms at the very least on the official level.[140] There is no record indicated that Nathan Bangs objected to the choirs of John Street Church. Emory preferred congregational singing to bad harmonies of the "singers." When the *Harmonist* (ca. 1837) was published as a supplement to the *Methodist Hymnbook*, Emory offered his measured commentary on the value of congregational singing. Emory was cautious about corrupting congregational singing with poor lyrics, harmonies, or instrumental music. Citing Dr. Adam Clarke, he warned losing the simplicity of Christian worship.

> *Melody*, which is allowed to be the most proper for devotional music, is now sacrificed to an exuberant *harmony*, which requires not only many *different kinds of voices*, but *different musical instruments*, to support it. And by these preposterous means, the *simplicity* of the Christian worship is destroyed, and all edification totally prevented.[141]

The Wesleyan predilection for congregational singing notwithstanding, American as well as British Methodists were eager to enhance their worship experience with improved music. The original disciplinary instruction for public worship suggested that the preacher, rather a "singer," give out the words of a hymn.[142] The improvements of music eventually removed the preacher from this role. The *Discipline 1856* advised that song leaders be chosen for the congregation and that "due attention be given to the cultivation of sacred music."[143]

Union Theological Seminary in New York took the lead in cultivating sacred music as an academic discipline. Presbyterians had long relied on "precentors" to give the pitch and lead the tunes. The trouble was that middle-class constituents, now quite familiar with stage performances and concert hall music, were not easily pacified by dull or substandard music.[144] In 1837, six months after the establishment of the school, Abner Jones was elected as Professor of Sacred Music. Several other notable figures followed in his footsteps. Students at Union formed the Haydn Society for the revival and study of classical sacred music. The Society remained active from 1841 to 1852. During this time composers Thomas Hastings and Lowell Mason energized and elevated the music of New

140. Tucker, *American Methodist Worship*, 160.

141. Emory, *Life of John Emory*, 347.

142. MEC, *Minutes of Several Conversations*, 22.

143. MEC, *Doctrines and Discipline*, 81.

144. Cashdollar, *A Spiritual Home*, 78, 80.

York churches. In 1852, George Frederick Root took the baton at the seminary. He pooled his fame by collaborating with Chauncey Marvin Cady and Fanny Crosby. In 1855, Root convinced the chancellor of New York University to confer the first doctor of music degree on veteran composer and music educator Lowell Mason. Under Mason's term, auditors were permitted to attend lectures on music.[145] Throughout this entire period, instruction in sacred music was widely disseminated among New York composers, choirs, organists, and pianists.[146]

Further evidence that congregational singing diminished in importance may be inferred by the change in the rules for singing in worship. To avoid formality, it was suggested that the [congregational] singing be limited. "By not singing too much at once; seldom more than five or six verses."[147] The *Discipline 1856* amended this rule by reducing the number of suggested verses to four or five.[148]

Prayer and Discipline

> The primitive Methodist preachers knew well how to accommodate themselves to the habits, as also to the fare of [settlers]. . . . The early memoranda before me afford not a few glimpses of this primitive life of the frontier—crowded congregations in log-huts or barns—some of the hearers seated, some standing, some filling the unglazed casements, some thronging the overhanging trees—startling interjections thrown into the sermon by eccentric listeners—violent polemics between the preacher and headstrong sectarists, the whole assembly sometimes involved in the earnest debate, some for, some against him, and ending in general confusion. A lively Methodist hymn was usually the best means of restoring order in such cases.[149]

Many Methodists prized the enthusiastic experiences associated with camp meeting religion. Therefore, they attempted to extend the revivalistic worship experience into the venue of established congregations. In some cases, as evidenced above, hymn singing could restore order to an unwieldy crowd. However, order came only by the enforcement of strict

145. Handy, *A History of Union Theological Seminary*, 41.

146. Skinner, *Sacred Music*, 12–17.

147. MEC, *A Form of Discipline*, 22.

148. MEC, *Doctrines and Discipline*, 81.

149. MEC, *Doctrines and Discipline*, 102–3.

discipline. This must have been a consideration when Wesley's "Rules for Congregational Singing" were reprinted in the *Methodist Magazine.*[150]

Although Bangs appreciated a genuine heart-felt worship, he did not tolerate disorder. As a pastor, he was horrified to observe excesses of demonstrative worship in the historic John Street Church in Manhattan. Bangs testified that he "witnessed . . . a spirit of pride, presumption, and bigotry, impatience of scriptural restraint and moderation, clapping of the hands, screaming, and even jumping, which marred and disgraced the work of God."[151] He quickly laid down the law to his parishioners, basing his action on a dream in which he slew the "snake" of disorder with the "whip" of the *Methodist Discipline.* One disgruntled congregant bemoaned Bangs' insistence on decorum. "Mr. Bangs had done more injury that evening to the cause of God than he could ever be able to make amends for."[152]

The importance of the *Discipline* in maintaining order in worship cannot be understated. Although the *Discipline* was published following the Christmas Conference of 1784, it did not at that time regulate the form of service. Such forms were passed on from preacher to preacher. Unquestionably, the *Discipline* surpassed Wesley's *Sunday Service* in this particular role in the critical year after Wesley's death in 1791. The *Sunday Service* was abandoned, and the "sacramental services" entered the pages of the 1792 *Discipline.*[153] The long form of Wesley's Sunday Service was reduced to singing, prayer, reading one chapter each from the Old Testament and the New Testament, and preaching. The rejection of the 1784 Sunday Service reveals a trend toward a uniquely American style of worship that maintained an interest in uniformity and classic Christian worship.[154]

Seeing the need for a formal book of worship, the General Conference of 1820 appointed Joshua Soule, Nathan Bangs, and Daniel Ostrander to assist the episcopacy to revise the *Discipline.*[155] The resulting *Doctrines and Discipline* (1824) had some of the most sweeping changes

150. Wesley, "Mr. Wesley's Rules for Congregational Singing," 189–90. Wesley's rules can be summarized as: (1) sing all; (2) sing lustily; (3) sing modestly; (4) sing in time; and (5) sing spiritually. *Works of John Wesley* (Bicentennial ed.), 7:765.

151. Stevens, *Life and Times of Nathan Bangs*, 183.

152. Stevens, *Life and Times of Nathan Bangs*, 185–86.

153. White, *Protestant Worship*, 158.

154. Wade, "A History of Public Worship," 223–24.

155. MEC, *Journal of the General Conference, 1820*, 239.

to church order in the denomination's history. It outlined a formal order of worship with the addition of the Lord's Prayer enjoined for all occasions. Methodist preachers were admonished to use this form "invariably" to avoid the temptation for free form of worship.

> In administering the ordinances, and in the burial of the dead, let the form of discipline invariably be used. Let the Lord's Prayer also be used on all occasions of public worship in concluding the first prayer, and the apostolic benediction in dismissing the congregation.[156]

The *Discipline* of 1828 also tried to enforce "uniformity" in worship. James F. White posits that the frequent language that the "ritual invariably be used" is "good evidence that it was not."[157] The difficulty, again, was enforcing new formal modes of worship. In preparation for a General Conference in Baltimore, Bangs visited some local churches, including an African American congregation. What he saw would stay with him for the remainder of his clergy career.

> I was particularly interested in the worship of the negroes, which I here witnessed for the first time. These poor people seemed ecstatic in their gratitude for the Gospel and their hope of a better life. They shouted and "leaped for joy;" they heard the word with intense eagerness, and their prayers and singing were full of animation.[158]

It is surprising that Bangs recorded so little contact with African Americans, considering his work for the Liberia mission and related conference committees. He was not overtly racist though at times his insensitive comments suggest he may have believed that White people were superior in some ways to people of color.[159] This did not prevent him for supporting the election of Francis Bums, an African American,

156. MEC, *Doctrines and Discipline*, 72.

157. White, *Protestant Worship*, 159.

158. Stevens, *Life and Times of Nathan Bangs*, 168.

159. Nathan Bangs wrote a series of articles on missions published in *Zion's Herald* and *Western Christian Advocate*. These articles were compiled into a book, *Emancipation*, in which this footnote appears: "According to the statistics of Mexico, lately published, it contains a population of 7,006,000, of whom 4,000,000 are Indians, 2,000,000 mulattoes, 6,000 Blacks, and 1,000,000 only are Whites; that is, only one-seventh part of the population are Whites! And perhaps about the same proportion prevails throughout the South American States; and the successive revolutions show the unsettled habits of the people generally, as well as the unfitness of the ignorant population to govern themselves." Bangs, *Emancipation*, 36–37.

to become the first missionary bishop to Liberia.[160] Such support demonstrated that Bangs was genuinely sympathetic to the social condition of African American people.

Worship styles of African Americans, both slave and free, often reflected their status of wealth and education. Slave religion was both otherworldly and worldly. That is, Christianity offered hope in deliverance for slaves who saw themselves as a type of the biblical Israel.[161] This combination of otherworldly and worldly religion is especially evident in this account of a Wesleyan watchnight service for emancipation in the British held Antigua in the West Indies in 1834.

> All was animation and eagerness. A mighty chorus of voices swelled the song of expectation and joy; and as they united in prayer, the voice of the leader was drowned in the universal acclamation of thanksgiving, and praise, and blessing, and honor, and glory, to God, who had come down for their deliverance. . . .
>
> At the instruction of the White missionary, they went to their knees in silence as the clock tolled twelve. Then, the celebration resumed in a greater measure than before. Shouts of "Glory!" and "Alleluia!" filled the room as the now free Africans clapped, hugged, laughed, and cried. When the excitement subsided, the missionaries exercised their control by "exhorting the free people to be industrious, steady, obedient to the laws, and to show themselves in all things worthy of the high boon which God had conferred upon them."[162]

Another incident involving jubilant worship of African Americans occurred in Ithaca in upstate New York. Methodists in Ithaca decided to hold their own prayer meeting and keep their Black members away from the indecorous trappings of camp meetings. "If the Methodists from the country become disorderly, we will not suffer, as the public can see the difference between the Ithaca Methodists, and the ranting Methodists from the country."[163] Thus, it is evident that Bangs was not alone in his effort to apply discipline to Methodist worship.

160. Barclay, *History of Methodist Missions*, 3:176–77.

161. Raboteau, *Slave Religion*, 318.

162. Thome and Kimball quoted in Channing, *The Works of William E. Channing*, 87–88.

163. Wigger, *Taking Heaven by Storm*, 124.

Summary

As respectability became the desired image in the MEC, tighter controls were placed on the order of worship. The results proved that church order was an effective means of establishing the MEC as a respectable denomination. The early successes of camp meeting and revival worship services guaranteed continuance as a denominational institution. This did not necessarily guarantee the continuance of the associated frenzied style of camp meetings and revivals worship services. The Gilded Age witnessed the "toning down" of emotionalism and reduction of camp meetings into Chautauqua meetings.[164] The criticism of excesses was replaced by criticisms of commercialism.[165] Another faction, following in the holiness tradition of Phoebe Palmer and John Inskip, formed camp meeting associations where they could combine holiness of body and mind.[166] Demands for regularity and order gave way to their replacement by quarterly meetings. In turn, the quarterly meeting worship diminished in enthusiasm until it became little more than miniature versions of annual conferences where reports dominated the floor. Religious fervor in the MEC cooled down and constituents adjusted to a more settled lifestyle. Preaching and singing were formalized. The Methodist penchant for spontaneity remained as a dormant subcurrent until it later emerged as Holiness and Pentecostal worship.

At the end of the day, Bangs considered the resulting formal mode of MEC worship closer to the original church of Christ than other denominations. "It is to be hoped that Methodists will cleave to their standards, maintain their spirituality, and be more solicitous for the inward purity and internal energy of their church, than they are for those outward decorations which may commend it to the approbation of the mere men of the world."[167] This statement reveals the ongoing tension between Bangs' desire to promote the lively evangelical religion and the quest for denominational respectability. These divergent streams of spiritual fervor and material respectability nurtured the rise of pulpit princes and formal church music. The simple Methodist chapel was no longer adequate for new forms of worship. As the next chapter will demonstrate, preaching palaces came into vogue as the sacred space of choice for respectable Methodists.

164. Maddox, "A Change of Affections," 24.

165. Moore, *Selling God*, 78.

166. Messenger, *Holy Leisure*, 12.

167. Bangs, *Rites*, 21–22.

Chapter IV

ELEGANT CHURCH ARCHITECTURE

> Brother Taylor, you need not think that any of us Western men are anxious about preaching to you in Boston; your way of worship here is so different from ours in the West, that we are confused. There's your old wooden god, the organ, bellowing up in the gallery, and a few dandified singers lead in singing, and really do it all. The congregation won't sing, and when you pray, they sit down instead of kneeling. We don't worship God in the West by proxy, or substitution. You need not give yourself any trouble about getting a Western man to preach in your church; we don't want to do it, and I do not think that I will preach in Boston any more, unless you permit me to conduct the services after the Western manner.[1]

THE ARRANGEMENT AND USE of sacred space of urbane Methodists in the mid-nineteenth century changed so much that the new form was almost unrecognizable to pioneer veterans such as Peter Cartwright. The place of the rustic log chapels and austere wooden meeting houses was supplanted by tall steepled stone and brick buildings with stained-glass windows. Congregational singing became less important than the sacred music led by song leaders, choirs, and organs. Cushioned slip pews replaced the crude bench seating. Prayer was conducted by a solitary leader while the congregation sat rather

1. Cartwright, *Autobiography*, 309.

than kneel. Following the Anglican tradition, Holy Communion was taken kneeling. Karen W. B. Tucker notes that the altar rail became a characteristic of Methodist interior design. "The rail—the point of encounter with the divine—marked the most sacred spot in the worship space and might itself be called 'the altar.'"[2] To the observer fresh from beyond the Appalachians, worship was more akin to a day at the theater than church. These "evils" smacked of formality to traditionalists. Thus, they were denounced as engendering pride and destroying spirituality. "It gives precedence to the rich, proud, and fashionable part of our hearers, and unavoidably blocks up the way of the poor; and no stumbling-block should be put in the way of one of these little ones that believe in Christ."[3] John Bangs denounced steeples and the inclusion of musical instruments in the church as "superfluity and needless expense."[4]

The subject of architecture, of little concern in the early lean years, became an important issue for upwardly mobile Methodists. This was especially true for those situated in proximity to the more affluent Unitarians, Episcopalians, Congregationalists, Presbyterians, and even Roman Catholics.[5] The interiors were expanded and remodeled to match the more ostentatious exteriors. The pulpit and organ split the congregation's focus in two during worship. By the early 1850s, as Cartwright found in Boston pulpits, congregations expected to be entertained by narrative preaching. Thus, they would no longer tolerate boring didactic sermons. Even during Bangs' tenure, the so-called "Pulpit Princes" were attracting crowds who preferred riveting narratives to dry doctrinal treatises. Galleries were built for the organs, singers, and seating. They were also used to segregate from the congregation those of lesser means and other races.

Improved Architecture

> Those who have been acquainted with our circuits and stations for twenty, thirty, and forty years past, and who can compare our

2. Tucker, *American Methodist Worship*, 241.

3. Cartwright, *Autobiography*, 310.

4. Bangs, *Autobiography of John Bangs*, 101, 102.

5. Roman Catholic property values increased threefold by 1860 making it second only to the Methodist Episcopal Church. This does not include the other RC properties such as schools, convents, seminaries, and monasteries. See Dolan, *Catholic Revivalism*, 29.

> houses of worship then with what they are now, will be struck with the contrast, and will praise God for the improvement in this respect. In former days, most of the preaching places, more particularly in the country villages and settlements, were private houses, schoolhouses, barns, and groves; even when a church edifice was erected, a site was generally selected in some obscure retreat, remote from the centre of population, as though the Methodists were ashamed to be seen and heard by their neighbours; and even this small edifice was frequently but half finished, and left to fall down under its own rottenness. In this respect, there is a mighty improvement, such an improvement as must be encouraging to the hearts of all God's people. Now there are large and commodious houses of worship, not only in our populous cities—where indeed many have been recently built or enlarged, and their number increased with the advancing population,—but in almost every village and considerable settlement throughout the country are found temples finished in a neat, plain style, in which the pure word of God is preached, and his ordinances duly administered.[6]

The long-standing admonition that Methodist preaching chapels should be "built plain and decent" no longer met the needs of the MEC.[7] Increased prosperity naturally led to the construction of exquisite churches. Furthermore, the burgeoning growth of the Methodist movement also created a demand for more churches with larger space. American cities buckled under the population explosion fueled by the lure of industry and settlement of new immigrants. For example, in 1838 the Methodist Episcopal Church in Lowell, Massachusetts found it necessary to divide itself into two congregations. Chapel Hill and Wesley Chapel were created to accommodate the influx of mill workers who either came to Lowell as Methodists or converted soon after. Wesley Chapel enjoyed the growth spurt. When it was rebuilt as St. Paul's (1839), it was considered the largest MEC sanctuary in New England.[8] By 1857, there were approximately eight thousand members and twenty-eight Methodist churches in New York City. Twenty-three of these churches were built between 1831 and

6. Bangs, *The Present State*, 32–33.

7. MEC, *Minutes of Several Conversations*, 32.

8. Mudge, *History of the New England Conference*, 220–21.

1854.[9] Money for construction was in good supply between 1831 and 1839 due to a rise in cotton prices and commodities.[10]

Bangs stated that a stationed ministry must be established to keep the converts from going to competing sects. This necessitated construction of new chapels and parsonages. For Bangs, new construction met a serious missional need in the MEC.

> You might as well go home and go to sleep, so far as Methodism is concerned, as to preach in the manner you do; for though your labors may be blessed, other sects will reap their results, and thus, so far as our own Church is concerned, you lose the fruit of your toils and sufferings. . . . We must . . . go to work and build churches in all the cities and populous villages, and have preachers stationed in them, that they may perform the duties of pastors, watching over the flock and building them up in holiness.[11]

Bangs openly supported the construction of new churches and the reconfiguration of existing churches. It is notable that Bangs was present in the construction of several prominent New York churches. In 1817, Manhattan's historic John Street Methodist Church underwent a building scheme while he served as their appointed pastor. Seven years earlier Bishop Asbury suggested that "this house must come down and something larger and better occupy its place."[12] Bangs organized and brought forward that vision for an improved building. Additional land was purchased, and the original building was razed. The new building exterior was in the style of Greek Revival, the typical fashion of the period.[13] The interior retained the plainness expected of a "meeting house." Bangs preached the morning dedication sermon recounting the brief history of Methodism in America that led to the reconstruction of John Street Church.

9. Vestry Street, Mulberry Street, and Forty-first Street moved uptown in 1833, 1835, and 1846, respectively. Madison Street and Cherry Street merged in 1844. The church-ship "John Wesley," a ministry to seamen, was replaced by "Bethel" ship after 1854. Wakeley, *Lost Chapters*, 589.

10. North, *Economic Growth*, 198.

11. Stevens, *Life and Times of Nathan Bangs*, 204, 205.

12. Streeter, *Past and Present*, 24.

13. Most MEC's were built or rebuilt in Greek Revival from 1820 to 1850, with the exception of some church buildings of mixed Greek and Gothic features toward the end of this period. Drummond, *Church Architecture of Protestantism*, 58–60.

> Notwithstanding God had so enlarged our borders, that six additional houses of worship had been erected, (including two for the people of colour), it was found that this, which is now rebuilt, was not sufficiently large to accomodate all who wished to convene for the worship of God in this place. For some time previous to the actual commencement of the work, it had been in contemplation. Having formed the resolution, you commenced on the 13th day of May last to demolish the former house. On the 22nd day of May, the foundation sermon was preached for this. Through the protection and smiles of our God, you have succeeded according to your wishes in completing a neat, elegant, and commodious house for divine worship, which we have now dedicated to the special service of Almighty God.[14]

Joshua Soule preached the evening dedication sermon. Whereas Bangs was more interested in history and statistics, Soule focused on the "object and nature of spiritual worship." This was perhaps an indication of an underlying hope for a more refined worship devoid of enthusiasm and superstition in the newly erected building.

> For want of such knowledge, enthusiasm and superstition have too often usurped the seats of christian moderation and charity. It is not the least affliction which the church has suffered, that many of her professed friends have substituted the impulses of their passions, or the strength of their prejudices for the unerring testimony of the oracles of God; and through an indiscreet zeal have broken down those sacred barriers which the gospel has erected to guard her rights.[15]

Soule's emphasis on a proper mode of worship was a point not missed by Thomas O. Summers who reprinted it as early as 1855 for the MEC, South under the title *Object and Nature of Religious Worship*. Rebuilding John Street Church created no small discord among the congregants. The location had become more commercial than residential. "Downtown" and "uptown" members, long-time opposing church factions, argued whether the new building should be "an improvement on the architectural style of the old one."[16] The preacher in charge, Daniel Ostrander, opposed the reconstruction plan, apparently in retaliation for not being invited to preach the dedication sermon. Despite this

14. Bangs, *The Substance of a Sermon*, 19–20.
15. Soule, *The Substance of a Discourse*, 24–25.
16. Stevens, *Life and Times of Nathan Bangs*, 225.

unfortunate episode, the church was rebuilt and even served as "a model for many later structures in the country."[17] The importance of John Street Church was elevated to a higher level, serving its most critical leadership role in the local community and the MEC nationally after the reconstruction.[18]

In several MECs proper preaching palaces were appointed with exquisite furnishings such as carved wooden pulpits, altar rails, and communion tables. Tall pulpits were also lowered to reduce the awkwardness of climbing steps.[19] The impression given was that of formality and solemnity. Even at John Street Church, largely unchanged on the outside, the atmosphere of opulence prevailed inside and out.

> Arriving at John-street, the corpse was taken into the Methodist church, which was filled to overflowing; an eloquent and impressive discourse was delivered by the Rev. T. Birch; and the service concluded by a solemn and affecting prayer from the Rev. Henry Chase. The procession was then again formed and proceeded to the steamboat ferry; where it crossed over to Brooklyn, Long-Island: here the corpse was again taken into the Methodist church, when the Rev. Nathan Bangs read the 15th chapter of 1 Corinthians, and concluded by reading the burial service, after which the body was silently committed to the grave. His voice, while living, had often been heard in this temple, and there "his body, precious even in death, sleeps near the spot where the doctrines of the Christian denomination to which he was attached were first preached in America:—there, it will await that morning of which he loved, when living, to speak, and of which he sometimes spoke in entrancing language—the morning of the resurrection."[20]

The 1825 funeral service for Rev. John Summerfield illustrates the link between formality of ritual and architecture. It is also significant that an inscribed black and white marble cenotaph was placed in John Street Church as a tribute to the deceased. It is described as "finely polished" and "elegantly sculptured."[21] The practice of installing cenotaphs was later abandoned. In time, memorials were given in the form of financial gifts

17. Stevens, *Life and Times of Nathan Bangs*, 225–26.

18. Streeter, *Past and Present*, 25.

19. Embury, *Early American Churches*, 138.

20. Holland, *Memoirs*, 332–33.

21. Holland, *Memoirs*, 334, 335.

and endowments. Increased cash flow from memorials enabled churches to upgrade their furnishings to suit the more refined tastes of congregants.

The general move from plain chapels to exquisite churches began about 1820. In the early days, the simple Methodist chapels served farmers, day laborers, and mechanics. The new stately churches were built to accommodate the expectations of prosperous Methodist lawyers, physicians, politicians, and merchants.[22] Yet, some Methodists stubbornly continued the tradition of building "plain and decent" houses of worship as a form of resistance against the appetite for formality in the class of upwardly mobile Methodists.[23]

Greek and Gothic Revival

> Although some persons aim most at intellectual purity and simplification, for others *richness* is the supreme imaginative requirement. When one's mind is strongly of this type, as individual religion will hardly serve the purpose. The inner need is rather of something institutional and complex, majestic in the hierarchic interrelatedness of its parts, with authority descending from stage to stage, and at every stage objects for adjectives of mystery and splendor, derived in the last resort from the Godhead who is the fountain and culmination of the system. One feels then as if in presence of some vast incrusted work of jewelry or architecture; one hears the multitudinous liturgical appeal; one gets the honorific vibration coming from every quarter.[24]

William James' definition of sacred space is descriptive of what became of the character of Methodists who were estranged from the faith of their pioneer fathers and mothers. Having moved up in social strata above the crises of the poor, they found more grace in aesthetics than in individual experiences. Thus, they were open to changes in fashion and architecture which were the domain of the refined elite.

Archaeological discoveries in the ancient Mediterranean cities of Herculaneum and Pompeii influenced European designers to create classical Greek motifs. The Greek revival in England was inspired by Stuart and Revett's *Antiquities of Athens* (ca. 1762). But it was the

22. Brekus, *Strangers and Pilgrims*, 285.
23. Tucker, *American Methodist Worship*, 247.
24. James, *Varieties of Religious Experience*, 349.

architect Benjamin Henry Latrobe who introduced the Ionic design of Philadelphia's Bank of Pennsylvania.[25] Greek styles were also imported to America in the form of fashion design books and furniture and art reproductions. Therefore, many of the rebuilt and new churches of the years between 1820 and 1850 were in the Greek Revival style complete with Doric columns and pediments suggestive of classical Greece.[26]

In response to an undercurrent of Anglo-Catholic thought, British architects and theorists rejected the pagan-based Greek style and began a series of discussions about the superior Christian attributes of pointed, or Gothic, architecture. In *The True Principles of Pointed or Christian Architecture* (1841), Augustus W. Pugin argued that Gothic was the true Christian form. However, Pugin was suspect because of his conversion to Roman Catholicism.[27] Critics were concerned that embracing Pugin's principles was tantamount to deferring to Edward Pusey's scandalous inclinations to reunite with Rome. At length, theorists were able to separate Puseyism from Gothic architecture. At the same time, a renewal of high church liturgy was being promoted in the Anglican church by John Henry Newman and the Oxford movement. This complex network of theorists and movements has been referred to *in toto* as the "Tractarian-Oxford-Anglo-Catholic Ritualistic movement."[28] Architects, theorists, and liturgist agreed that Gothic was the legitimate historical heritage of the Anglican Church.[29]

It is unclear how the Gothic Revival entered the mainstream of Methodist thought. However, it is certain that the Gothic, or ecclesiological, movement made its way to America by way of publications and increased international exchanges with Britain. Ecclesiological societies sprang up promoting the renaissance of Gothic architecture. The Cambridge Camden Society was formed in 1839 by students J. M. Neale and Benjamin Webb and their tutor Rev. T. Thorpe to "promote the study of Ecclesiastical architecture and the restoration of mutilated architectural remains." The society produced several pamphlets including: *Hints for the Practical Study of Ecclesiastical Antiquities* (1839); *Church Enlargement*

25. Andrews, *Architecture, Ambition, and Americans*, 71–72.

26. Drummond, *Church Architecture of Protestantism*, 58.

27. Stanton, *Gothic Revival & American Church Architecture*, 20–21.

28. Willimon, *Word, Water, Wine and Bread*, 110–11.

29. Clarke, *Church Builders of the Nineteenth Century*, 74–75. For more information on the Gothic Revival in North America, see Wilson, *The Gothic Cathedral*; Smith, *Gothic Arches, Latin Crosses*.

and Church Arrangement (1842); *Twenty-three Reasons for Getting Rid of Church Pues*; and *Hints to Workmen Engaged in Churches.*[30] By mid-century the Ecclesiological Society had become sufficiently powerful to intimidate architects into building Gothic style buildings.[31]

In America, one of the most influential publications on Gothic architecture was Bishop John Henry Hopkins' *An Essay on Gothic Architecture* (1836). It was the first such book published in the United States.[32] Hopkins, and other thinkers sympathetic to the Oxford Movement, suggested a return to Gothic architecture as the true Christian form of the art. John Summerson has suggested that the movement "represents a surgence of that hard bourgeois Puritanism half-hidden in the 18th century which had never expressed itself emotionally but at last seized the opportunity to do so" in literature and architecture.[33] Whatever the reasons, the idea made a great impression on Bishop William Rollinson Whittingham, Protestant Episcopal Bishop of Maryland, who began promoting construction of parish churches with deep chancels and a half-Georgian, half Gothic style.[34]

Most notable of the American neo-Gothic edifices was Trinity [Protestant Episcopal] Church, located in New York City only a few blocks from John Street Methodist Episcopal Church. Richard Upjohn, a British architect influenced by Pugin's designs, began building Trinity Church in 1839 and completed it in 1846. His first buildings were in the Greek Revival style. He was influenced toward Gothic architecture by the writings of famed British architects Pugin and Britton. Reverend Jonathan Mayhew Wainwright, a high-ranking Protestant Episcopal cleric, also guided Upjohn in thinking in terms of High Church Anglicanism.[35]

The lavish Gothic design of Trinity Church epitomized the Anglican desire for returning to authentic "Catholic" architecture. "Its sanctuary was paved with coloured [*sic*] marble, and contained an altar of panelled oak, backed by an elaborate oak reredos, the panels of which were painted with the Lord's Prayer, the Creed and the Ten Commandments."[36] It

30. Clarke, *Church Builders of the Nineteenth Century*, 74–75.

31. White, *The Cambridge Movement*, 180.

32. Stanton, *Gothic Revival & American Church Architecture*, 59.

33. Summerson, *Heavenly Mansions*, 173.

34. Stanton, *Gothic Revival & American Church Architecture*, 216–19.

35. Brown, "Quest for the Temple," 13.

36. Anson, *Fashions in Church Furnishings*, 68.

was fashioned in eighteenth-century English Perpendicular Gothic. By contrast, James Renwick built New York City's St. Patrick's Roman Catholic Cathedral in French Gothic style.[37]

One reason why low church Protestants were attracted to the Gothic Revival in architecture may have been a growing appetite for refinement, education, and taste. Another is that the Gothic form was it was not sectarian but "simply Christian."[38] It is significant that up to the Civil War, American Protestants often purchased a set of architectural plans and contracted a builder rather than hire an architect.[39] In Ottawa, Canadian Methodists were advised to consult with architects. They concluded that Gothic architecture was necessary to insure survival of the Methodists in their upwardly mobile community.[40]

The downside of the Gothic plan was the long chancel hindered the hearing of the preacher by the congregation. This did not go without notice to Methodists who preferred to hear the sermon. The following except from the *Christian Advocate* is anything but irenic.

> Most of our readers have never had the inconvenience of worshipping in a church in which they could not hear the preacher. . . . It is so outrageous that it can be called doing nothing less than the work of the devil. In the very place where, of all others, God's kingdom is to be enlarged and Satan's power overthrown, there to be occupied in speaking to the air! It does seem as if the devil was engaged in the structure of many of our church buildings. One of the best contributions to the spread of the gospel would be, to tear down every such structure, and then to take good care that the architect of the new building was not possessed of a demon, that he should do the same folly over. Then let him build a church in which all can see, all hear, and all be comfortable.[41]

Bishop Matthew Simpson, enthused by the growing wealth of Methodists, encouraged the construction of Christ Church, Pittsburgh which began in 1853 and was completed in 1855. Simpson described it as "a beautiful edifice, and the first church of more modem architecture built

37. Drummond, *Church Architecture of Protestantism*, 90.
38. Kilde, *When Church Became Theatre*, 57, 58.
39. Greenagel, *The New Jersey Churchscape*, 30.
40. Bennett, *Sacred Space and Structural Style*, 219.
41. McTyeire, "Houses for Worship."

by the Methodists in America."[42] Indeed, it was the first Gothic Revival Methodist church in America.[43] The MEC's experiments with Gothic were not widespread. By the time the MEC entered the Gilded Age, the Romanesque exterior with the creative Akron plan theater-inspired sanctuary became the preferred form of architecture.[44] Although the MEC architecture took a different direction, the Romanesque, the construction of Gothic churches in proximity of their churches both provoked and inspired better architecture for public worship.

Preaching Palaces

In 1832, Lewis Tappan, Charles Grandison Finney's chief financier, leased the opulent Chatham Theatre in New York for its excellent acoustics and stage presence. He refitted the auditorium with an enlarged pulpit and large windows. Otherwise, it retained much of the character of the original theater space.[45] The auditorium had three tiers of galleries with adjoining rooms for prayer meetings and lectures. The success of this first preaching palace was quickly realized. Despite a devastating cholera epidemic, which also infected Finney, the Second Free Presbyterian Church, or Chatham Street Chapel, fostered seven new churches. Although rich patrons paid most of the bills, their converts consisted mostly of middle class and lower class. According to Finney, "This was what we aimed to accomplish, to preach the Gospel especially to the poor."[46] In only two years, against the objections of his architect, Finney himself designed the first purpose built preaching palace known as Broadway Tabernacle.[47]

Revival meetings had a nice benefit for New York Methodists. A protracted revival at Allen Street Church, MEC, resulted in the erection of seven new and two rebuilt churches.[48] As congregations became more middle-class, so the desire increased for conspicuous wealth in their church architecture. The earlier protests against the Gothic renewal

42. "Pittsburgh," in Simpson, *Cyclopaedia of Methodism*, 722.

43. Marti, "Rich Methodists," 266.

44. Rowe, "Redesigning Methodist Churches," 118. For more on Romanesque, see Allsopp, *Romanesque Architecture*.

45. Loveland and Wheeler, *From Meetinghouse to Megachurch*, 26–27.

46. Finney, *Memoirs*, 323, 324, 325.

47. Finney, *Memoirs*, 326.

48. Stevens, *Life and Times of Nathan Bangs*, 292.

may have slowed down updating plain chapels into exquisite churches. However, it did not prevent others from zealously pressing forward in the construction of Methodist preaching palaces. In 1835, Second Wesleyan Chapel in New York was built in the same design as First Wesleyan Chapel on Vestry Street. Nathan Bangs preached the morning dedicatory sermon. The building boasted seating for nine hundred, carpeting, cushions, and a custom mahogany pulpit. In 1856, Second Wesleyan Chapel accepted an offer to sell their property to St. Philip's Protestant Episcopal Church. The chapel was sold and moved to Fourth Avenue and Twenty-second Street the site of the old wooden chapel known as Calvary Protestant Episcopal Church. The new church was now known as St. Paul's Methodist Episcopal Church. Nathan Bangs laid the cornerstone for a more ambitious building.[49] St. Paul's MEC was constructed of white marble in Romanesque architecture with a 210-foot spire and "comfortable seats" for thirteen hundred. J. B. Wakeley described it as "chaste and simple."[50] The "Cathedral of Methodism" became the site for the Centenary Jubilee of American Methodism.[51]

Methodists living in Washington, DC, had lamented the palpable absence of any notable Methodist church building of respectable architecture in the nation's capital. In response, they formed a committee to study the possibility of constructing a proper memorial to American Methodism. The report was delivered to the General Conference of 1852 to address what they considered a national problem.

> Every one who feels a just and jealous concern for the respectability and success of our fondly-cherished Methodism, must see and regret the same deficiency, and desire to supply it by every justifiable means at his disposal. . . .
>
> *Resolved*, 1st, That we cordially approve of the erection of a new house of worship for the Methodist Episcopal Church in the city of Washington, as contemplated by our brethren in their memorial.
>
> *Resolved*, 2nd, That, regarding the success of this enterprise as of high importance to the interests of Methodism throughout the country, we will give it our individual influence in our

49. Seaman, *Annals of New York Methodism*, 323–25.

50. Wakeley, *Lost Chapters*, 593.

51. It is fitting that the funeral service for Nathan Bangs was held at St. Paul's MEC. Sitterley, *The Building of Drew University*, 15.

> respective annual conferences, and by all appropriate means aid in its promotion.[52]

The construction plan for the national church was approved at the General Conference in 1852. This was the last General Conference which Bangs sat as a delegate, though he was not a member of the memorial committee. Nevertheless, the acceptance of this proposal embodied Bangs' fifty-year travail for respectability.[53] Frank M. Bristol, a contemporary Methodist preacher, noted that the "National Church of Methodism" was a special project of Bishop Matthew Simpson. "From the foundation stone, laid before the Civil War, to its completion and final redemption from all debt, the great Bishop took a pride and interest in it as the child of his brain."[54] Bishop Simpson took up the cause for respectability from this time forward. He preached the dedication sermon on October 23, 1854. When Metropolitan Memorial Church was completed in 1869, it was strikingly different from nearby Lovely Lane Chapel. The new church boasted a 220-foot spire and towering members such as President Ulysses S. Grant, who once served as chair of the trustees. It was the ultimate monument to respectable Methodism in America.

Congregational Furnishings

Promiscuous Seating

> It was determined to build a new house, which by persevering exertion was effected; the new house was completed and dedicated in the spring of 1822. It is built of brick, on the northwest comer of the public square, or green, 68 by 80 feet, and has a basement story of about 67 feet square. It is plain and convenient, and reflects much honour upon the builders. The only objection that can be made to it is, the slips have doors, and part of them are either sold, with the privilege of redeeming them after ten years, or rented- but the whole of the gallery is free, and both sides of the lower part, with exception of one or two seats.

52. Committee on the Memorial from Washington City, *Journal of the General Conference*, 202.

53. Stevens claimed that Bangs was the "chief actor in the most important measures of" all except one General Conferences from 1808 to 1852. Stevens, *Life and Times of Nathan Bangs*, 380.

54. Brown, *A Living Centennial*, 7.

> This by many is thought a very great convenience, as they can have their families sit together.[55]

Changes in social mores stretched the boundaries of male/female relationships, even in church seating. The historic MEC rules did not permit the sexes to sit together in chapels. "Q. Is there any Exception to the Rule 'Let the Men and Women sit apart.' A. There is no Exception. Let them sit apart in all our Chapels."[56] Actually, Wesley provided for an exception in certain cases. "In those galleries where they have always sat together, they may do so still. But let them sit apart everywhere below, and in all new erected galleries."[57] Methodist chapels were arranged so that men and women entered in separate entrances and sat opposite each other in the sanctuary. However, as American Methodists prospered, the inconvenience of separating the families became less tolerable. Furthermore, the egalitarian aspect of Methodist camp meetings helped to change the popular attitude toward a more inclusive seating arrangement in chapels. In fact, it was so inclusive that it was an object of criticism by Presbyterian minister William Annan.

> Because they [Methodist camp meetings] afford to the mixed multitude who attend them, unusual and most abundant advantages for the practice of wickedness in many of its foulest forms. It is well known that whilst the mass of the steady, orderly, and influential men of the community, who give tone to society, and impart a healthful direction to the current of its manners and customs, take little or no interest in such assemblages [camp meetings], seldom attend, and then for a very short time—on the other hand, persons of almost every shade of color and character are advertised, invited, and expected to attend; and it is of these for the most part that Methodism calculates her gain . . . Is it the best way to bring together in dangerous combination for many days and nights, men and women in mixed multitudes, where, it cannot be denied, great facilities are presented, to kindle unholy fires in the soul, and practice iniquity in many of its vilest shapes?[58]

55. Bangs, "Rise and Progress," 265.

56. MEC, *Minutes of Several Conversations*, 32.

57. John Wesley, "Minutes of Several Conversations," in *Works of John Wesley* (Jackson ed), 3:332.

58. Interesting to note that the book was endorsed by Archibald Alexander, president of Princeton Seminary. Annan, *The Difficulties of Arminian Methodism*, 203, 204.

Critiques against mixed seating notwithstanding, Methodists were becoming intolerant of the separate seating in their ever-improving houses of worship. About 1830, an alternative seating plan was proposed by Rev. J. Kennaday for a church in Newark. Kennaday's plan permitted men and women to sit in alternating parallel rows separated only by aisles and arranged perpendicular to the altar rail and pulpit. Although the seating arrangement was not readily accepted in Newark, a few years later it was introduced to New York City churches. By 1837, promiscuous seating became acceptable in those New York City churches.[59]

The Pew System

The earliest rustic Methodist chapels employed simple benches for seating. They were little more that crude wooden planks supported by stumps, barrels, or the most available item. However, as chapels became more sophisticated, they graduated to square pews. These, in turn, were eventually replaced by the more fashionable slip pews.[60]

In 1824, the *Discipline* introduced the rule that churches should be built with free seats.[61] This rule was repeated with each subsequent *Discipline* until 1852. In that edition, the wording was changed to "free seats wherever practicable."[62] Seating became more comfortable and expensive. Unfortunately, it was discovered that the desirable slip pews became a saleable commodity. Endeavoring to defray construction and operation costs, many churches rented and sold church pews. This was a common practice in many other denominations. For example, historic St. John's Protestant Episcopal Church in Savannah, Georgia was erected in 1853 according to C. N. Otis' High Gothic plan. Their construction cost, originally budgeted for $25,000, rose to $40,000. To cover the shortfall, the church sold their pews at auction for $100 to $500 each.[63]

In New York City, the Protestant Episcopal Church and the Presbyterians dominated the elite classes. High pew prices insured their social exclusivity. In 1852, pew prices were fetching from $100 to $700 plus

59. Seaman, *Annals of New York Methodism*, 268–69.

60. Embury, *Early American Churches*, 138.

61. MEC, *Doctrines and Discipline*, 160.

62. MEC, *Doctrines and Discipline*, 169.

63. Eight pews, four each, were later set aside as free seats for Black and poor White members. Weeks, *St. John's Church in Savannah*, 21, 24.

additional ground rent of 8 percent per annum.[64] The sale and rental of pews created no small controversy in the connection. In 1852, the old circuit rider Peter Cartwright called out the pew system for its degrading treatment of the poor.[65] This was an unexpected causality of the wealth and numerical growth of the MEC.

> The pew system is inevitably at war with the best interests of the Church, for no honorable, high-minded man, who is poor, and unable to buy or rent a pew, but will feel himself degraded to intrude himself into a pewed church; and that form of worship adopted in any Church which goes to exclude the poor, contravenes the Divine law, and prevents the realization of that blessedness that God has provided for the poor. Fifty years ago there was not a member or preacher among the thousands in the Methodist Episcopal Church that thought of having a pewed church. But since the Church has risen in numerical strength, and become wealthy, this system of pewed churches is fast becoming the order of the day.[66]

In 1863, John E. Risely, a Methodist preacher, observed that because of the pew system the poor "are virtually shut out of the house of God by having a tax imposed upon all the seats, in the form of pew rent, which they are not able to pay; so that supposing they had the disposition to enter these houses of worship, it would be impossible for them to do so."[67] The issue of pew rent was the object of particular scorn for sectarian Benjamin Titus Roberts. Roberts, a pastor of the Genesee Conference, was an avid promoter of Wesleyan perfectionism, abolition, and more stringent discipline. The campaigns for newer and more elaborate church buildings financed by pew money ran contrary to his notion of Methodism as a religion for common folk.[68] By 1860, Roberts publicly denounced the MEC for promoting the alienation of the poorer class by the pew system.

> The pew system, wherever it prevails, not only keeps the masses from attending church, but alienates them, in great degree, from Christianity itself. They look upon it as an institution for the

64. Beckert, *The Monied Metropolis*, 59.
65. Cartwright, *Autobiography*, 312–13.
66. Cartwright, *Autobiography*, 312–13.
67. Risely, *Some Experiences of a Methodist Itinerant*, 122–23.
68. Dieter, *The Holiness Revival*, 45–46.

> genteel, and the fashionable; and upon Christians as a proud and exclusive class.[69]

That same year Roberts and other like-minded clergy were forced out of the MEC. They reorganized their sect of Free Methodists mostly from the "burned-over district" in upper New York. Roberts charged that the MEC was no longer the same church begun by John Wesley and Francis Asbury. The evidence of this departure from tradition was the apparent deteriorated concern for poor constituents. The formation of the Wesleyan denomination confirmed that the MEC had finally "secularized."[70] However, this does not mean that wealthy churches abandoned the idea that they could help the poor. Rather, it demonstrated that respectable congregations felt justified in "excluding the poor from beautiful buildings because the beautiful worshippers were the ones who counted."[71]

Galleries

The practice of including galleries in sanctuaries may have originated from the rood lofts in sixteenth-century English churches. They were used primarily as a place for choirs, musicians, and private seating.[72] They were not unknown in the preaching houses of Wesley's day. Wesley approved of the construction for The New Room in Bristol and the much later City Road Chapel in London. Both were built with gallery seating to accommodate seating and enhance eye contact with the preacher.

The American Methodist experience with chapel galleries has a more ignominious past. In late eighteenth-century Delaware, a young African slave by the name of Richard Allen, a member of the "invisible church," was awakened by the preaching of a Methodist itinerant preacher, Rev. Freeborn Garrettson. Inspired to better himself and others, Allen and his brother threw themselves into the backbreaking work of wood splitting to purchase their freedom. They were able to purchase their freedom and accumulate modest personal wealth. Richard Allen's desire to help the local community of African descent led him to consider

69. "Benjamin T. Roberts Laments Methodism's Upward Mobility," in Richey et al., *A Sourcebook*, 320.

70. Finke and Stark, *The Churching of America*, 153.

71. Bushman, *The Refinement of America*, 352.

72. Bond, *Screens and Galleries*, 149.

the options available for free Blacks. In 1787, Allen, Absalom Jones, and other prominent Africans established the Free African Society in 1787 "for the benefit of each other." He continued social work until 1794 when his church work demanded more attention.[73]

Allen developed a reputation as a popular local preacher for the Methodist Episcopal Church. "Crazy" Lorenzo Dow, the flamboyant Methodist lay preacher, suggested that Francis Asbury "jealous of his power, noticed Allen with a watchful eye."[74] Allen was offered the opportunity to travel with Bishop Francis Asbury and "Black Harry" Hosier. Instead, he chose to remain at St. George's Methodist Episcopal Church in Philadelphia. Allen and his associate the Rev. Absalom Jones gathered fellow African Americans for private prayer and Bible study at the predominantly White St. George's. No small controversy occurred over the matter of receiving Holy Communion.

> A number of us usually attended St. George's church in Fourth street; and when the colored people began to get numerous in attending the church, they moved us from the seats we usually sat on, and placed us around the wall, and on Sabbath morning we went to church and the sexton stood at the door, and told us to go in the gallery. He told us to go, and we would see where to sit. We expected to take the seats over the ones we formerly occupied below, not knowing any better. We took those seats. Meeting had begun, and they were nearly done singing, and just as we got to the seats, the elder said, "Let us pray." We had not been long upon our knees before I heard considerable scuffling and low talking. I raised my head up and saw one of the trustees, HM . . . , having hold of the Rev. Absalom Jones, pulling him up off of his knees, and saying, "You must get up—you must not kneel here." Mr. Jones replied, "Wait until prayer is over." Mr. HM . . . said "No, you must get up now, or I will call for aid and force you away." Mr. Jones said, "Wait until prayer is over, and I will get up and trouble you no more." With that he beckoned to one of the other trustees, Mr. LS . . . to come to his assistance. He came, and went to William White to pull him up. By this time prayer was over, and we all went out of the church in a body, and they were no more plagued with us in the church.[75]

73. Alexander, *Richard Allen*, 78–79.

74. Lorenzo Dow, quoted in Singleton, *The Romance of African Methodism*, 9.

75. Allen, *Life Experiences*, 25.

The custom at St. George's was to serve communion to the White members first, while the Black members waited in the gallery or some other fringe area.[76] Before St. George's added a second-floor gallery, there had been a more egalitarian seating arrangement. At the very least, African Americans were allowed to sit in the perimeter on the first floor. The presence of the new gallery changed the spatial dimensions along racial lines without any prior notice to the African American members, who were also partakers in funding St. George's.

There is some debate about the historical accuracy of this episode since the gallery was built later. Whatever occurred prior, the group staged a walkout from St. George's in 1792.[77] Although they had a substantial spiritual and financial investment into the church, they could not consign themselves to return. A proposal for a new place of worship was sought. Allen purchased the land on Sixth and Lombard Street that formerly belonged to the Church of England.[78] The building dedication took place on Sunday 29 July 1794. Although Bethel Methodist Church was built as a reaction to racism, worship services there were open to people of all races.

> The Rev. John Dickens sung and prayed, and Bishop Asbury preached. The house was called Bethel, agreeable to the prayer that was made. Mr. Dickens prayed that it might be a bethel to the gathering in of thousands of souls. My dear Lord was with us, so that there were many hearty "amen's" echoed through the house. This house of worship has been favored with the awakening of many souls, and I trust they are in the Kingdom, both white and colored.[79]

Asbury never mentioned the unfortunate incident at St. George's in his journal. However, he recorded his participation in the dedication service of the new church called Bethel. "I preached at the new African church. Our coloured brethren are to be governed by the doctrine and

76. Singleton, *The Romance of African Methodism*, 9.

77. James Varick led a similar walkout from John Street Church in 1796. In 1821, he organized and founded the African Methodist Episcopal Church, Zion. The Colored Methodist Episcopal Church (now known as the Christian Methodist Episcopal Church) grew out of the "Colored" conferences of the Methodist Episcopal Church, South in 1870.

78. Allen, *Life Experiences*, 31.

79. Allen, *Life Experiences*, 31.

discipline of the Methodists."[80] Asbury mentioned Allen specifically only one more time in his journal. Apparently, Allen once bought a fresh horse for him to continue his long travels.

As early as 1771, Methodists in Georgia were utilizing seating to segregate Black people from White people. They recognized that free seating implied social equality, a difficulty for middle-class White people. Blacks were segregated at camp meetings, often behind the preaching stand. In the plain preaching houses White people sat in front and Black people sat in the back rows. The construction of more elaborate churches initiated the practice of seating Black people in the galleries.[81]

Pipe Organs

> At the cathedral we had a useful sermon, and the whole service was performed with great seriousness and decency. Such an organ I never saw or heard before, so large, beautiful, and so finely toned; and the music of "Glory be to God in the highest," I think exceeded the Messiah itself.[82]

It is clear from John Wesley's *Journal* that he appreciated the aesthetic value of a good pipe organ played well. Wealthy Methodist churches on both sides of the Atlantic valued organ music in their worship services. They discovered that galleries in the newer buildings made ideal locations for organs and choirs. Predictably, the introduction of organs and choirs in worship was the source of no small controversy in Methodist chapels.

Church organ music reputedly goes back as early as the twelfth century. The first two organs used in America churches were Thomas Brattle's in the Queen's Chapel, Boston (ca. 1713), and Dean Berkeley's in Trinity Church, Newport, Rhode Island (ca. 1733).[83] But it would take considerably more time for organs to enter Methodist chapels. While John Wesley lauded organ music in the Church of England, he was reticent to permit organs in his chapels. "Let no organ be placed anywhere, till proposed in

80. Asbury, *Journal of Rev. Francis Asbury*, 2:231.

81. Owen, *The Sacred Flame of Love*, 17–18.

82. John Wesley, *Journal*, August 29, 1762, in *Works of John Wesley* (Jackson ed.), 3:111.

83. Thompson-Allen, "The History of the Organ," 136.

the Conference."[84] It had been a favorite instrument of Charles Wesley's sons, Charles and Samuel, who performed their music before the Royals and other social elites.[85] Samuel Wesley, a renowned organist himself, was said to have been particularly impressed by the singing of the congregants at Leeds. "Those Leeds folks made me play second fiddle."[86] It is evident that some resistance to organs existed among the British Wesleyans from the beginning. Contemporary Daniel Isaac wrote against instruments of all kinds in worship, but especially the organ. "Organs are undoubtedly the worst; because they make most noise, nearly drown the voice of those who sing, and render the words quite inaudible."[87] Thus, the main objection to the organ in the sanctuary was that it distracted from congregational singing, the hallmark of Methodist worship. Objections aside, the organ became a part of modem worship. British churches that could not afford an organ or musicians were offered "barrel-organs" which could be played simply by turning the crank. Such devices served for up to fifty years in the galleries of British Methodist churches.[88]

In MEC churches, pipe organs were often placed either in the galleries above the entrance or behind the pulpit. The former arrangement created the additional problem of splitting congregation's attention between preacher and musician. Thus, organ music often competed against the pulpit princes in the grand churches. Bangs did not seem to have any particular prejudice against musical instruments. However, he did have an incident in which a disruptive fiddler attempted to lure Bangs' congregants to dance rather than pray. After a stern public rebuke from Bangs, the "devil's musician" went home and burned his fiddle.[89] The divisive topic of organ music was rivaled only by the controversy of slavery.[90] Pipe organs and choirs were still controversial throughout the 1830s. Yet, they both became "omnipresent" as churches increased in wealth.[91]

84. John Wesley, "Several Conversations," in *Works of John Wesley* (Jackson ed.), 8:319.

85. Olleson, "The Wesleys at Home," 139–58.

86. Gregory, *Side Lights*, 63.

87. Isaac, *Vocal Melody*, v.

88. Whitely, *Congregational Hymn-Singing*, 149–50.

89. Stevens, *Life and Times of Nathan Bangs*, 104.

90. Stevens, *Life and Times of Nathan Bangs*, 316.

91. White, *Introduction to Christian Worship*, 126.

Summary

Historic churches such as John Street and St. George's, incapable of changing with the times, became more important as remnants of denominational and local history. Surviving "plain and decent" preaching house became either shrines or odd relics of the past. Such shrines were immortalized in legend and verse.

> Hail JOHN STREET's venerable shrine!
> Hallowed and crowned with joys divine!
> At thought of thee what memories rise,
> What praise, like incense, fills the skies![92]

The rude log cabins and rustic meeting houses used by class leaders and circuit riders were snubbed for the more elaborate ambiance of the Greek and Gothic Revival churches. Three churches stand out as representative of the architectural landmarks of the MEC during Bangs' era: John Street Church as the model church with elements of Greek Revival; Christ Methodist Episcopal Church as the first Gothic Revival experiment; and Metropolitan Memorial Church as the apex of Gothic Revival preaching palaces.

Interiors were adorned with fine woods, organs, galleries, and exclusive seating arrangements. Members could now occupy the posh sanctuary seats, insulated from the poorer class, and enjoy worship in a multidimensional experience with a preacher at one end and musicians at the other. Critics of the new form were apt to say, "When I look away to the 'land of steady habits,' where they have pews, and organs, and pay the choir to do their singing—where the itinerant is snugly fixed in the village station, and the local preacher doing what little itinerant work is done, my fears come on."[93]

This ever-refining worship changed the character of American Methodist life to better serve the more respectable members of the urbane communities. The issue of pew rents, widely used by other respectable denominations, would simply not be ignored by Methodists concerned for the mission of the church.[94] The MEC's newfound respectability did

92. Excerpted from Taylor, "A Centennial Rhyme," 114.

93. Anonymous letter to John F. Wright, in Wright, *Sketches*, 267.

94. Pew rents became harder to collect, even in stylish churches such as St. James' Episcopal Church in New York City. By 1868, an incentive was created permitting the Sexton to keep 5 percent of collected pew rents. Lindsley, *A History of St. James Church*, 37.

not occur without strident cries for justice and reform. The next chapter will give further details of the impact of respectability on society both inside and outside of the church.

Chapter V

METHODIST MIDDLE CLASS

> In the view we have taken of the present state of the Church, compared with what it was formerly, we have seen the vast improvements which have been made in temporal, intellectual, and spiritual enjoyments—how God has mercifully enlarged our borders, increased our substance, and in a variety of ways, multiplied our resources and capabilities of doing good. These certainly have proportionately augmented the amount of our responsibility, imposed upon us new and higher duties, and that in exact proportion as we have increased in wealth, in knowledge, and spiritual attainments.[1]

AT MID-CENTURY, NATHAN BANGS reviewed the history of the Methodist Episcopal Church and marveled at the dramatic changes he witnessed over his fifty years of ministry. His summary of the situation boiled down to three main areas of increase: church growth; status; and new responsibilities to "do good," Methodism's second General Rule.[2] Fifteen years later, Abel Stevens detailed Bangs' third point. Methodism should do these five things.

1. Enlarge its means of ministerial education.
2. Minister to the public culture by improvement of its architecture.
3. Consolidate with the other branches of American Methodism.

1. Bangs, *The Present State*, 223.
2. Wesley, *The Nature*, 7.

4. Concentrate on "securing" the children in membership.
5. Maintain "apostolic piety" in the land and spread it over the world.[3]

These goals all resonate with the legacy of progressive thinking left by Nathan Bangs. In his 1862 eulogy of Bangs, Bishop Edmund S. Janes commented that Bangs considered change in the MEC was as necessary as it was inevitable.

> Unlike most old men, [Bangs] was, to the last, progressive in his views. He sympathized with all well-considered measures for the improvement of his Church. To him its history was all providential, and the very necessity of changes was the gracious summons of providence for it to arise and shine still brighter. This hearty, resolute love of his friends and his cause was one of the strongest, noblest traits of the war-worn old hero.[4]

While Bangs helped foster institutional resources previously unavailable to Methodists, the changes which he considered "improvements" were not universally beneficial. There were others both within and without the MEC who did not fare as well as the wealthy, educated, and spiritual elites of Methodism. It had come to fit H. Richard Niebuhr's typology of a middle-class church in the final phase of development.

> This is not the religion of that middle class which struggled with kings and popes in the defense of its economic and religious liberties but the religion of a bourgeoisie whose conflicts are over and which has passed into the quiet waters of assured income and established social standing. Yet it remains the religion of a middle class which excludes from its worship, by the character of its appeal, the religious poor as well as those who live within the lower ranges of economic and cultural respectability.[5]

It is certain that much of the external conflict had ceased for the MEC. However, internal conflicts created incidents of marginality for the poor and others outside the expected norm of respectability. This became more evident as the MEC expanded respectability into the several spheres life by way of missions and women's role in society and religion. It is necessary at this juncture to rehearse the national historical context which provided the fecund environment for respectable religion.

3. Stevens, *The Centenary of American Methodism*, 232, 233, 236, 238, 240.
4. Janes, *Sermon on the Death of Nathan Bangs*, 26.
5. Niebuhr, *The Social Sources of Denominationalism*, 105.

National Context

> I think that in no country in the civilized world is less attention paid to philosophy that in the United States. The Americans have no philosophical school of their own; and they care but little for all the schools into which Europe is divided, the very names of which are scarcely known to them. Yet it is easy to perceive that almost all the inhabitants of the United States conduct their understanding in the same manner, and govern it by the same rules; that is to say, without ever having taken the trouble to define the rules, they have a philosophical method common to the whole people. To evade the bondage of system and habit, of family-maxims, class-opinions, and, in some degree, of national prejudices; to accept tradition only as a means of information, and existing facts only as a lesson to be used in doing otherwise and doing better; to seek the reason of things for one's self, and in one's self alone; to tend to results without being bound to means, and to aim at the substance through the form;—such are the principal characteristics of what I shall call the philosophical method of the Americans. But if I go further, and seek amongst all the rest, I discover that, in most of the operations of mind, each American appeals only to the individual effort of his own understanding.[6]

Alexis de Tocqueville observed that the American philosophical tradition was one where individualism reigned supreme. Indeed, it was in this national context that Nathan Bangs was nurtured. He was born May 2, 1778, just after the American Revolution and died May 3, 1862, shortly after the start of the Civil War.[7] American territories stretched the country out over the continent in an unprecedented wave of imperialistic fervor. In 1803, American diplomats gained control of the strategic Mississippi River by negotiating the Louisiana Purchase for the paltry sum of fifteen million dollars. The War of 1812 settled once and for all the independent status of the rebel Americans. It also secured the boundaries between British Canada and the United States. The next year Congress passed the Indian Removal Act. By 1838, the US Army forced over one hundred thousand Cherokees, Choctaws, Chickasaws, Creeks, and Seminoles out of the Southeast in the infamous Trail of Tears death march. In 1835,

6. Tocqueville, *Democracy in America*, 143.

7. For an excellent overview of this period of cultural history, see Matthews, *Toward a New Society*. For a more prosaic account, read Daniel J. Boorstin's Pulitzer Prize winning *The Americans: The Democratic Experience*.

White settlers in Texas aggravated their Mexican hosts by declaring independence. The United States 1945 decision to annex Texas resulted in the Mexican-American War. On January 24, 1848, only one week before the Treaty of Guadalupe Hidalgo, General Johann Augustus Sutter announced the discovery of gold in California. By 1849, over one hundred thousand Americans and new immigrants, goaded by gold fever, made the long trek westward to California.

Rural families abandoned the harsh conditions of farm settlements for the attractive new urban industrial centers. They were introduced to new ideas and opportunities for pecuniary gain. But they were also introduced to the greatest social issue of the time—slavery. William Wilberforce's success in abolition in Britain in 1807 brought hope to slaves and abolitionists in America.[8] At the same time, such news increased the resolve of slave holders to maintain their position. Individuals who did not find their fortune or were striving to understand the upheavals of the day were especially vulnerable to promises of a better life.

Visionary American prophet Joseph Smith seized upon the instability of the times by publishing *The Book of Mormon* in 1830. By 1839, Smith managed to lead a few thousand followers on an exodus to establish the city of Nauvoo, Illinois. The newly organized Church of Latter-day Saints, popularly known as the "Mormons," did not find many willing neighbors and often faced violent evictions. Against all odds, the Mormons eventually found a permanent home to build their utopian society in Utah. The Mormon experience illustrates the religious consciousness of the period as well as the eventual marriage of religion with expansionism.[9] The phenomenon of the rural Cane Ridge Revival in 1801 signified the inception of a religious fervor that surpassed even the Great Awakening. The latter constituents were located mostly in New England and the middle colonies. The Second Great Awakening extended to a greater population and larger geographic area. This was a tempting opportunity for the many upstart groups who were competing for the souls of men and women.

8. William Wilberforce's work for social reform included a tract on Christian morals which was first published England, ca. 1797. A second edition appeared in 1837 which was reprinted in as many as twenty-six editions in America. He argued that while Christianity had a history of humanitarian treatment of the "poor and weak," middle and upper classes experience proves that "prosperity hardens the heart," thus, making it necessary to seek "a thorough change and renovation of our nature." Wilberforce, *A Practical View*, 23.

9. See Bushman, *Joseph Smith and the Beginnings of Mormonism.*

The effects of newfound respectability within the MEC were perhaps less obvious among Native Americans and Mexicans than African Americans. The exception, of course, was that increased encroachment applied pressure to their respective ways of life. For Native Americans, the paternalistic imperialism of the Methodist Mission Society reached its peak when it created the Oklahoma Indian Missionary Conference in 1844. Missionaries had the task of "Christianizing" and teaching them "customs requisite for citizenship."[10] Several Indian schools were already in place across the states in answer to the government's plea "for the civilization of the Indian." Henry Rowe Schoolcraft captured the growing sentiment toward the American Indians during the 1850s.

> Whatever defects may, in the eyes of the most ardent philanthropist, have at any time marked our system of Indian policy, nothing should, for a moment, divert the government or people, in their appropriate spheres, from offering to these wandering and benighted branches of the human race, however often rejected by them, the gifts of education, agriculture, and the gospel.[11]

At the request of President Ulysses S. Grant, the Missionary Society assumed administration of the Indian Service, at least for a brief period.[12] The missionaries received government money and support while the government received low wage workers willing to acculturate the Indians. The millennial hopes of Christian missionaries were easily married to the idea of the superiority of the (White) American way of life. Yet, they were disappointed when the massive conversion to Christianity did not occur.[13]

As the American penchant for expansionism swelled the minds of White Americans, the pressure on cultural survival increased to the same degree. Pioneers and robber barons gobbled up their lands as prime sites for farming, ranching, lumbering, mining, and railroad easements. Resistance and force resulted in bloody skirmishes which continued well into 1870.[14] The problem of "Indian trouble" notwithstanding, the push westward carried on. An unsigned editorial, later attributed to editor John L. O'Sullivan, strongly supporting the annexation of Texas appeared in

10. Bowden, *American Indians and Christian Missions*, 167.

11. Henry Rowe Schoolcraft, quoted in Pearce, *Savagism and Civilization*, 241.

12. Barclay, *History of Methodist Missions*, 3:326.

13. Berkhofer, *The White Man's Indian*, 150–51.

14. Danziger, "Native American Resistance and Accommodation," 164–65.

the July-August 1846 issue of the *United States Magazine and Democratic Review.* The article criticized the British and French resistance to the annexation proposal as attempts to obstruct "the fulfillment of our manifest destiny to overspread the continent allotted by Providence for the free development of our yearly multiplying millions."[15] The US-Mexican War ended 2 February 1848 with the Treaty of Guadalupe Hidalgo conferring over one million acres of Mexican territory to the United States. Garrisonian abolitionists were concerned that some antislavery "Conscience" Whigs, antislavery "Barnburner" Democrats, and Liberty men joined to form the Free-Soil party. The Free-Soilers agreed only to curb the expansion of slavery, not to abolish it.[16] As late as 1860, slaves living in the South fled to Canada rather than nearby Mexico for fear it would become a slave region subservient to the South, per Senator John J. Crittenden's compromise plan.[17]

Along with the spoils came persons still living on their recently expropriated lands. During the early days of the Texas Republic, White settlers sent word back to the Missionary Society asking for Methodist preachers. Mission districts were formed to minister to the needs of Anglo and German settlers.[18]

Methodist Colonialism

> It is the peculiar office of Christianity to inspire in the breasts of its notaries an ardent desire for the happiness of man. Expanding the soul with the purest benevolence, wherever its influence is felt, it expels that selfishness which is fed and strengthened by avarice. And this divine principle, occupying the heart, prompts its possessor to the selection of the most suitable means to accomplish the object of his desire. Ever active, and directing his activity to exalt the glory of God, and to effect the present and future happiness of man, whenever suitable means are presented,

15. See Howe, *What God Hath Wrought*, 702–8.

16. Sterling, *Ahead of Her Time*, 248.

17. Conrad, *Harriet Tubman*, 152.

18. Bangs' slowness to respond adequately to the missionary needs of German immigrants is cited in Douglass, *The Story of German Methodism*, 25. For a detailed history of Methodist missions in Texas, see Vernon et al., *The Methodist Excitement in Texas.*

> they are applied with assiduity and with certain hop of success. Such, we trust, are affects of the patrons of this society.[19]

In the 1839 centenary of Methodism, Bangs cited the remarkable growth of global Methodism as proof of God's favor on the Wesleyan message. He noted that both the British and American connections managed to increase themselves by means of missionaries "over the four quarters of the globe, in the states of Europe, in Asia, in Africa, in the islands of the sea; in South America, in Texas, in Liberia; among the aboriginal tribes of America, extending even beyond the Rocky Mountains."[20] Bangs suggested that personal evangelism could potentially quintuple the membership. At the very least the Methodist influence would be multiplied.

> If to each of these 1,151,829 church members we add four, as the probable number of hearers to one communicant, we shall have the number of 5,759,145, who are brought, less or more, under the influence of the Methodist doctrine and usages; and all this in the space of one hundred years! Has not God borne testimony to the labours of his servant, his helpers and successors?[21]

Missions

Methodists on both sides of the Atlantic were always dependent on a missionary spirit to promote their evangelical enterprise. Evangelism under Asbury was organized as a system of itinerant preachers setting up class meetings in their circuits. Their determination to give themselves wholly to the work reflected the "disinterested benevolence" popularized in the devotional *The Life of David Brainerd.*[22] Since the time of Asbury and Coke American Methodists were known for their missionary spirit. Asbury was not reticent to remind critics that the Methodist Episcopal Church was a missionary movement from its inception. Responding to the reports of expanding Baptist missions, Asbury replied that "the Methodist preachers, who had been sent by John Wesley to America, came as missionaries; some of them returned, but all did not. And now,

19. Bangs, "[Chairman's] Address."

20. Bangs, *Centenary Sermon*, 24.

21. Bangs, *Centenary Sermon*, 25.

22. For a discussion on "disinterested benevolence," see Conforti, *Jonathan Edwards*, 80, 85.

behold the consequences of this mission!"[23] Methodist missionaries were already enjoying a respectable reputation in English society. The social acceptability of evangelical missionaries even prompted Jane Austen to pen these flattering words in her 1814 novel *Mansfield Park*. "When I hear of you next, it may be as a celebrated preacher in some great society of Methodists, or as a missionary into foreign parts."[24] In 1816, *The Life of David Brainerd* was serialized in the Anglican *Missionary Register*.[25] David Brainerd had become the "principal model of early British Missionary spirituality" as his mission was supported by the Society in Scotland for the Promoting of Christian Knowledge. Asbury lamented the failure of the MEC to publish Brainerd's biography in America as "painful."[26] He only stopped reading Brainerd because of his failing eyesight.

> I have lately read the Life of David Brainerd—a man of my make, such a constitution, and of great labours; his religion was all gold, the purest gold. My eyes fail; I must keep them for the Bible and the conferences.[27]

Bangs recognized the power of spiritual biographies to launch Methodist missions. He recommended that young ministers read *The Life of Brainerd*, but not exclusively. He also recommended biographies of other exemplars including Wesley, Fletcher, and Asbury. He commended them all for their "instructive piety and persevering zeal."[28] This is most telling in his reflection on the spiritual value of Asbury's journal, which he reprinted in 1821.[29]

Methodist missionaries idealized the suffering and hardship in their spiritual biographies. However, not all missionaries were willing to live their lives in the same sacrificial fashion. Peter Cartwright resented the unscrupulous tactics of some missionaries. They would come from the eastern states as missionaries totally unprepared for the work and unwilling to acknowledge the hard work of the earlier pioneer preachers. Then they would report back in unflattering terms about the "moral wastes

23. Asbury, *Journal of Rev. Francis Asbury*, 3:459.
24. Walls, *Missionary Movement*, 80.
25. Walls, *Missionary Movement*, 80.
26. *General Minutes*, in Barclay, *History of Methodist Missions*, 1:200–201.
27. Asbury, *Journal of Rev. Francis Asbury*, 3:208.
28. Bangs, *Letters to Young Ministers*, 74.
29. Asbury, *Journal of Rev. Francis Asbury*.

and destitute condition of the west."[30] Worse yet, they would use these distorted facts to raise financial support for their "missions."

> These letters would be read in their large congregations, stating that they had traveled hundreds of miles, and found no evangelical minister, and the poor perishing people were in a fair way to be lost for the want of the bread of life; and the ignorant or uniformed thousands that heard these letters read would melt into tears, and their sympathies be greatly moved, when they considered our lost and heathenish state, and would liberally contribute their money to send us more missionaries, or to support those that were already here. Thus some of these missionaries, after occupying our pulpits, and preaching in large and respectable Methodist congregations, would write back and give those doleful tidings.
>
> Presently their letters would be printed, and come back among us as published facts in some of their periodicals.[31]

Bangs encouraged the publication of missionary reports as a tool for propagating new missions. He wrote many personal letters to missionaries with instructions regarding their mission. Bangs served as corresponding secretary of the Missionary Society until May 19, 1841, when his resigned to take the presidency at Wesleyan University.[32] A sampling of his many letters reveals that his tone was pastoral, but firm in the requirement to send reports to the Missionary Society in New York.

> My dear bro, . . . I rejoice much to hear of your prosperity in Texas, & we shall do our best to sustain you in your noble interprise. I hope you will not neglect to communicate regularly the status of prospects of your mission.
>
> With prayers for your welfare, I remain, yours affectionately,
>
> N. Bangs[33]

At the turn of the century, published reports of possible gains in territory were a bit more controversial than mission reports. The New York *Outlook*, the Boston *Congregationalist*, and the *Catholic World* all reluctantly supported the taking of the Philippines from Spain. However, the *Methodist Review of Missions* remained quiet on the subject until

30. Cartwright, *Autobiography*, 236.

31. Cartwright, *Autobiography*, 236.

32. Barclay, *History of Methodist Missions*, 1:312.

33. Nathan Bangs to Littleton Fowler, January 17, 1840.

after President McKinley ruled on the annexation.[34] Though the MEC and other mission boards did not openly suggest annexation of extra territories, they resigned themselves to the reality of the opportunity for missions they presented. Neither did many openly oppose the Mexican War. Rather, Baptists and Methodists considered it a just crusade against Roman Catholicism.[35]

In 1837, Nathan Bangs wrote to H. K. W. Perkins that a proposal to colonize the Pacific Northwest would not necessarily conflict with the missionary goals of Methodism. "If the mission prospers, a colony will rise up, so we hope a foundation will be raised thus early for its future prosperity."[36] Clearly, the organization of Methodist missions encouraged an ordered social climate on the fringe areas. One of the great claims of Methodist itinerants was that Methodism brought order to the frontier. The successes of new missions were interpreted as God's favor for the new systems of control. Missions were used to expand respectability by converting and educating indigenous and borderland peoples in the ways of Anglo-Christian culture. Missionaries often confused the adoption of Western ideals of clothing and customs with conversion to Christianity. The sad case of the paternalistic missions to Hawaiians is a well-known example of a several failed attempts to "civilize" non-Western and indigenous cultures.[37] German Methodists were also busy reaching fellow immigrants.

Cultural Imperialism

> Here I introduced him [William Nast] to the "first families" of pious Methodists, all of whom took a deep interest in his welfare, and many an ardent prayer was offered for his conversion. During his stay with me he translated our Articles of Religion and the General Rules of our Discipline, and wrote in English characters so that I could read it. When he came to the translation of the sacramental services he hesitated very much, saying

34. May, *Imperial Democracy*, 256–57.

35. Crouse, "Methodist Encounters," 161.

36. Nathan Bangs to H. K. W. Perkins, January 16, 1837, Perkins Collection, WSHS, quoted in Loewenberg, *Equality on the Oregon Frontier*, 108.

37. This event of culture clash was popularized in twentieth-century pop culture by James Michener's novel *Hawaii* and romanticized by Rogers and Hammerstein's *South Pacific* musical. MEC missions to the Sandwich Islands, or Hawaii, began in 1855. Reid, *Missions and Missionary Society*, 2:143.

> that he was too great a sinner and too unworthy to translate and write those solemn words. At my earnest request, however, he proceeded and finished the translation.[38]

Bangs published his assessment of progress at midcentury in *The Present State, Prospects, and Responsibilities of the Methodist Episcopal Church.* Only fifteen years later MEC historian Abel Stevens was asked to comment on the one hundredth anniversary of Methodism in America.[39] What he presented was the logical conclusion of Bangs' earlier work. Methodism in America had triumphed both spiritually and economically. Therefore, their incumbent duty was to manage American interests. Stevens' tone sounds astoundingly arrogant to twenty-first-century readers. "As the leading Church of this country, it bears, before God and man, the chief responsibility of the moral welfare of the nation."[40]

It is important to note that Stevens published his book after the Civil War. His only mention of African Americans was in his comment that the "question of slavery" was "now practically obsolete." In other words, Stevens made no provision whatsoever for the future of African Americans in postbellum America. By postmodern standards, Stevens' work may be interpreted as a xenophobic, misogynistic, and elitist blueprint for White male privilege. He excluded all people of color, but most especially those descending from Africans, Native Americans, Mexicans, and others he referred to as "semi-barbarous foreigners."[41] In his own words: "The destiny of the country is then in the hands of its [White] educators."[42] On the other hand, those who proffered a vision for a White America could not discount the presence of people of color. As early as 1820, William Ryland reported to the General Conference that the Committee on the State of Missions recommended mission work to "our Western frontiers generally, having regard for those who use the French, Spanish, or other foreign languages" and the "Indian tribes."[43]

Nineteenth-century church historian Robert Baird was embarrassed that news of race riots and trouble had reached the *intelligentsia*

38. Miller, *Experience of German Methodist Preachers*, 62.

39. Stevens, *The Centenary of American Methodism*.

40. Stevens, *The Centenary of American Methodism*, 15.

41. Stevens, *The Centenary of American Methodism*, 227, 228.

42. Stevens, *The Centenary of American Methodism*, 231.

43. William Ryland, quoted in Youngs, *A History of the Most Interesting Events*, 398.

of Europe. Seeking to exonerate White Anglo-Americans, he blamed Black people and immigrants of German and Irish origin for the troublesome reports.[44] Isaac M. Wise was more generous when he referred to America as an "heiress of the European civilization" encompassing "English, Irish, French, Dutch, German, Polish, Spanish, or Scandinavian" peoples.[45] Methodists in New York City accommodated the immigration of non-English speaking Methodists by setting up districts to minister to Germans (1842), Swedes (1845), French (1838), Welsh (1853), and, toward the end of the century, Italians (1889) and Chinese (1888).[46] Both the Evangelical Association and the United Brethren in Christ, close followers of the MEC discipline and theology, specialized in ministry to German speaking folk.[47] This segregationist mode of Methodist missions continued well into the Gilded Age. At the 1873 dedication of Philip Embury's tomb, AME Bishop Jabez Pitt Campbell demonstrated that segregationist ideas were not limited to White people when he argued that missions should be carried out by people of their respective racial group. "The Chinese for China; the Japanese for Japan; the German for Germany; the African for Africa."[48]

In North America, Africans (both slave and free), Native Americans, Mexicans, Chinese, and other immigrant communities were subjected to objectification as exotic targets for the missionary enterprise. At mid-century, people of African heritage comprised the largest non-White ethnic group in America. The African American history of respectability runs parallel to that of the predominantly White MEC. African Americans who chose to remain in the MEC were not forgotten by the 1824 General Conference. Three main clauses were added to the Discipline that directly dealt with African American ministry needs including: an exhortation to teach slaves to read the Bible and worship; allowance for Black preachers to have the same privileges as White preachers, where legal; and authorization for the Annual Conference to appoint Black preachers according to the rules of the *Discipline*.[49] However, it was not

44. Baird, *Religion in America*, 296.

45. Isaac M. Wise, "Our Country's Place in History," lecture delivered before the Theological and Religious Library Association of Cincinnati, January 7, 1869, in Cherry, *God's New Israel*, 226, 227.

46. Seaman, *Annals of New York Methodism*, 391–401.

47. See Behney and Eller *History of the Evangelical United Brethren Church*.

48. Reynolds, *The Birth of Methodism in America*, 47.

49. Graham, *Black United Methodists*, 21.

until March 30, 1864 that John Newton Mars was received into the New England Conference on probation, distinguishing him as the first Black preacher admitted into a White annual conference. That same year the Delaware Conference was organized in Philadelphia as the first Black mission conference of the MEC.[50]

In 1861, the MEC had fifteen thousand seven hundred African slave adherents compared to the MEC, South with over two hundred thousand African slave adherents. Over 47 percent of these members were a result of evangelistic efforts led by Methodists.[51] After the US emancipation and after the middling of American Methodism, the hegemony of Northern Black missionaries migrating south to save and educate Southern Blacks created no small conflict. Former AME ministers who rejoined the MEC, South prevented rival AME missionaries from entering plantation missions.[52] There was also a problem of class conflict within worship styles. In one incident, a certain Northern Black minister with theological education was ridiculed by his Southern Black congregation who thought his undemonstrative preaching resembled the Presbyterians.[53]

Not much happened by way of Methodist missions with Spanish speaking people on the borderlands until the 1870s. The primary reason was that the Missionary Society focused their efforts on Latin America rather than Spanish-speaking people living in the borderlands. The ethnic variety of borderland peoples included Anglo and European colonists, African Americans, unassimilated Native Americans, Spaniards, Canary Islanders, and "Mexicans." Roman Catholic priests maintained an elaborate level of caste distinctions for their parishioners assigned according to ethnic background and parentage, such as "*espanol*, indio, negro, meztizo, *mulato*, *coyote*, *lobo*, and *coyote*."[54] Attempts to successfully missionize borderland peoples would have to deal with this complexity.

In 1845, Melinda Rankin, under the auspices of the Western Presbytery of the Presbyterians established the Rio Grande Female Institute in Brownsville, Texas. It survived for only a few years. Following the 1848 General Conference, the MEC expanded their boundaries into the newly annexed western territories. In 1850, an English speaking MEC mission

50. Graham, *Black United Methodists*, 34.

51. Lakey, *The History of the CME Church*, 98–99.

52. Whelchel, *Hell without Fire*, 99.

53. Foner, *Reconstruction*, 92.

54. Chipman, *Spanish Texas*, 250.

was established in Sante Fe, New Mexico under the supervision of Enoch G. Nicholson.[55] Shortly after his arrival Benigno Cardenas, a suspended Roman Catholic priest offered his services to Nicholson and the Methodists. Although Nicholson was charged to explore Spanish missions, he refused the offer. He did not desire to interfere with the Roman Catholic in-house dispute. Cardenas went to Rome to answer to the authorities for his rebellion. On his return voyage he stopped over in London. He was befriended by William H. Rule, a veteran British Wesleyan Methodist missionary to Spain. Rule did not mention Cardenas in his memoirs. However, Rule recorded that he provided letters of introduction for Don Angel Herreros de Mora, an ex-priest from Spain, for employment in the American Bible and Tract Societies.[56] It is reasonable to assume that Rule would do the same for another priest. Cardenas remained with Rule for ten weeks of personal mentoring. Cardenas arrived in New York with letters from Rule to the Methodist Missionary Society. Cardenas encountered Nicholson who was there to discuss the New Mexico mission. Walter Hansen, a resident of New Mexico, joined the mission team. Nicholson returned to New Mexico as a superintendent. Hansen and Cardenas were assigned to assist as colporteurs and preachers. Ignoring the Roman Catholic bishop's threats of excommunication, Cardenas boldly delivered his message under the portals of the Governor's Palace on November 20, 1853.[57] Cardenas is often celebrated for delivering the first Spanish Methodist sermon preached in America.[58]

Walter Hansen abandoned the mission after a few months. Nicholson also returned to New York in less than a year. Cardenas, still only a colporteur, was left on his own in New Mexico. He made several converts and successfully formed congregations in both Socorro and Peralta. In 1855, the mission was terminated after pejorative reports were received

55. The earliest known Protestant mission in Sante Fe was established by a Baptist named Hiram W. Read in 1849. William J. Kephart also came in 1850 to set up a Presbyterian mission. See Sylvest, "Hispanic American Protestantism," 296–304.

56. Rule, *Recollections*, 232.

57. Nañez, *History of the Rio Grande Conference*, 5–7.

58. This popular claim does not adequately consider John Wesley's journal entry of April 4, 1737, which stated: "I began learning Spanish, in order to converse with my Jewish parishioners." Spanish speaking Georgia residents included Sephardic Jews, Native Americans and *Mestizos*. Wesley also used the term "converse" prior to learning German and Italian to preach to the local immigrants. It follows that John Wesley may very well have preached the first Methodist sermon in Spanish in the Americas. *Works of John Wesley* (Jackson ed.) 1:47.

by the Missionary Society from Dallas D. Lore, the new superintendent.[59] The Methodist work among Spanish speaking people of New Mexico languished under the care of Ambrosia Gonzalez, a lay exhorter.[60] Methodist work among Spanish speaking people was sporadic in the years following. The next major push did not occur until 1869 with the bilingual efforts of Thomas Harwood in New Mexico.[61] The Mexican Mission began in Texas in 1873 when Alejo Hernandez, an aspirant for the Roman Catholic priesthood, was received as a Methodist preacher under the authority of the MEC, South.[62]

It is helpful to review the 1855 report of General Missionary Committee. It reflects ambitious plans for the expanding mission of the MEC in the coming quadrennium. Funds allocated for foreign missions included: $31,000 for Liberia; $8,500 for China; $10,500 for foreign German work; $5,000 for France; $1,000 for Norway; $1,000 for Norway or Sweden; $400 for Sweden; $7,500 for India; $5,000 for Turkey; $2,750 for Argentina; $3,000 for northern South America; and $1,500 for Central America. The General Missionary Committee also made financial provision for future expansion into the territories and domestic ethnic missions. Regarding the latter, they allocated $48,000 for German Domestic Missions, $13,250 for Indian Missions, $1,000 for a mission to the Jews in New York City, and $1,250 for "concluding" the New Mexico mission.[63]

New Gender Roles

> While we contend that it is not absolutely necessary for the itinerant's wife to be instructed in the languages, or mathematics, or to be skilled in instrumental music, we *do* contend that she ought to have a good English education, such as is taught in our public schools. *More* she *may* have to advantage; this amount she must have, or she will often find herself in a very awkward and unpleasant position in society, as she will be called

59. Barclay, *History of Methodist Missions*, 3:237.

60. Barton, "Inter-ethnic Relations," 65–67.

61. Barclay, *History of Methodist Missions*, 3:239.

62. Alejo Hernandez was ordained a deacon by Bishop Enoch Marvin on December 24, 1871. Barton, *Hispanic Methodists*, 203–4n79.

63. MEC, *Journals of the General Conference*, 3:264–65.

> to mingle not only with the poor and ignorant, but also with the better informed, and more refined portion of community.[64]

Male ministers often spoke to women as a sex with peculiar powers and responsibilities. As women, they were expected to perform certain biological and social functions, but the latter being under the guidance of the minister.[65] Women also instructed other women to stay in their sphere. In *The Mother's Practical Guide*, the author takes a sharp aim at women as responsible to the church and the world for the education of their children.

> Her words, her actions, the tones of her voice, the expression of her countenance, have all a powerful influence in forming the youthful mind. On her efforts depends, under God, the future well-being of her children, and her children's children. Her prayers, her example, her instructions are to educate the parents and teachers of another generation; to her exertions may the world be indebted for some of its brightest ornaments, and the church for some of its most valuable members and most devoted ministers.[66]

One of the unexpected results of industrialization was the expansion of gender spheres within the family structure. Men were sent off to work in factories, leaving their wives in charge of the homes. Freed African American women left the field for work in the home while their husbands engaged themselves in factory labor. Black women, already experienced in navigating social and economic inequities, were suddenly confronted by stronger patriarchy in Black families. Furthermore, the separate gender spheres became institutionalized.[67] This shift in gender roles was already happening in White families near industrial towns. In the antebellum South, dominated by an agricultural economy, men were permitted to stay home with the family. Thus, Southern women were less likely to be the spiritual leader in the home.[68]

One of the elements rural folks found appealing in revival and camp meetings was its leveling effect on social strata. It offered both inclusion of

64. Eaton, *The Itinerant's Wife*, 15.
65. Cott, *The Bonds of Womanhood*, 148.
66. Bakewell, *The Mother's Practical Guide*, 16.
67. Foner, *Reconstruction*, 87.
68. Foner, *Reconstruction*, 158–59.

all races and offered near egalitarian gender participation.[69] In the camp, neither class nor race nor gender excluded a person from participation in the spiritual exercises or phenomena. It is not surprising that Michael Chevalier (ca. 1839), referred to American camp meetings as "festivals of democracy."[70]

This leveling effect also assisted the expansion of the social sphere of women in religion. Many women reported experiences of conversion or sanctification at these meetings.[71] Some evidence of these experiences may be found in the testimonies of Hannah Bunting, Elizabeth Lyon, Mary W. Morgan, Jarena Lee, Annie Taylor, Rebecca Fisher, Amanda Berry Smith, Clementina Butler, and Phoebe Palmer. These women would challenge the order of discipline which was exerting incremental restraints around the camp meeting's spirit of freedom.

Hannah Bunting described her camp meeting experiences in ecstatic terms. She reported receiving the gift of sanctification at a camp meeting. She found herself ministering, rather reluctantly, to other women in her own tent during another camp meeting in Belleville, New Jersey.

> The severest cross was yet to be lifted: I was soon required to raise my feeble voice in prayer. The hundreds who surrounded me did not daunt me or prevent my trust in God. While I endeavored to apply to promise to a sincere female, who for two nights and days had been wrestling in an agony for full redemption, the answer came. Her soul was filled with pure seraphic joy. She rose on her feet, and, with feeling and clearness, declared what God had wrought. To my surprise the day dawned. So sweetly had the moments rolled, I had not ever wished to close my eyes in sleep. The loud blast of the trumpet summoned us to the last meeting. . . . Why should anyone dispute the utility of camp meetings?[72]

Hannah Bunting's response to the call to public prayer was not altogether different from that of the earlier Susanna Wesley. Bunting responded to a situation which was immediate and pressing. Susanna

69. Raboteau, *Slave Religion*, 132.

70. Quoted in Hatch, *Democratization*, 58.

71. Schmidt, *Grace Sufficient*, 46.

72. The "tarrying" testimony in the anecdote was typical of the holiness movement. This is distinguished from Phoebe Palmer's "altar theology," which eliminated the need for tarrying for sanctification. Schmidt, *Grace Sufficient*, 41, 42.

Wesley acted out of a long-held conviction prompted by reading some accounts of Danish missionaries.

> At last it came to my mind, though I am not a man nor a minister of the gospel, and so cannot be employed in such a worthy employment as they were; yet if my heart were so sincerely devoted to God, and if I were inspired with a true zeal for his glory and did really desire the salvation of souls, I might do somewhat more than I do. I thought I might live in a more exemplary manner in some things; I might pray more for the people and speak with more warmth to those with whom I have an opportunity of conversing.[73]

Although Susanna Wesley remained a woman of her time, the opportunity for female leadership in the church was a significant hallmark of Methodism. The Methodist movement was the realm of women from the beginning.[74] Starting with the initial input of Susanna Wesley women served vital roles as leaders and supporters of the Wesleyan revival. Thus, the early Methodist Societies were chiefly women's organizations.[75]

In America, a vestige of the Puritan society relegated women's sphere to teaching in the home. Oddly enough, Southerners eagerly chose to adopt the Puritan position. This presented a strange option for the "cult of domesticity." Middle-class Yankees identified the home as "a church" where wives took charge of religious training.[76] Though there was widespread acceptance in the South of the "cult of domesticity," Southern homes never became the women's religious sphere as it did in the North. This middle-class ideal applied to married women in the home and volunteer associations and to single women performing in-home services. As such, it "constituted a guiding image for domestic servants, both immigrants and freed slaves, who sought economic security and upward mobility."[77]

Some women found that Christian ministry was another way to improve one's lot in life. As Methodism expanded nationwide, doors opened for women to respond to ministerial calls, even in the South. This was no less true for women of color. Jarena Lee found an open door for ministry

73. Susanna Wesley to Samuel Wesley Sr., February 6, 1711/12, in *Susanna Wesley: The Complete Writings*, 80.

74. Chilcote, *She Offered Them Christ*, 24.

75. Chilcote, *She Offered Them Christ*, 25.

76. Heyrman, *Southern Cross*, 158.

77. Browning et al., *From Culture Wars to Common Ground*, 85.

in the African Methodist Episcopal Church to preach the gospel. She was converted under the preaching of Rev. Richard Allen. About five years later, she answered a call to preach, though without much support.

> I now told him [Richard Allen], that the Lord had revealed to me, to [I] must preach the gospel. He replied, by asking, in what sphere I wished to move in? I said, among the Methodists. He then replied that a Mrs. Cook, a Methodist lady, had also some time before requested the same privilege; who, it was believed, had done much good in the way of exhortation, and holding prayer meetings; and who had been permitted to do so by the verbal license of the preacher in charge at the time. But as to women preaching, he said that our Discipline knew nothing at all about it—that it did not call for women preaching.[78]

Accounts of Nathan Bangs' interactions with women preachers and exhorters are few, but significant. His missionary tour in Lower Canada and at John Street Church connected him indirectly to the legacy of Barbara Heck. Although he never met Heck, her testimony made such a deep impression that in later years he referred to her as "a pious matron."[79] Abel Stevens compared her role in the Wesleyan revival to that of Susanna Wesley and Countess Selena of Huntingdon. Looking back on the earlier days at the rigging loft, which became Wesley's Chapel and then John Street Church, Stevens credited the expansion of Methodism in North America to Barbara Heck. "Philip Embury justly ranks as founder of American Methodism, but Barbara Heck may even take precedence of him as its foundress."[80] She may have found more opportunities to express her faith on the Canadian frontier. Certainly, Nathan's own sister, Elinor Bangs Gatchell, established her own reputation as an effective exhorter in Canada. One admiring witness said her exhorting was "like a streak of red-hot lightening!"[81]

Phoebe Palmer represented a higher profile connection between Bangs and women ministers. Palmer enjoyed a reputation as the most celebrated of American women preachers or exhorters of the nineteenth century. Notably, Nathan Bangs served as her childhood catechist in New York.[82] The mutual admiration enjoyed between Palmer and Bangs

78. Lee, *Religious Experience*, 11.

79. Bangs, *Life of Freeborn Garrettson*, 2.

80. Stevens, *The Women of Methodism*, 184.

81. Carroll, *Case and His Contemporaries*, 224.

82. Stevens, *Life and Times of Nathan Bangs*, 350.

was long-lasting. Palmer composed a hymn celebrating the golden anniversary of the Bangs.[83] In his Last Will and Testament, Bangs named Palmer as one of his friends identified to receive a copy of his posthumously published memoirs.[84] Their close relationship may suggest space existed for ongoing conversations on the subject Christian perfection. This is possible without diminishing Palmer's genius.

Palmer wrote *Promise of the Father* (1859) in defense of the female response to the ministerial call. However, Palmer did not advocate that a woman should preach using the technical technique common to male preachers of the mid-nineteenth century.[85] Citing Dr. Francis Wayland, Palmer maintained that a preacher is "a messenger of good news." Thus, she was suggesting that preaching in the nineteenth century was not faithful to the scriptural model. "If this be the true scriptural idea of *preaching*, to this we believe *every* individual called, whether male or female, who has been brought to an experimental knowledge of the grace of Christ, as the Savior of sinners."[86]

Phoebe Palmer is best remembered for her relentless promotion of Christian perfection. She led a standing "Tuesday Meeting" in New York City as an ongoing discussion group focusing on Christian perfection. They were well attended by denominational luminaries such as Stephen Olin, Leonidas Hamline, and Nathan Bangs.[87] Bangs was a regular at the Tuesday meetings. Discussions at the meetings contributed to the body of her book, *The Way of Holiness* (1843). The popularity of this book gave Palmer an international platform. Written in the third person, it promoted Palmer's "altar theology" based on her personal experience of receiving sanctification.

> And by the determination to consecrate all upon the altar of sacrifice to God, with the resolve to "enter into the bonds of an everlasting covenant to be wholly the Lord's for time and eternity," and then acting in conformity with this decision, *actually laying all upon the altar*, by the most unequivocal Scripture testimony, she laid herself under the most solemn obligation to *believe that the sacrifice became the Lord's property; and by virtue*

83. Palmer, "Semi-Centennial Marriage Hymn," 22–23.

84. Nathan Bangs, last will and testament dated July 16, 1862, Letters of Testamentary, County of New York, vol. 142, 162.

85. Leclerc, "Two Women Speaking 'Woman,'" 196–97.

86. Palmer, *The Promise of the Father*, 330.

87. Stevens, *Life and Times of Nathan Bangs*, 352.

> *of the altar upon which the offering was laid, became "holy" and "acceptable."*[88]

The upshot of Palmer's "altar theology was the eradication of sin, understood in the Wesleyan holiness sense, no longer required agony and soul searching.[89] Bangs objected to Palmer's "altar theology" on the use of semantics. However, he found some common ground in the opposition to the Reformed view of gradual sanctification. "Those who teach that we are gradually to grow into a state of sanctification, without even experiencing an instantaneous change from inbred sin to holiness are to be reputed as unsound, anti-scriptural and anti-Wesleyan."[90] Perhaps due to his own commitment to the Wesleyan doctrine of sanctification Bangs found something good in Palmer's message.

> Some object to her phraseology. I do not pledge myself to the correctness of every word she may utter any more than I can expect every other person to agree with me in all my words and phrases. But why should I dispute about words so long as the substance is retained? I care not by what name this great blessing be designated, whether holiness, sanctification, perfect love, Christian perfection, so long as is meant by it an entire consecration of soul and body to God, accompanied with faith that he accepts the sacrifice through the merits of Christ alone.[91]

By the time Palmer's popularity crested, Bangs' national influence was greatly diminished. Putting their slight differences aside, he was not reticent to defend her ministry. Considering his track record for bureaucratic control, Bangs may have been tempted to place limits on female ministry. Near the close of his own ministry, he offered a lively support of her ministry.

> And why should anyone oppose another, even though a female, so eminently owned by the Head of the Church in the conversion of sinners and in the sanctification of believers? For my part I dare not. I cannot but rejoice in whatever instrumentality God shall use in the salvation of souls. And I have abundant reason to believe that this devoted woman has been thus used of

88. Palmer, "The Way of Holiness (1843)," in Oden, *Phoebe Palmer*, 179.

89. Pugh, "The Wesleyan Way," 11.

90. Nathan Bangs, *Guide to Perfection* (1854), quoted in Haney, *The Inheritance Restored.*

91. Stevens, *Life and Times of Nathan Bangs*, 351.

> God as an instrument of good to others. She possesses the happy art of winning their confidence, and of pointing them directly to the Lord Jesus for life and salvation.[92]

Nathan Bangs left his mark on nineteenth-century American Methodism, much of it faded at the turn of the twentieth century. On the other hand, Palmer's teachings significantly influenced theology and practice for Wesleyan, Holiness, Pentecostal, and charismatic traditions beyond her own time.[93] Her influence as a female leader and theological innovator continues as a force to be reckoned with into the twenty-first century.

Summary

Despite the best efforts to emulate John Wesley's ideals of egalitarianism, the MEC at mid-century more closely resembled Nathan Bangs' respectable White middle-class ideal. African Americans created their own niche in American Methodism by dire necessity and creative genius. At the same time, the wealth of middle-class America continued to expand with the territories by shrewd purchase and aggressive conquest. It is ironic that the MEC, founded as a working-class movement, became less a church of the common people and more a church for the middle class. American Methodism at the end of the antebellum period remained firmly under the control of privileged White men. Whether poor Whites or non-Whites, immigrants or colonized peoples, the phenomenon of respectability in the MEC translated into unhappy legacy of marginalization and neglect. Yet, these outsider groups were not left without hopes and dreams. Their suppressed Wesleyan religious fervor later emerged in the myriad forms of Holiness and Pentecostal movements of the late nineteenth century and continue to expand in the twenty-first century.

92. Stevens, *Life and Times of Nathan Bangs*, 351.

93. Oden, *Phoebe Palmer*, 5.

Chapter VI

ANTISLAVERY

> Whoever has had opportunity of acquaintance with society in New England, during the last twenty-five years, with those middle and with those leading sections that may constitute any just representation of the character and aim of the community, which have been struck with the great activity of thought and experimenting. His attention must be commanded by the signs that the Church, or religious party, is falling from the church nominal, and is appearing in temperance and nonresistant societies, in movements of abolitionists and of socialists, and in very significant assemblies, called Sabbath and Bible conventions,–composed of ultraists, of seekers, of all the soul of the solidiery [*sic*] of dissent, and meeting to call in question the authority of the Sabbath, of the priesthood, and of the church. In these movements, nothing was more remarkable than the discontent they begot in the movers. The spirit of protest and of detachment drove the members of these Conventions, their independence of their colleagues, and their impatience of the methods whereby they were working. They defied each other, like a congress of kings, each of whom had a realm to rule, and a way of his own that made concert unprofitable. What a fertility of projects for the salvation of the world![1]

THE TRANSCENDENTALIST RALPH WALDO Emerson succinctly described the social context of New England in the mid-nineteenth

1. Emerson, "New England Reformers," 253.

century as one filled with elements of discord. Indeed, there were a variety of forms of both secular and religious dissent. As the church became more respectable, constituents turned their attention to perfecting the social order. The most pressing issues were slavery, temperance, and suffrage. However, by far the most heated of these subjects was slavery.[2] Nathan Bangs recognized reform movements dealing with these issues as unwieldy and divisive. He preferred the limits of the *Discipline* for managing order. The authority of such was acceptable enough for local congregations. Unfortunately, it was insufficient for controlling popular opinion on divisive issues. Bangs was in a precarious position. On the one hand, his contemporaries judged him harshly for his apparent political neutrality. On the other, it would be said of him that the "two great errors of position in his life were his opposition to the temperance organizations and to the antislavery movement."[3] Regarding temperance, Bangs used the press to speak out against temperance societies. At length, the temperance advocates won him over.[4] He even wrote a letter recommending Rev. W. Armstrong for his sermon on temperance.[5]

Bangs resisted taking a partisan stance with either the abolitionists or the slave holders. He believed that neutrality on the issue would be the most irenic position. Indeed, Bangs considered it safest to side with the African colonization project. But he was not neutral. Rather, he leveraged his influence in publishing to curb dissent in the MEC. The volatile issue of slavery became the battleground for maintaining respectability.

Abolition

> DEAR SIR,– Unless the divine power has raised you up to be as *Athanasius contra mundum*, I see not how you can go through your glorious enterprise in opposing that execrable villainy, which is the scandal of religion, of England, and of human nature. Unless God has raised you up for this very thing, you will be worn out by the opposition of men and devils. But if God be for you, who can be against you? Are all of them together

2. Bangs cites this as the most heated topic of discussion in the 1836 General Conference. Bangs, *History of the Methodist Episcopal Church*, 4:242.

3. Review of *Life and Times of Nathan Bangs*, 173.

4. Mudge, *History of the New England Conference*, 298.

5. Bangs, "Recommendation of Rev. W. Armstrong."

> stronger than God? O be not weary of well doing! Go on, in the name of God and in the power of His might, till even American slavery (the vilest that ever saw the sun) shall vanish away before it.[6]

Clearly, the most divisive issue of the nineteenth century was slavery. John Wesley's stance against slavery was made clear with the 1774 publication of *Thoughts upon Slavery.* Significantly, his last written letter (cited above) was addressed to the British abolitionist William Wilberforce. Typical of his visionary leadership, he endorsed the abolition movement while forecasting a bitter struggle ahead. Wesley may have expected that abolition would be the default position embraced by American Methodists. This was not the case. Even John Street Church, the "Mother Church" of American Methodism, owned a slave named Peter Williams.[7] Parliamentary legislation outlawed slave merchanting in Britain as early as 1807. However, abolitionists continued crusading another grueling six decades afterward for similar legislation in America. At length, the federal government finally took a firm stand by issuing the Emancipation Proclamation on January 1, 1863. Even though Francis Asbury held a dim view of slavery, American Methodists failed to promote the official antislavery position stated in the *Discipline.* In 1809, Asbury complained of the impediment which the MEC's antislavery reputation represented in their efforts to bring the Gospel to slaves.

> We are defrauded of great numbers by the pains that are taken to keep the blacks from us; their masters are afraid of the influence of our principles. Would not an *amelioration* in the condition and treatment of slaves have produced more practical good to the poor Africans, than any attempt at their *emancipation?* The state of society, unhappily does not admit this: besides, the blacks are deprived of the means of instruction; who will take the pains to lead them into the ways of salvation, and watch over them that they may not stray, but the Methodists? Well; now their masters will not let them come to hear us.[8]

In his bid to win the confidence of slave owners, Asbury fell into the trap of emphasizing the results of conversion rather than the prospects

6. John Wesley to William Wilberforce, February 24, 1791, in *The Letters of John Wesley*, 265.

7. Streeter, *Past and Present*, 22–23.

8. Francis Asbury, February 1, 1809, in *The Journal of Rev. Francis Asbury*, 3:298.

of emancipation.[9] Although he opposed slavery, he was not adamant on immediate abolition. Frederick Douglass, while still a slave, was hopeful that the conversion of his master to Methodism would mean an immediate end to his bondage.

> I had read somewhere, in the *Methodist Discipline*, the following question and answer: "Question. What shall be done for the extirpation of slavery?" "Answer. We declare that we are as much as ever convinced of the great evil of slavery; therefore, no slaveholder shall be eligible to any official station in our church." These words sounded in my ears for a long time, and encouraged me to hope. But, as I have before said, I was doomed to disappointment.[10]

It is necessary at this point to distinguish the varieties of abolitionism. There were two main types of abolitionism: "gradualism" and "immediatism." Gradualism was the predominant type of antislavery movement in the eighteenth century. "Gradualism, in the sense of a reliance on indirect and slow-working means to achieve a desired social objective, was the logical consequence of fundamental attitudes toward progress, natural law, property, and individual rights."[11] By contrast, "immediatism" besides its temporal reference, had a very wide semantic range which was the source of no small confusion to the public. For some abolitionists, the term suggested rejection of the intermediary agencies which delayed complete freedom from slavery. Thus, colonization and apprenticeship were considered affronts to immediatist abolitionists.

A person conscious of the sinfulness of slavery could consider themself an immediatist. The same could be said for another who actively boycotted produce from slave labor. This fuzzy definition was detrimental to the cause of antislavery. "The doctrine of immediacy, in the form it took in the 1830s, was at once a logical culmination of the antislavery movement and a token of a major shift in intellectual history."[12] In part, "immediatism" was a product of the natural rights arguments of Louis de Jaucourt, Anthony Benezet, and Granville Sharp. George Keith, Society of Friends, reminded Quakers to judge slavery by the Golden Rule.[13] John

9. Raboteau, *Slave Religion*, 145.

10. Douglass, *Life and Times of Frederick Douglass*, 109.

11. Davis, "The Emergence of Immediatism," 142.

12. Davis, "The Emergence of Immediatism," 140.

13. Davis, "The Emergence of Immediatism," 140–41.

Wesley's writings were strongly "immediatist." Significantly, John Wesley appended the third verse of Charles Wesley's hymn *For the Heathens* to the end of his *Thoughts upon Slavery*.[14] Unfortunately, this gave unintended credence to the "curse of Ham" myth that Africans were destined to be slaves.

> The servile progeny of Ham
> Seize as the purchase of thy blood;
> Let all the heathens know thy name;
> From idols to the living God
> The dark Americans convert,
> And shine in every pagan heart![15]

Nathan Bangs prided himself as a faithful follower of John Wesley. He reported that early in his ministry he dreamed that Wesley passed by on a chariot of light and threw him a shining sword saying, "Take this and conquer!"[16] However, unlike Mr. Wesley, Bangs was definitely a "gradualist." In addition, he was an active supporter of the American Colonization Society.

> Slavery in the United States may be considered the remote, and Christian philanthropy the proximate, cause of establishing the colony in Africa, now known as Liberia, under the auspices of the American Colonization Society. This society was formed in 1816, by some benevolent individuals, with a view to transport to Africa such free people of color from the United States as might consent to emigrate, and establish them as a colony, with all the rights and privileges of freemen. Though at first the society was viewed with suspicion by some, fearing it was designed chiefly to rivet the chains of slavery yet tighter on the slave, by removing the free colored people out of the land; yet as its character was gradually developed, the public confidence was acquired, and its friends and supporters were daily increased.[17]

The American Colonization Society, founded 1816, promoted a scheme to help free African Americans emigrate to Africa. The ACS presented itself as a respectable alternative to civil war, servile insurrection,

14. Wesley, *A Collection of Hymns*, *Works of John Wesley* (Bicentennial ed.), 7:609n432.

15. See Wesley, *Thoughts upon Slavery*, 23.

16. Stevens, *Life and Times of Nathan Bangs*, 61.

17. Bangs, *History of the Methodist Episcopal Church*, 4:111.

and Black equality.[18] By 1830, besides receiving grants from benevolent agencies and the state legislatures, the ACS enjoyed endorsements by Presbyterians, Methodists, Baptists, and Dutch Reformed Churches nationally and by Episcopalians, Congregationalists, and Quakers regionally.[19] The editorship of the *Methodist Magazine and Quarterly Review* was decidedly in favor of the scheme. The quote below illustrates a respectable appeal to both patriotism and the Christian virtue of disinterested benevolence.

> There is no institution of benevolence, among all those which are now before the public, which is so strictly national in its character as the American Colonization Society. In its origin it engaged the hands and hearts of the purest patriots, the most exalted philanthropists, and the most enlightened Christians. And in its progress thus far, in furtherance of the grand and sublime purposes of its organization, it has called forth and exhibited an extent of labor, privation, suffering, and sacrifice, which Christianity alone could inspire, and to which Christian heroism can alone furnish a parallel in this world's history. And we may add, that, to the present hour, this society has had a success which far exceeds the hopes of its founders; and promises a rich harvest of blessing both to the African continent and to our own land.[20]

The ACS was not well accepted by either free African Americans or by slave owners.[21] There were several weaknesses of the scheme. The financial impracticality of the venture was looming. Slave owners opposed it as a personal assault to their honor. Former slaves opposed it as racist plan formulated and promoted by White supremacists.[22] As a countermeasure William Wells Brown, a fugitive slave living in Europe, was commissioned to thwart the fundraising efforts of the ACS overseas.[23]

One of the more radical "immediatist" abolitionists was David Walker, a freeborn Black man from Wilmington, North Carolina. He was a frequent contributor to William Lloyd Garrison's *Freedom Journal.*

18. Stewart, *Holy Warriors*, 30.

19. Brown, *The Travels of William Wells Brown*, 3, 17.

20. See the editorial, "American Colonization Society," 353.

21. For a detailed discussion on Free Black resistance to the ACS, see Kendi, *Stamped from the Beginning*, 143–58.

22. Stewart, *Holy Warriors*, 29–30.

23. Brown, *The Travels of William Wells Brown*, 4.

Perhaps the most disturbing of his writings was a tract entitled *Our Wretchedness in Consequences of the Preachers of Religion.* In it, he lambasted America's religious hypocrisy and alluded its impending apocalyptic violent end.

> What the American preachers can think of us, I aver this day before my God, I have never been able to define. They have newspapers and monthly periodicals, which they receive in continual succession, but on the pages of which, you will scarcely ever find a paragraph respecting slavery, which is ten thousand times more injurious to this country than all the evils put together; and which will be the final overthrow of this government, unless something is very speedily done; for their cup is nearly full. Perhaps they will laugh at it, or make light of this; but I tell you Americans! That unless you speedily alter your course, *you* and your *Country are gone!!!!!!* For God Almighty will tear up the very face of the earth!!!![24]

Compare this with the later "gradualist" words of Daniel Alexander Payne, presiding bishop of the African Methodist Episcopal Church. In 1862, the venerable preacher responded publicly to the Emancipation Proclamation urging African American people to respond in like manner with prayers.

> To make supplications, prayers, intercessions, and thanksgiving for these authorities, is the peculiar privilege of the Colored People in the United States. They are not permitted, as in the days of the Revolution and the war of 1812, to take up arms in defence of the Government. Some, both among Anglo-Saxons and Anglo-Africans, complain of this prohibition. For my part, I am glad of it, because I think I see the hand of God in it. The present war is a kind of family quarrel. Therefore, let a stranger take heed how he meddles, lest both parties unite to drive him out of the house. "Why shouldst thou meddle to thy hurt?"[25]

Payne preferred to emphasize nonviolence, religious and civil duties, and hard work. Though he was reared a freeborn person in Charleston, South Carolina, his position represented his professional New York constituency. He refrained from entering the dispute which split the MEC

24. David Walker, "Our Wretchedness in Consequences of the Preachers of Religion," in Sernett, *African American Religious History*, 197.

25. Daniel Alexander Payne, "Welcome to the Ransomed," in Sernett, *African American Religious History*, 238.

along the boundary of North and South. Southern ministers concentrated on evangelization while Northern ministers supported colonization.

The emphasis on abolition and reform did not reappear in great numbers until the 1830s.[26] By no means was pro-slavery confined to the South. On the contrary, it occurred in some surprising places in the North. Some of this sentiment was flushed out by at least one issue of Charles Grandison Finney's New York newspaper, the *Evangelist.* Joshua Leavitt, the editor, published articles promoting antislavery. He misjudged the position of his subscribers. The newspaper suffered a severe backlash. Leavitt later wrote an apology to Finney.

> Brother Finney, I have ruined the *Evangelist.* I have not been as prudent as you cautioned me to be, and I have gone so far ahead of public intelligence and feeling on the subject [of abolition], that my subscription list is rapidly falling; and we shall not be able to continue its publication beyond the first of January, unless you can do something to bring the paper back to public favor again.[27]

Finney saved the *Evangelist* by publishing reports of his revival experiences as a series of lectures. In 1835, it was edited and published under the title, *Lectures on Revival.*[28] In lecture fifteen, Finney pronounced slavery as a sin. He refused to permit membership to any who engaged in any part of the merchandising of slaves. When a rumor surfaced that his proposed Broadway Tabernacle in New York would be "an amalgamation church" with integrated seating, it was burned down by arsonists. After the fire, the church was built, and the congregation practiced segregated seating.[29]

When Finney was offered a teaching position at Oberlin Collegiate Institute, one of his conditions was that no one would be denied admission based on race or sex.[30] Yet, Black students continued to be seated separately from White students. Finney's chief benefactor Lewis Tappan called him to task on the segregation issue. Under accusations of lacking Christian charity, Finney responded that social equality was not a

26. Schmidt, "Reexamining the Public/Private Split," 76.

27. Finney, *Memoirs*, 329.

28. Finney, *Memoirs*, 330.

29. Finney, *Memoirs*, 328.

30. Drummond, *Charles Grandison Finney*, 165.

Christian duty. To drive home his point, Finney asked Tappan, hypothetically, whether he would consent to his daughter's marriage to a Black man.[31]

Despite struggles within the administration of Oberlin, it became a haven for abolitionists. During Lyman Beecher's term as president of Lane Seminary, the trustees acted against a group of student abolitionists.

While Beecher and his son-in-law, Calvin Stowe, were away on summer vacation, the trustees passed some resolutions to suppress all conversation on abolition in the school.[32] "Societies or associations were prohibited, as well as all public meetings, discussions or addresses upon the troublesome topic. It was forbidden even to dwell upon the subject at meals or in ordinary conversation. Especially was the Anti-slavery Society, already existing, to be at once abandoned on pain of dismissal from the seminary." The dissidents fled to Oberlin College.[33]

This Northern strain of racism was typified by the sad case of Charles B. Ray, the first Black student at Wesleyan University. The situation was so oppressive that Mr. Ray was forced out within seven weeks after matriculating in 1832. To ensure that this would not happen again, the Wesleyan board of trustees officially resolved that "none but white male persons shall be admitted as students at this institution."[34] Four years later, at a New York Anti-Slavery Society meeting, Ray lamented his lost opportunity to receive a college education. He judged the spirit which drove him out as "cruel, unnatural and awfully wicked prescription which turns us away from the useful arts, and from places of profit and responsibility. . . . O! This heartless prejudice!"[35]

Some abolitionists were taken in by the millennial teachings which were being promoted by such influential preachers as Charles G. Finney and William Miller. Finney predicted that Christ would return sometime in 1838. Miller's predictions that Christ would return on March 21, 1843, was later known as "The Great Disappointment."[36] Despite these failed prognostications, many evangelicals continued to believe that the

31. McLaughlin, "Charles Grandison Finney," 103–4.

32. Calvin Stowe was the husband of Harriet Beecher Stowe, author of *Uncle Tom's Cabin* (1852), which depicted the evils of slavery on a Southern plantation. Unfortunately, it portrayed African Americans as childlike and naturally subservient.

33. Hayward, *Lyman Beecher*, 75–77.

34. Swift, "O! This Heartless Prejudice," 13.

35. Swift, "O! This Heartless Prejudice," 16.

36. For a compact analysis of the Millerite movement, see Doan, *The Miller Heresy*.

millennium was near, and so was an end to human bondage. Transfixed on the pending millennium, many abolitionists misjudged the entrenched racism in the North and the tolerance for the same in the South.[37]

Nathan Bangs rejected the pessimistic views of the Millerites. Rather, Bangs held to a postmillennial view. Methodists and Finney conveniently rolled their perfectionism into postmillennialism.[38] He saw the church as conquering the world for Jesus Christ rather than subjecting society to Christian ideals.[39] This eschatology left little room for a proactive public theology. Bangs was turned off by the strident cries of the abolitionists. The "conquering" sanctified church motif left little room for social reform and even less for "the abolition excitement."[40]

Opposing Viewpoints

> Take, for example, the temperance reformation. Its entire realization would free the world from an untold amount of misery and crime, and yet it would fall short of reaching the seat of the world's disease. Take, again, the great anti-slavery movement; and suppose the shackles of every slave knocked off, and the very idea of ownership in man stricken from the mental calendar; still evil exists—you have not even brought to an end oppression and wrong.[41]

The growth and popularity of Methodism made it difficult for the MEC to establish a singular public opinion regarding abolition. There were simply too many opposing views within the denomination. Originally, Bangs held the position that statements in the *Discipline* were sufficient in themselves. Thus, he maintained that there was no need to engage in dialogue outside of the General Conference. However, this position was shortsighted. Public debate was not preventable. The *Christian Advocate* printed red hot debates that led to accusations of libel and misconduct.

When Bangs became editor of the *Christian Advocate*, he was appalled by the previous record of church journals to involve themselves in

37. Stewart, *Holy Warriors*, 48–49.

38. There were exceptions to this eschatological view among perfectionists. The Keswick Movement and other holiness people adopted a premillennial view which negatively portrayed society's decline. Moorhead, *World without End*, 14.

39. Whidden, "Eschatology, Soteriology, and Social Activism," 98–99.

40. Whidden, "Eschatology, Soteriology, and Social Activism," 99.

41. Clark, *The Cross of Christ*, 15–16.

torrid debates or *ad hominems*. He set an official policy to restrict stories or editorials of controversial nature or dubious authorship.

> That all the editors and correspondents of periodicals under the patronage of this General Conference be instructed to avoid, as far as practicable, all personalities in controversies which may arise, and in no case to admit an anonymous writer to assail any man's character, either in or out of the Church.[42]

This policy effectively silenced the voices of opposition within the Methodist Episcopal Church. Still, Bangs' effort to control the verbal war using his editorial powers did not prevent them from communicating in other media. It did manage to earn Bangs a tarnished reputation for not supporting abolition. Abel Stevens offered an overly ameliorating interpretation of his actions.

> From his infancy he had been trained to abhor slavery. His Church had always considered it a legitimate subject remonstrating testimony; but of late years it had become a question of rife controversy, especially in the north-eastern Conferences, and it seemed to him so badly managed, and so menacing to the unity of the denomination, as to justify his persistent opposition to the antislavery leaders, whom he considered destructives rather than reformers.[43]

In 1835, La Roy Sunderland wrote and published a letter on behalf of the New England Wesleyan Anti-Slavery Society. It stated that slavery is a sin in the sight of heaven and should cease at once and forever. Abel Stevens' own position is evident by the presence of his signature, with others, on a rebuttal letter prepared by Willbur Fisk and Daniel Whedon. They denounced the New England Wesleyan Anti-Slavery Society's position by denying that all slaveholding is sinful and recommending political neutrality. At the General Conference, Fisk unsuccessfully challenged the character of those who signed the first letter on behalf of the New England Wesleyan Anti-Slavery Society. On September 4, 1835, Bangs signed and published a letter in *The Christian Advocate* supporting Fisk for facing down the abolitionists at the General Conference.[44]

The slavery controversy severely tested Bangs' publishing policy restricting articles on divisive issues and *ad hominems*. In 1834, La Roy

42. Stevens, *Life and Times of Nathan Bangs*, 376.

43. Stevens, *Life and Times of Nathan Bangs*, 313–14.

44. Mudge, *History of the New England Conference*, 280–81.

Sunderland became one of the main founders of the Methodist Anti-Slavery Society in New York City. In 1836, he established *Zion's Herald* as the society's official voice. Concurrently, he began to publish *Zion's Watchman* for the New York Wesleyan Society. The first issue of the *Zion's Watchman* was issued January 1, 1836. The *raison d'etre* for the second publication was somewhat vague at first. The first edition proclaimed it was to be "devoted to the interests of the Methodist Episcopal Church–Revivals of Religion–Doctrinal Discussion, and General Intelligence . . . a substantial medium through which they may address the world--upon each of the great moral enterprises of the day."[45] The true motive was clearer when the editor posed the rhetorical question, "Why do we publish?" Quite pointedly he answered: "Because there are nearly three million of our fellow citizens enslaved in this land and no less than sixty or seventy thousand of our own brethren and sisters, members of the Methodist Episcopal Church, who are 'in bonds' and violently deprived of their right to themselves."[46]

Sunderland's *Zion's Watchman* met with a mixed reaction. According to Edward D. Jervey, numerous death threats were leveled against him in the South, some even offering cash rewards up to $150,000 for him dead or alive.[47] Abolitionist Orange Scott considered *Zion's Watchman* responsible for convincing the Maine Conference to hold the abolitionist position.[48]

Sunderland was severely criticized, and his paper was suppressed by members of the New York Conference. Nathan Bangs convinced the New York Conference to pass a resolution censuring any member of their conference who read or supported *Zion's Watchman*.[49] June 20, 1836, he was charged by the New England Conference for slander and falsehoods toward Bangs and New York Conference and for "publishing profanity."[50] In 1837, Bangs accused him of slander and falsehood over an unsigned article, "Methodist Missionary Society in Debt."[51] The Conference granted Sunderland a supernumerary relation. In 1838, Bishop

45. Quoted in Jervey, "La Roy Sunderland," 21.

46. Jervey, "La Roy Sunderland," 21.

47. Jervey, "La Roy Sunderland," 22.

48. Jervey, "La Roy Sunderland," 23.

49. Jervey, "La Roy Sunderland," 24.

50. The profanity charge referred to Sunderland's publication of a letter to the editor using the word "damned." Jervey, "La Roy Sunderland," 24.

51. Jervey, "La Roy Sunderland," 25.

Hedding charged Sunderland with publishing injurious falsehoods. As before, charges were dropped but his conference relation was reduced to superannuated. That year, Bishop Hedding also brought charges against Orange Scott who was summarily acquitted.[52]

In this way, Bangs was able to suppress the voices of abolitionists in the arena of his denominational control. Consequently, newspapers such as William Lloyd Garrison's the *Liberator* (1831) were founded for the express purpose of representing the views of abolitionists. The *Colored American*, owned and operated by Charles B. Ray, a Methodist Episcopal Church minister in New York, reflected a broader social commentary from the perspective of the Black community.

> Mankind generally act towards a people, as they feel towards them, and feel in accordance with their views of them, and the views they entertain are measured by what they know or do not know of their character, their virtues or their vices. We are convinced that the greatest amount of the prejudice in our country, which exists against our people, has its foundation in wrong views of them, and that such views are predicated upon ignorance, or upon what the people do not know of what is meritorious, and virtuous, and consistent amongst them, and that contact by our people, in every possible way, will be a very efficient method to change the views and the feelings of the public, and the course they pursue towards us; because, it will develope the whole people, and the whole character of the people. We know of no better way to effect this, than to develope through the press, the mind of the people, and those institutions existing among them, which of themselves are an index to the moral character and condition of any people.[53]

Bangs' editorials against Orange Scott's speeches and writings in 1838 precipitated Scott to prefer misconduct charges against him. Bangs was brought to a ecclesiastical trial before the New York Conference. After his acquittal, Bangs recorded in his journal: "God enabled me to vindicate my conduct against these charges in a manner perfectly satisfactory to myself, and I think also to my friends, as well as to the confusion of my adversaries. The motive of my accuser I leave to himself and

52. Mudge, *History of the New England Conference*, 284–85.

53. Charles B. Ray, "Colored Churches in this City," in Sernett, *African American Religious History*, 218–19.

to the Judge of all, hoping he may find acceptance in that day which shall disclose the secrets of all hearts."[54]

In 1844, Orange Scott published, *The Methodist Episcopal Church and Slavery*, presumably intended to deride the denomination. Scott's comments regarding the way Bangs handled himself at the 1836 General Conference were not so forgiving.

> Rev. Nathan Bangs, D.D., of New York. This gentleman did not propose to divide the Church, but sacrifice the colored population, and Silas Comfort to keep it together. He said: "We were on a snag, and he believed he could help us off. He perceived a way to get out of the difficulty, and proceeded to read three resolutions, one of which went to *affirm* the decision of the Missouri Conference in the Comfort case."[55]

In 1840, the case against Silas Comfort was sustained. They accepted a resolution suggested by Ignatius A. Few "that it is inexpedient and unjustifiable" to permit a Black person "to give testimony against white persons in any State where they are denied that privilege in trials at law."[56]

Compromise

> I do not wish them [ministers of religion] to lift up their voice in bold, dogmatical denunciations against slavery and the slaveholder; nor to spend their strength in mere boisterous declamation on the evils of the system, sending all to hell, indiscriminately, who either hold slaves, or apologize for those that do; bestowing offensive epithets with unmeaning profusion, upon all who may dissent from them in their views.[57]

Bangs agreed that emancipation should be offered to slaves. However, he did not approve of the harsh attacks launched by the abolitionists. The antislavery issue became extremely intense as early as the Methodist Episcopal Church General Conference of 1836. Orange Scott and William Winans, both members of the New England Conference, spoke about slavery. The reaction was so bitter that they were both censured and abolition was officially condemned. The resulting resolution disclaimed

54. Stevens, *Life and Times of Nathan Bangs*, 315.

55. Scott, *The Methodist Episcopal Church and Slavery*, 67.

56. Sherman, *History of the Revisions*, 46.

57. Bangs, *Emancipation*, 65–66.

"any right, wish or intention to interfere in the civil and political relations between master and slave."[58]

> The General Conference of 1840 marks the end of an era in Methodist history. In the strenuous controversy which had begun in 1831, those who favored abolitionism had attempted by a process of education, radical though it may have been, to change the thinking of the Methodist Episcopal Church on the question of slavery. . . . Southerners and abolitionists alike showed the courage of their full strength against the abolitionists, and the theories of the South were accepted as the will and law of the Church. If slavery were triumphant in 1836, it was supremely so in 1840.[59]

Bangs responded by publishing *A History of the Methodist Episcopal Church* (1838–41). A possible motive for writing the *History* was to serve as an apologetic aimed against "denominational rivals" and "ambitious reformers."[60] Confronted by attacks from both outside and inside of the Methodist Episcopal Church, Bangs was determined to publish evidence of God's favor for the denomination. The fourth volume of four was completed by 1841. His defense utilized copious notes of the 1828 General Conference to counteract distortions and membership reports to dissuade denominational defections. Bangs' carefully edited church history of the MEC was the standard work for a quarter of a century.[61]

Bangs could not prevent the defections from the MEC which were already in progress. In 1843, Orange Scott led delegates from nine Northern conferences to form the Wesleyan Methodist Church. This was one of the few denominations founded in response to a social issue.[62] This is inclusive of the prior defections of the Union Church of Africans (1813), the African Methodist Episcopal Church (1817), and the African Methodist Episcopal Church, Zion (1821).[63]

58. Bangs, *Emancipation*, 44.

59. Swaney, *Episcopal Methodism*, 99–100.

60. Rowe, "Counting the Converts," 13.

61. Rowe, "Counting the Converts," 13.

62. Donald W. Dayton's claim that the Wesleyan Methodist Church was the only denomination founded because of a social issue did not consider denominations founded by Black leaders such as the AME, the AMEZ, UCA, and later the COGIC. See Dayton, *Discovering an Evangelical Heritage*, 73.

63. These are the generally accepted dates for the founding of these denominations. See McEllhenney et al., *United Methodism in America*, 59–60.

To stop the migration from the MEC, the *Christian Advocate and Journal* began publishing articles condemning slavery.[64] The new policy endorsing abolition was too little too late for the "Scottites." Furthermore, the expansiveness of the MEC made enforcement of any ecclesiastical law condemning or restricting slavery rather difficult. The authority of the General Conference was severely tested when a ruling made in 1816 came back decades later to haunt slaveholding bishops. The long-ignored addition to the *1816 Discipline* made slaveholders ineligible to hold office where the State allowed emancipation and permitted liberated slaves to enjoy their freedom.[65]

The new pro-abolitionist posturing of the northern Methodists was evident in the controversial case of Rev. Francis Harding who inherited slaves by marriage. The Baltimore Annual Conference suspended Harding for failing to free his slaves. Harding appealed to the 1844 General Conference of 1844 but lost in a vote of 117 to 56. According to Donald G. Matthews this was the first time Southerners lost a vote in the MEC.[66]

The issue of slave-holding clergy rapidly escalated.[67] The Harding affair predicated a near similar case of Bishop James O. Andrew. In 1832, he had been elected to the office partly because he was a non-slaveholding Southerner. However, it was found later that the new bishop inherited slaves by marriage. They were two youths from his first wife's estate and several others from his second wife. Under Georgia law, Andrew could not free them from his trusteeship. He was unintentionally violating the 1816 prohibition against slaveholders being elected to office. There was some sympathy for the bishop's legal conundrum.[68] However, Peter Cartwright was less sympathetic to the bishop's plight.

> I never had anything against Bishop Andrew; but this does not alter my mind in this matter, and I will forbear noticing his pacific relation to slavery; I will do this in view of the information of this large and respectable body of ministers. But while I do this, I must beg leave to repudiate the heretical doctrines advanced by southern men on this floor, that if you take a man in

64. Mathews, "Orange Scott," 96.

65. Sherman, *History of the Revisions*, 38.

66. Mathews, *Slavery and Methodism*, 254.

67. Barton Stone, leader of the Disciples, also inherited slaves, but cured the problem by moving to a state where he could legally free them. See Williams, *Barton Stone*, 76–78.

68. Richey et al., *A History*, 183–87.

> the south and elect him without slaves, he is liable to become a slaveholder, and he cannot get rid of it. Why, my dear sir, this is all humbuggery, and nothing else. It was once my misfortune to become by heirship the owner of slaves. I could have pled with truth, and certainty of sympathetic responses, the disabilities of the law: but no, sir, I did not do so; I shouldered my responsibility, and resolved to be, like Cesar's wife, beyond suspicion. I took them to my state, set them free, gave them land, and built them a house, and they made more money than ever I did by my preaching.[69]

Cartwright reduced the objections against freeing slaves to the legal requirement to remain responsible for their welfare. In defiant testimony he stated that he himself had pledged himself surety for over two hundred freed slaves. Furthermore, these manumitted slaves prospered and became "respectable men."[70]

Thomas Emerson Bond led another gradualist group in offering a five-point proposal at compromise over the issue. It tried to use neutral terminology which would be acceptable to all parties, North and South. Yet, it was decidedly weighted in Bishop Andrew's favor.

1. 1st, That the slave holding Conference agree whenever a slave holding Bishop should be elected to purchase his slaves and do with them as directed by the General Conference.
2. 2nd, That no Abolitionist be eligible to, or be permitted to remain in the Episcopacy.
3. 3rd, That hereafter the Bishops be selected from the slave and non-slave holding Conferences in ratio proportioned to the number of ministers attached to each.
4. 4th, That the General Conference yield to the annual Conferences all right to legislate on the subject of slavery.
5. 5th, That the above regulations be incorporated be incorporated into the Constitution of the Church.[71]

The anti-abolitionist language of the compromise proposal led to its rejection. The situation could not have been predicted nor could it be

69. Peter Cartwright, "Speech in General Conference, 1844," in Stevens, *Dr. Cartwright Portrayed*, 23–24.

70. Cartwright, "Speech in General Conference 1844," 25.

71. Bond, "To the Methodist Conservatives."

easily forgotten. A "Committee of Nine" drew up a "Plan of Separation" as an emergency provision outlining the separation of those members in slaveholding states.[72] Five years later, Bangs published a compilation of articles originally written and published, circa 1846, in *Zion's Herald* and the *Wesleyan Journal*. The collection was appropriately entitled, *Emancipation*. Bangs admitted that he had resisted speaking out against slavery until he "dare resist no longer." "Life is fast ebbing out with me, and I shall soon be called to 'give an account of my stewardship,' so that whatever I would say or do must me said or done soon, or not at all."[73] Bangs traced the history of slavery from ancient civilizations to his contemporary North American context.[74] His conclusion states that slavery has always been evil, but never as evil as in the American form. At first it seemed as if Bangs had a change of heart. However, the content revealed the author hawking the same old gradualist rhetoric.

> For myself, I would not advise that immediate and unconditional emancipation should take place. Laws could be so framed and enacted, as to provide for a gradual emancipation; say, all at such an age should be free, from time to time, until finally an era would be fixed when slavery should cease to exist in such a State, and then another, until all should proclaim freedom to their slaves. And what a glorious era would this be to the State that should thus propose liberty to its slaves![75]

From the twenty-first-century perspective, it may seem strange that ethics of enslaving fellow human beings was so difficult to grasp. Northern Methodists supported the caste system while southern Methodists supported slave owners. These both gained social respectability within their own contexts of White hegemony. Southern evangelicals parlayed

72. Richey et al., *A History*, 189–92.

73. Bangs, *Emancipation*, 3.

74. Bangs garnered much of the historical data for his argument from George Bancroft, *History of the United States*. Justification for African slavery was deeply rooted in European literature which dehumanized and hypersexualized Africans. Such works included Gomes Eanes de Zurara's *The Chronicle of the Discovery and Conquest of New Guinea* (1453), Bartolome de Las Casas' *A Short Account of the Destruction of the Indies* (1542), and Leo Africanus' *Description of Africa* (1526). Italian freethinker Lucilio Vanini (1616) and French theologian Isaac La Peyrére (1655) both made cases for polygenesis suggesting that White and Black people had distinctly different origins. The "curse of Ham" myth was also propagated by Reverend Thomas Cooper in Ireland and Virginia. See Kendi, *Stamped from the Beginning*, 22–30, 37, 51.

75. Bangs, *Emancipation*, 17.

their new respectability with plantation owners into enterprises of evangelism targeting slaves. During the 1840s, Methodists, Baptists, and Presbyterians took a hard line against antislavery agitators. Furthermore, they redoubled their efforts to secure the trust of slave holders by providing biblical arguments for slavery.[76]

Summary

All hopes for a peaceful settlement over the slavery issue were dashed when the Methodist Episcopal Church enacted the Plan of Separation, 1844. Orange Scott, an abolitionist and holiness advocate, made his break to form the Wesleyan Church in 1845. Sixteen years later, Benjamin Titus Roberts, a former student of Wesleyan University, 1845–48, took Northern Methodists a different way. Influenced by abolitionism, Finney's revivalism, and Palmer's perfectionism, B. T. Roberts founded the Free Methodist Church in 1860.[77] Palmer may well have decided to put her lot with schismatics Roberts and Scott, both comrades in the holiness movement. Rather, she chose to minister ecumenically and remain faithful to the Methodist Episcopal Church.[78] By the time Bangs tried to make amends it was too late. His heavy-handed bureaucratic tactics smacked of elitist respectability to the abolitionists. The latter eventually defected from the MEC to form the blossoming holiness movement. At the end of the day, Bangs found himself the odd fellow out as the rare "holiness gradualist."

76. Touchstone, "Planters and Slave Religion in the Deep South," 100.

77. Snyder, "Formative Influences on B. T. Roberts," 177–99. See also Snyder, *Populist Saints.*

78. Oden, *Phoebe Palmer*, 21.

Chapter VII

THE LEGACY OF METHODIST RESPECTABILITY

> Revd. Dr. Bangs, permit me to assure you that the company here assembled are your warm and devoted friends, and as such, most heartily and cordially covered in the sentiments of our worthy and expert Bishop. Many have known you from our childhood, and we learned to venerate and respect you in early life. For years we have listened to your instructions from the pulpit, and greatly to our profit we have read your books and other productions of your pen; and now, Sir, after a long life of labor and toil as a faithful and devoted minister of the Lord Jesus Christ, we thought it but fitting and proper to present you a trifling testimony of our personal respect.[1]

In late January 1859, three hundred friends gathered in the New York City home of Rev. Dr. M'Clintock. From there they marched to the Bangs family home in Irving. Bishop Janes called the crowd to order and began delivering remarks on the legacy of Bangs to the MEC. A succession of speakers spoke and prayed while those gathered affirmed their words with holy "amens." They were honoring the eighty-one-year-old Rev. Dr. Nathan Bangs. A fine walking stick, the great symbol of a respectable nineteenth-century gentleman, was presented

1. "A Surprise Party," *New York Times*, January 24, 1859, 1. This story was corroborated by Stevens, *Life and Times of Nathan Bangs*, 407–9.

to him as a token of their high esteem. This was a very special gentleman's walking stick.[2] This one was finely crafted of ebony, hollowed out, and filled with four hundred five-dollar gold pieces. Considered expensive for the time, it was valued at two thousand dollars.[3] Thus, Bangs received his unexpected reward for his decades of labor for the MEC.

Bangs legacy of respectability passed on to a new generation of educated Methodists who learned strict religious discipline as one of their core values. Those fortunate enough to afford MEC related private schools benefitted tremendously from this highly structured educational system. Such discipline extending to the Christian Sabbath gave them the basis for entering respectable society.[4] Even those who received a modest education in Sunday School and grammar school became industrious workers. This drive for personal perfection lent itself to material gain and social accomplishments. In worship, grape juice replaced wine for Holy Communion.[5] Along with their newfound respectability, Methodists benefitted financially from improvements in power, class, and industrial economics. Children in respectable homes were taught that they should not be ashamed of their Methodist heritage. Rather, they should be proud of how far they had come.

> *John.* Look at our Book Concern—the greatest religious publishing house in this country, and, for aught I know, in the world.
>
> *Edwin.* Really John, you are placing things in a new light to me. To tell you the truth, I have sometimes been almost ashamed that my parents belonged to the Methodist Church.
>
> *John.* You have much greater reason to be ashamed of your own ignorance, my dear boy. Study the history of Methodism and you will feel thankful that you were born under its influence.[6]

The humorous description of the presiding elder Samuel Parker as a "homely, awkward frontier preacher, clad in an ill-fitting, homespun preacher garb" was typical of the popular conception of Methodist

2. The importance of walking-sticks in the nineteenth-century urban culture is discussed in Andersson, "The Walking Stick in the Nineteenth-Century," 275–91.

3. Stevens, *Life and Times of Nathan Bangs*, 408.

4. Bylaw 18 of 23 in Genesee Wesleyan Seminary, *Catalogue*, 32.

5. See Tait, *The Poisoned Chalice*.

6. Wise, *The Children's Centenary Memorial*, 82.

preachers prior to gaining respectability.[7] Such was an embarrassment to their descendants, even the second generation who engaged in the pastime of mocking Methodist itinerants as "fanatics."[8] Respectability was not the driving issue on the rural American frontier. The early Methodist preachers were more concerned "to reform the Continent, and to spread scriptural Holiness over these Lands."[9] They had no time for improving their position in society. Itinerant James B. Finley related the story of Bishop Asbury's visit to a Methodist family indulgent in fashion and gaiety.

> We stopped with a Methodist family. As we passed through the parlors we saw the daughter and some other young ladies dressed very gayly. The daughter was playing the piano, and as we moved through the room we doubtless elicited from those fashionable young ladies some remarks about the rusticity of our appearance; and the wonder was doubtless excited, where on earth these old county codgers have come from? The Bishop took his seat, and presently in came the father and mother of the young lady. They spoke to the Bishop, and then followed the grandfather and grandmother. When the old lady took the Bishop by the hand he held it, and looking her in the face, while the tear dropped from his eye, he said, "I was looking to see if I could trace in the lineaments of your face, the likeness of your sainted mother. She belonged to the first generation of Methodists. She lived a holy life and died a most happy and triumphant death. You," said the Bishop, "and your husband belong to the second generation of Methodists. Your son and his wife are the third, and that young girl, your granddaughter, represents the fourth. She has learned to dress and play on the piano, and is versed in all the arts of fashionable life, and I presume, at this rate of progress, the fifth generation of Methodists will be sent to dancing-school."[10]

For the post-Asbury generation, the rustic ideal of pioneer Methodist life faded with the social improvement of the more prosperous constituents of the MEC. The middling class rejected the stereotypical backwoods Methodist preachers in favor of professionally trained preachers. Urbane Methodists in America and Britain had developed

7. Sweet, *The Rise of Methodism*, 44.

8. Stevens, *Life and Times of Nathan Bangs*, 28–29.

9. MEC, *Minutes of Several Conversations*, 4.

10. Finley, *Autobiography*, 276.

their own sense of style and taste.[11] As early as 1820, British Methodists were recognized as "an *imperium in imperio* . . . avowedly members of the English Episcopal Church, and differing in few particulars from the faith of the majority of their fellow-citizens, have yet their own seminaries, their own hierarchy, their own regulations, their own manners, their own literature."[12] Likewise, higher social status was now a reality in American Methodist circles. American Methodists were not only going on to spiritual perfection, but they were also gaining a firm toehold in affluent social circles.

The Wesleyan movement had begun as a champion of the proletariat. It offered a disciplined and simplified way of life that was attractive to the new working class of the industrial revolution. The movement's simplicity of message and plainness of presentation spelled success for the growth of Methodism among factory workers.

Methodist preachers had several advantages over other Protestant ministers. For example, their minimal education was recognized as a point of identification with workers. As discussed in chapter 3, early Methodist preachers placed greater emphasis on religious experience and emotional response than on doctrine. Teaching doctrine to new converts and seasoned members was a key function of the class leader. The internal structures of Methodist class meetings and bands offered an added sense of strength in community. The working poor interpreted "perfection" in material terms. Thus, the doctrines of spiritual equality and behavioral restraint did not detract from the radical potential of Methodism for personal improvement.[13]

The popular attraction to American Methodism quite naturally expanded to the middling class. Upward mobility was perceived as an obvious outcome of Christian perfection. Some Americans, less motivated by a thirst for spirituality, joined the church for personal gains. MEC congregations benefited from these prosperity seekers. The numerical growth of the movement and the economic strides of the members were connected in an almost organic way.[14] One Baltimore congregation, High

11. Material history of America during this period indicates that cultural refinement permeated many aspects of society; thus, influencing Methodist communities in the areas of taste, fashion, and architecture. See Bushman, *The Refinement of America*, 319–48.

12. Review of *The Life of Wesley*, 1.

13. Lazerow, *Religion and the Working Class*, 85–86.

14. Wigger, *Taking Heaven by Storm*, 174.

Street MEC, demonstrated this connection by making high-quality quilts with religious motifs as gifts for their ministers.[15]

The financial gains for the Methodist Episcopal Church started improving during Asbury's episcopacy and continued steadily to mid-century. The record indicates that the Methodists were increasing both in wealth and status. Growth statistics for Methodists indicate that "between 1774 and 1860 the richest 10 percent of free wealth holders increased their share of total American assets from a little less than 50 percent to 73 percent, and the richest 1 percent more than doubled their holdings from about 13 percent of all assets to 29 percent."[16] Thus, Methodists gained substantial prominence as an emerging middle class.

The industrial revolution was a godsend for the Methodist Episcopal Church. The proliferation of factories created new wealth and economic power in a relatively short period of time. The upward mobility of Methodists and rich benefactors sparked a demand for professional preachers and shunned rough homespun itinerants. Urbanization, fueled by the industrial revolution and expansion to new markets via the railroad, created new community centers and built up existing ones. Methodists in these upwardly mobile communities were under increasing pressure to compete with other historic churches of higher social status such as the Unitarian, Congregational, Presbyterian, and Episcopal churches. In a relatively short period of time the Methodist Episcopal Church was no longer the powerless little revivalist sect ridiculed by the elitist denominations. Seemingly overnight, the young upstart sect became a highly structured denomination commanding national attention.

Methodist lay people acquired offices of high profile in state and federal government. Congregations moved forward in constructing neo-Gothic monuments to their increasing prestige. Their increased presence in state and federal government positions attests their newfound influence. Nathan O. Hatch refers to this turning point as a "metamorphosis."

> By mid-century, the early republic's populist religious movements were undergoing a metamorphosis from alienation to influence. Eleven of thirteen congressmen from Indiana in 1852 were Methodists, as were the governor and one senator. As Methodist and Baptist churches grew wealthier, they built

15. Porter, "Through the Eye of the Needle," 71–85.

16. Wigger, *Taking Heaven by Storm*, 175.

> substantial sanctuaries, installed organs, rented out pews and demanded college-trained ministers.[17]

The new generation of respectable Methodists was profoundly different from earlier constituency known to Asbury. Few areas were immune from the influences of the process of *embourgeoisement*.[18] This term suggests a process of adopting middle-class or *bourgeois* values into the community life of the church. Popular British novelist Sir Edward Bulwer-Lytton Bart deftly summarized that refinement and religion had finally come together. "The art of design have been more appreciated—the Beautiful has been admitted into the pursuits of labor as a principle—Religion has been regaining the ground it lost in the latter half of the last century."[19]

The economic condition of the general population within American Methodism improved substantially. Bangs considered these "improvements" as results of the General Rule to "do good." He enumerated good deeds as building churches, founding and endowing colleges, supporting professors and students, establishing and sustaining missions, printing and circulating Bibles and "other good books," conducting Sabbath schools, and supporting ministers.[20] The middling class was the strongest supporter of these programs. Bangs was unable to counteract resistance of the "richer classes" to embrace these middle-class ideals. He observed that "the poor" laborers readily contributed to institutional building concerns and benevolence. Furthermore, he concluded that inability to meet institutional needs, despite the obvious enrichment of some members, was an indication of their unwillingness to shoulder the load. "I think it highly probable that the fault is more among the richer class than among those in middling circumstances."[21]

It would be helpful at this point to restate the *embourgeoisement* thesis. The *proletariat* embraced the values of the *bourgeoisie* and worked together for the collective goals of the MEC. This runs contrary to Max Weber's observation of working-class northern European Calvinist

17. Hatch, *The Democratization*, 193.

18. Dayton, "Presidential Address," 15. Dayton further defines this term as "a form of upward social mobility that draws the movement more and more into the bourgeois middle classes and forms of church life." See Donald W. Dayton, "'Good News to the Poor': The Methodist Experience after Wesley," in Meeks, *The Portion of the Poor*, 71.

19. Bart, *Pelham*, xv.

20. Bangs, *The Present State*, 224.

21. Bangs, *The Present State*, 232–33.

Protestants who were "earning of more and more money, combined with the strict avoidance of all spontaneous enjoyment of life" as an end of itself. American Methodists had definite goals of individual and collective nature.[22] Liston Pope rated the labor discipline via moral supervision of workers as "the greatest contribution of the industrial revolution in the South."[23] The opposition of Southern gentry against working-class values kept Southern Methodists at odds with the elites.[24]

As demonstrated in the chapters above, change did not come wholly without internal resistance. In the area of worship, traditional Methodists still preferred to cling with nostalgia to forms reminiscent of Asbury's glory. G. W. Henry's book, *Shouting in All Ages of the Church* (1859), defended the "old way" of "shouting" in the tradition of John Wesley, Edwards, Christmas Evans, Benjamin Abbott, Peter Cartwright, and J. B. Finley.[25] On the other hand, the practice of omitting the preaching to save time for the sacraments became common even in the station churches.[26] The progressive minded working-class Methodists were eager to strive for the collective goals of advancing higher education, foreign missions, and spirituality. By sheer numbers, they overwhelmed the MEC by mid-century. The result was a denomination dominated by middle-class values.

In England, where the same middling phenomenon was occurring, rude miners who joined the Methodist class meetings learned to read and write. Not only did they become literate, but they also felt obligated to improve their appearances as well.

> He took to going to Chapel, and, finding it necessary to appear decent there, he got new clothes and became what is termed respectable. . . . They took away his gun, his dog, and his fighting cock. They gave him a frock coat for his posy jacket, hymns for his public house ditties, prayer meetings for his pay-night frolics. They drove into the minds of the naturally improvident race that extravagance was in itself a sin.[27]

22. Weber, *The Protestant Ethic*, 53.
23. Pope, *Millhands & Preachers*, 29.
24. Lyerly, *Methodism and the Southern Mind*, 74.
25. Taves, *Fits, Trances, & Visions*, 233–34.
26. Tucker, *American Methodist Worship*, 132.
27. Wearmouth, *Methodism and the Working-Class*, 183–84.

The working class living in industrial cities were able to participate in the capitalistic opportunities afforded them by a steady flow of discretionary income. In growing numbers of workers settled in cities built with the perfectionist optimism offered by a market driven religion. However, many of them had to live in the reality of substandard housing.[28] The phenomenon of slums filled with working-class people was not unique to America. In Britain, Friedrich Engels noticed that unfortunate factory workers were forced to live in detestable squalid conditions.[29] The Five Points area in New York City gained a national reputation for its moral decadence and crime. At the center was a tenement in a building called the Old Brewery. At one time it was considered the most densely occupied building in the city with over one thousand two-hundred persons in residence. In 1838, the city of New York built a prison known as "the Tombs," styled in ancient Egyptian architecture, to regulate the criminal element in Five Points.[30] The turning point for this pit of social and moral corruption came with the demolition of the Old Brewery and the construction of Five Points Mission. This was perhaps the Ladies' Home Missionary Society most high-profile faith-based attempt to reform society.[31]

Secular and religious reformers intent on improving the conditions of factory workers labored under the unrealistic belief that "the Kingdom was about to come and that poverty could be abolished along with the rest of the world's evils."[32] Nevertheless, Houses of Industry were established to house and feed indigent people in exchange for labor.[33] Besides the poor housing conditions, middle-class Methodists relentlessly sought the opportunity to live the American dream of prosperity. However, they experienced commonality with the poor when they accepted the restrictions on leisure placed on them by traditional moralists. Recreation that marked the success of landed gentry was not only out of their league, it was also off limits. As contemporary Mike Walsh lamented: "The gloomy,

28. Philadelphia factory workers did not get decent housing until after the Civil War. See Fones-Wolf, *Trade Union Gospel*, 24.

29. Marcus, *Engels, Manchester, and the Working Class*, 184–86.

30. Hornberger, *The Historical Atlas of New York City*, 84.

31. Phoebe Palmer was one of the women leading the Five Points Mission via the Ladies' Home Missionary Society. Not surprising that Nathan Bangs was chosen to pronounce the benediction at the setting of the cornerstone June 18, 1853. Ladies of the Mission, *The Old Brewery*, 72.

32. Walters, *American Reformers*, 192.

33. Matthews, *Toward a New Society*, 144.

churlish, money-worshiping, all pervading spirit of the age has swept all the poetry of life out of the poor man's sphere. . . . Ballad singing, street dancing, tumbling, public games, all are either prohibited or discountenanced, so that Fourth of July and election sports alone remain."[34] Leisure of this sort wash not the right of the poor working class, but a luxury of the wealthier middle-class.

> And yet pure religion naturally leads to wealth. By inspiring a spirit of industry and economy, leading to a retrenchment of all extravagance in living, unless the religious man have some outlet for his surplus wealth, he must hoard it up for "those who come after him, whether they be wise men or fools." Unless, therefore, this man give in proportion to the increase of his property, his riches will eat out his religion, and thus destroy its own existence by the very means it furnishes its disciples with to accumulate wealth.[35]

Clearly, Nathan Bangs encouraged industrious living and the accumulation of wealth. Revisiting the main thesis, Bangs managed to link the MEC with the impulse of upward mobility in antebellum America. The industrial revolution in the resource rich young republic catapulted the social status of artisans to middle-class values. The class consciousness conflict predicted by Engels and Marx never occurred in America.[36] Rather, John H. Goldthorpe's *embourgeoisement* theory when applied antebellum American Methodism demonstrated that the working class assimilated the values of the *bourgeoisie.*[37] By mid-century, those who refused to improve socially found less accommodation in the MEC. Those who preferred to resist change were dealt with accordingly with the order of the *Discipline.* Church leaders, including Bangs, felt perfectly in the right in applying disciplinary or corrective measures to the populace. They proved E. J. Hobsbawm correct in his observation that "religion

34. Mike Walsh quoted in Moore, *Selling God*, 95.

35. Bangs, *An Original Church of Christ*, 376–77.

36. Karl Marx and Frederick Engels far underestimated the potential and lure of the capitalistic system to proletariats. Rather, they predicted a gloomy conflict: "The more openly this despotism proclaims gain to be its end and aim, the more petty, the more hateful and the more embittering it is." Marx and Engels, *Manifesto of the Communist Party*, 16.

37. Goldthorpe's *embourgeoisement* thesis is an intriguing alternative to Marxism. See Goldthorpe et al., *The Affluent Worker*, 26.

could be a powerful moral prop" for the rising middle-class.[38] Thus, the rigidity of Bangs' form of Methodism gave license to legitimize the regimentation of worship and spirituality in the MEC. Furthermore, it encouraged expansion of social controls in the areas of education, publishing, worship, and missions.

In a relatively short time, the MEC had achieved what H. Richard Niebuhr called "the religion of a bourgeoisie whose conflicts are over and which has passed into the quiet waters of assured income and established social standing." On the other hand, it was also "the religion of a middle class which excludes from its worship, by character of its appeal, the religious poor as well as those who live within the lower ranges of economic and cultural respectability."[39]

Any potential downside for the lower classes was a necessary sacrifice for the drive for respectability. Thus, people of African, Mexican, and Native Americans descent as well as women and poor Whites felt the brunt of upward mobility. Strangely enough, many of the "outsiders" did not despise middle-class values. Many actually coveted them. Not meeting up to the standards of respectability meant they would remain at the margins. The MEC, as an institution, was not as interested in cultivating respectability in the lower classes. Rather, it concentrated efforts on keeping rich White men and women in the church.[40]

The result was that daily life in the MEC community reflected the shift from Asbury's intuitive management style to Bangs' new formalism. Bangs effectively raised the status of the denomination by perfecting the patterns of worship, establishing public theology, and raising educational standards for clergy. Unfortunately, the MEC leadership's failure to recognize the problems of racism and classism precipitated defections of some of their most valued social reformers. The denomination never fully recovered from this schism in 1844, but the desire for respectability remained strong among its adherents. Even after Reconstruction, longing words for respectability pointed to the success of the upstart denominations.

> Take courage from the example of all religious denominations that have sprung up since Martin Luther. Each in its turn has been oppressed and persecuted.

38. Hobsbawm, *The Age of Revolution*, 272.

39. Niebuhr, *The Social Sources of Denominationalism*, 105.

40. Andrews, *Methodists and Revolutionary America*, 242.

> Methodists, Baptists, and Quakers have all been compelled to feel the lash and sting of popular disfavor—yet all in turn have conquered the prejudice and hate of their surroundings.[41]

Some felt alienated by the remodeled religious home as an institution focused on education, moral compromises, and respectability.[42] On the positive side, Bangs' efforts helped the second generation of American Methodists to break free from the roughhewn model of Francis Asbury. The legacy of respectable Methodism is a strong genetic trait inherent in the descendants of the Methodist Episcopal Church. This is evident in the formal patterns of worship, the social and religious nature of denominational publishing, and educational requirements for ministry.

Methodism offered relief from the feeling of alienation brought on by urbanization and industrialization. The internal power of the camp meeting was its ability to create an atmosphere of *communitas*. The massing together of separate people worked to overcome their feelings of isolation and alienation.[43] Within this social dynamic, intense ritually generated human connections were made manifest. The institution of camp meetings helped to sustain this social connectedness, but at a much "milder" level than spontaneous revivals.[44]

The *communitas* universally experienced in formalized Methodist ritual, such as the frequent use of the Lord's Prayer, aided in unifying the movement. The resulting democratization was due primarily to the "incarnation of the church into popular culture."[45] The unique substructures of Methodism, such as class meetings, naturally organized a subculture of Methodist disciples. Preaching to the more sophisticated congregants was a more difficult than before. In one case, it was reported that church fellowship meals were often more interesting than the preacher.[46] As a populist movement, the MEC gained powerful organizational momentum in the early nineteenth century. The organizing process gave meaning and direction to people under the growing social duress of a new

41. Frederick Douglass in a speech delivered August 1, 1880, in Elmira, New York, to celebrate the West Indies emancipation, in Douglass, *Life and Times of Frederick Douglass*, 493.

42. Doan, "John Wesley Young," 29.

43. Elsinger, *Citizens of Zion*, 225.

44. Elsinger, *Citizens of Zion*, 225–26.

45. Hatch, *Democratization*, 9.

46. Ferguson, *Organizing to Beat the Devil*, 145.

nation.[47] Furthermore, the spiritual underpinnings of perfectionism, found in hymnody and preaching, were fundamentally determinant in the development of the organization of the MEC. In other words, evolutionary growth in all areas of Methodist society was fully expected as the denomination moved toward perfection.

Although Bangs and Asbury were of the same religious spirit, there was less continuity between them than appears on the surface. Bangs was as quick to honor Asbury's memory as he was to encourage revivals of religion. Yet, he was uneasy about permitting indecorous enthusiasm in the normal life of the church. His discomfort was compounded by the upward mobility of untutored Methodists. Their numbers were being fueled by the explosive population growth and soaring economic prosperity. Bangs' solution was to raise the value of its social stock by perfecting the patterns of Methodist thought and practice. Unfortunately, respectability also brought about social stratification. This was the result of multiple failures to recognize the impending marginalization of members based on gender and race. The latter were especially vulnerable as casualties of the expansion of bourgeoisification. These oversights precipitated fragmentation within the denomination for which they forfeited seeds of the holiness movement and created the undercurrent which later manifested as the social gospel.[48]

Nathan Bangs presented himself a follower of Christ in the tradition of John Wesley. Theologically, he was fundamentally correct in this self-assessment. However, his desire to move the MEC toward middle-class values contradict the social ethics of Wesley which favored presenting the plain gospel for plain folk. Bangs' own social location embodied the new "Methodist" preference for the *bourgeoisie.* His career may be likened to a massive public relations campaign promoting the potentials of respectable religion. His early forays into apologetics and polemics helped form a Methodist tradition distinct from the American strain of the Puritan tradition, but just as "respectable." Bangs had an enormous influence on Methodist spirituality, public theology, and theological education. His efforts helped the second generation of American Methodists to break free from the rough-hewn model of Francis Asbury. This is evident in its formal patterns of worship, the social and religious nature of denominational publishing, and educational requirements for ministry.

47. Mathews, "The Second Great Awakening," 27.

48. This is the central thesis of Dayton, *Discovering an Evangelical Heritage.*

> The capabilities of American Methodism, for continued and increased usefulness, have already been shown in the historical view of its practical methods, its theological teachings, and its actual results. It stands strong to-day in its essential doctrines and methods; and it has the additional ability and responsibility of greater financial resources than it has ever had before. Its people, originally the poorest of the land, have become, under its beneficent training, perhaps the wealthiest.[49]

Nathan Bangs' legacy to the MEC and its several descendant Wesleyan denominations also included the "Methodization" of the secular doctrine of Manifest Destiny. Those who could not embrace the middle-class values were marginalized into obscurity or into the many splinters of the MEC family tree. Bangs worked the system to transform the MEC into a denomination dominated by middle-class values.[50] The eventual disappearance of the doctrine of sanctification from late nineteenth-century Methodism may indicate that their core values had changed from inward spirituality to outward materialism.[51]

Movements borne out of primitivism, in due time, often succumb to the tendency to accumulate wealth as they gain acceptance and respectability. Other Wesleyan denominations, such as the Nazarenes, have themselves experienced defections from their own ranks as a reaction against *embourgeoisement*.[52] Vinson Synan observed that third generation often become the "social arbiters" with vested interests against newcomers into their movements. Classical Pentecostals experienced the respectability phenomenon in the late twentieth century.[53] In the twenty-first century, Pentecostals have become "mainline" in the sense that they are now included in national conversations on social and political issues.

The late twentieth-century revival of Wesley studies coupled with the influence of Liberation Theology had the surprising effect of restoring discussions on Methodism's obligation to minister to the poor.[54] In the twenty-first century, the theological and historical discussions of the heirs of the Wesleyan tradition, including the The United Methodist

49. Stevens, *The Centenary of American Methodism*, 225.

50. Wigger, *Taking Heaven by Storm*, 193.

51. Dieter, *The Holiness Revival*, 177.

52. Thornton, "Behavioral Standards," 172–97.

53. Synan, *The Holiness-Pentecostal Tradition*, 295.

54. See Jennings, *Good News to the Poor*; Meeks, *The Portion of the Poor*; Heitzenrater, *The Poor and the People Called Methodists*.

Church, have largely focused on the neglect of poor and marginalized people rehearsed in the prophetic celebration of Holy Communion, that "we have not loved our neighbors, we have not heard the cry of the needy."[55] The inability to address the needs of vulnerable people of the LGBTQ+ communities has festered without resolve so that the UMC of the twenty-first century is now poised for a major schism. Unlike the 1844 Plan of Separation, this will not be easily defined geographically. Rather, the political polarizations of the nation may be the most reliable indicator for mapping the future fractures.

American Methodists marveled at their good fortune in the first hundred years. John Wesley warned against the dangers of increasing riches. He feared even amassing a sum for your descendants invited trouble. "Leave them enough to live on, not in idleness and luxury, but by honest industry."[56] In a free-market system, "honest industry" has the potential of producing wealth and upward mobility. Nathan Bangs guided the MEC during this opportune moment in history so that by mid-century they enjoyed widespread recognition as a denomination come of age. At the same time, faithfulness to the original spirit of Methodism's preferential option for the poor weakened as they increased in social legitimacy.

55. Service of Word and Table I and II in UMC, *The United Methodist Hymnal*, 8, 12.

56. John Wesley, "The Danger of Increasing Riches," in *Works of John Wesley* (Bicentennial ed.), 4:186.

APPENDIX A

NATHAN BANGS AT GENERAL CONFERENCE, 1808–1852 (EXCLUDING MOST ROUTINE MOTIONS)

1808

(No Motions or Actions recorded)

1812 MOTIONS	ACTIONS
Appoint committee to examine and report on Book Concern	carried
Above committee take into consideration whatever may related to Book Concern.	carried
Appoint a committee to revise the hymn book	carried
Amendment to chapter 2, sect. 7 of Discipline	tabled
Present address from James Evers on hymn book	tabled
That Book Steward and editor be elected	carried

1816 MOTIONS	ACTIONS
Representatives of each conference to examine conference addresses for administration and state of episcopacy be elected by their own conference	carried
The Discipline be incorporated with the rule that Presiding Elders' decision not to grant license of local preacher could be overturned by a vote of 2/3 majority	tabled

1816 MOTIONS	ACTIONS
Appoint a committee to consider parts of Discipline relating to local preachers	carried
That case of legality and constitutionality of Philadelphia Conference, regarding the expulsion of Joseph Samson for denying the divinity of Jesus Christ, be referred back to Philadelphia Conference	lost
Amendment to rules of Presiding Elders' election	accepted
Amend Ways and Means resolution to discourage taxation or legal assessment	carried
That all motions lie on table to consider 6th resolution of Ways and Means	carried
Resolution that Book Committee relating to editing of a magazine be recommitted to appoint two editors to magazine and general Book Concern leaving it to NY Conference to assist them	withdrawn
That NY Annual Conference lend assistance to Book Agents "if they judge it necessary"	carried
That editors and general book stewards submit a prospectus for editing a magazine and presiding elders and preachers collect subscribers	carried
That disposing of Sutcliffe's grammar and realization of the property of Book Concerned be referred to Book Committee	carried

1820 MOTIONS	ACTIONS
That further consideration of 29th rule be postponed until amendment be prepared by Cooper	carried
That a committee be appointed to superintend the printing of the list of preachers and residences	carried
That local preachers be permitted to take seats as spectators	withdrawn
That documents relating to revision of Discipline be referred to a select committee	carried
That memorial meeting in Baltimore be referred to a select committee	carried
Memorial as referred to local preachers be referred to a select committee	carried

Memorial on subject on subject of dress referred to a select committee	carried
That report of Missionary and Bible Society of MEC be committed to Committee on Missions	carried
That Book Committee inquire after the papers of Bishop Whatcoat and take them to make a report	carried
That a committee be appointed to revise the Discipline to harmonize parts in separate sections	carried
That the case of Morris Howe be taken up, who was located without his request by Baltimore Conference	carried
That report of the Book Agents with documents be referred to committee on the Book Concern	carried

1820 MOTIONS	ACTIONS
That resolution forbidding pewed worship houses be postponed Resolutions on Canada Affairs be taken up	withdrawn
That members desiring election of Presiding Elders be appointed to a committee to confer with Bishops	carried
Amendment to resolution that property of the Book Concern permanently owned by MEC	carried
That preachers who obtain subscriptions to magazine be responsible to their Presiding Elder for the numbers	carried
That Presiding Elders are advisory council to the Bishop or President of the conference	carried
That the sum of one thousand dollars be paid out f the funds of the Book Concern to Joshua Soule as additional remuneration for his services as Book Agent for four years past	carried

1824 MOTIONS	ACTIONS
That the Committee on the Episcopacy be instructed to inquire into all matters necessary for office, duties, and possible increase in the number of Bishops	carried
That a committee be appointed to inquire about alterations to rule of Discipline on admission and trial of members and on baptism and authority to call on other committees for papers on subjects	carried
That Canadians be permitted to speak on mission when Canadian Affairs are brought to conference	tabled

1824 MOTIONS	ACTIONS
That Secretary of the NY Conference furnish committee on the Book Concern with several reports of Book Committee of NY and acts for the last four years	carried
That Committee on Education inquire to expediency and practicability of establishing a general seminary of learning, or college, under superintendency of General Conference	carried
That the sections of the report of the Committee on Boundaries of the conferences relating to the Genesee and Canadian conferences be tabled until committee on Canada Affairs report	carried
That the report on John Emory's mission to the British Conference relating to Canada Affairs be referred to Committee on Canada Affairs	carried
That the report from the Committee on the Revision of the Discipline be read	tabled
That the fourth resolution on the Episcopacy be recommitted	lost
Amendment on the above to divide the connection into episcopal departments	withdrawn
That preachers discourage teaching Sunday School during hours of church services	lost
That report from Committee on Revision of the Discipline to be read	tabled
Amendment that votes in annual and general conferences be by ballot	admitted
That vote by ballot be allowed for a question on the floor	lost
Report from the Committee on the Admission and Trial of Members	tabled

1824 MOTIONS	ACTIONS
Request to permit Rev. John Hannah from the British conference to preach a sermon	adopted
That the Committee on the Book Concern inquire whether a more equitable apportionment of avails of Book Concern and Chartered Fund	carried
Committee on memorials report read	tabled
To strike out $2000 and insert $1000 on report of Committee n Expenses of delegates	lost
Request for leave of absence on account of indisposition of family	granted

1828 MOTIONS	ACTIONS
That a Committee on Education be appointed	carried
That a Committee on the Book Concern inquire into the expediency of taking measures for forming a Bible Society of the MEC	carried
That the Committee on Revisal and unfinished business take the Discipline into consideration and suggest alterations in phraseology	carried
That the hearing of Joshua Randall, expelled for holding and discharging doctrines contrary to Articles of Religion, be with closed doors	lost
Amendment to the Discipline after "among Indians" to insert "and those preachers who may be appointed to labor for the benefit of seamen, except in regard to such places as, in the judgment of any annual conference, may render a longer term necessary"	tabled

1828 MOTION	ACTIONS
That the pamphlets distributed by E. Little of Philadelphia be withdrawn	lost
That Committee on Temporal Economy inquire about alterations in allowance of retired preachers in the apportionment of avails of Book Concern and Chartered Fund	carried
To reverse the decision of the Baltimore Conference in case of William Houston	carried
Report from Committee on Canada Conference	tabled
Take up motion from table about time a preacher continue to labor among seamen	carried
Report from Committee on Missions that they be discharged from petition of James Gilrath and that he withdraw petition	granted and carried
Report from the Committee on Missions	tabled
Request to be excused from voting on statements of sums from agents of their traveling expenses, pensions, and salaries	not granted
That the General Conference act on the report of the Committee on Canada Affairs	withdrawn
To amend the report of the Book Concern	admitted
That Book Concern pay salary of William Capers during his trip to England	affirmed
That preachers in Charleston City station estimate amount of money needed for care of Caper's family	carried

That if Canada Conference be separated from the MEC, then the Board of Managers be allowed to appropriate funds to sustain Indian missions	carried

1828 MOTIONS	ACTIONS
To appoint a committee to prepare address to British Conference	carried
Report of the Committee on Education be accepted and printed in the Christian Advocate and Journal	carried
That provision for expulsion be made in the Discipline regarding person found guilty of a crime expressly forbidden by the word of God sufficient to exclude a person from the kingdom of grace and glory, by decision of a majority of members by trial	tabled
That the bishops be respectfully requested to prepare a biography of Bishop Asbury	carried

1832 MOTIONS	ACTION
Seconded motion to inquire of state of buildings and parsonages, including questions about mixed sex seating, free seats, and music in worship	carried
That Committee on Revisions of Discipline be instructed to inquire whether any more equitable method of avails of the Book Concern and Chartered Fund be allowed for retired preachers, widows, and orphans	carried
Seconded motion to include language in Discipline forbidding "indulging in sinful tempers, works, buying or selling lottery tickets, or disobedience to the order and discipline of the Church, &c."	tabled
That the Committee on the Itinerancy be instructed to consider modifications in the trial of traveling preachers to prevent appeal from being brought to General Conference	carried
Seconded motion to make it the duty of the bishop or a committee appointed by him to organize a course of study in the annual conference for four-year probation required by Discipline	tabled

1832 MOTIONS	ACTIONS
That Discipline be amended to change the procedure on appeals	tabled
That Discipline be amended after the words "missionaries among the Indians" with "missionaries to our people of colour and on foreign stations."	adopted
To appoint a bishop for MEC in Upper Canada and to permit U.S.A. bishops to appoint and ordain until then	tabled
Seconded motion authorizing Superintendents to appoint preachers to college not under direction of the MEC	carried
To authorize Book Committee of NY to make temporary provision for editing Christian Advocate and Journal until Editor and Asst. Editor are prepared to enter duties	carried

1836 MOTIONS	ACTIONS
That rules of the conference be referred to Editor of the Western Christian Advocate with instructions to have two hundred copies printed and distributed, with names of the members of conference	carried
That everyone presenting memorials state the contents of the papers and whether it ought to be read	carried
That representatives Lord and Chase, British Wesleyans, be invited to take honorary seats and feel at liberty to speak	carried
That a select committee be appointed to consider the section of the Discipline regarding allowance of ministers, preachers, wives, widows, and children and report on support of the ministry	carried
That Lord and Chase furnish their address for publication in official journals, with copies available to this conference	carried

1836 MOTIONS	ACTIONS
That a committee of seven be appointed on Bible, Sunday School and Tract Societies, and all related matters	carried
That a select committee of three be appointed to inquire about the retired ministers living outside the bounds of the conference where they have membership	carried
That a committee of three be appointed to respond to the British Wesleyan address and appoint a delegate to the Wesleyan Methodist Conference	carried

That a committee of five be called the Judiciary Committee to refer all appeals or complaints of character and it is the duty of the same to decide whether they are legally entitled to be heard before the conference	carried
That reply to the Wesleyan Methodist Conference be signed by the bishops and secretary	carried
That the Committee on the Allowance of Preachers be instructed to inquire whether further provision should be made for the support of bishops, their widows, and children	carried
To print the address of the Methodist Conference with the response	lost
Read the address form the MEC in Canada, motion that the letter be referred to a committee of five to consider the report	carried
That thanks to Rev. Dr. Edwards, Corresponding Secretary of American Temperance Society, for his address and recommend that members of the conference obtain a copy of his book	carried
That the words "United States of America" in the deed of settlement be stricken out for the sake of Canadian MEC	tabled
That Committee on Canada Affairs reconvene to consider above	carried

MOTIONS	ACTIONS
That report of Committee on Missions be taken up	carried
That proposed amendments to constitution of Committee on Missions be called up	carried
That suggestion to address the Wesleyan Methodists on the subject of temperance be referred to a committee	carried
That adjustment of the debts of the Canada Conference to the Book Concern be referred to the Book Agents and Book Committee for final settlement	carried
That the secretary be requested to furnish Canadian representatives with copy of all the papers respecting the Canada claim presented at conference	carried
That the Book Concern and Book Agents of NY shall have the authority to employ additional help in the editorial department until the editors are ready to enter work	carried
That a copy of the third resolution regarding the Chartered Fund be sent by the secretary to each annual conference	carried
That Bishops Beverly Waugh and Thomas Morris be consecrated and Dr. Fisk, as soon as he accepts	carried

Report of the Missionary Committee on South America, resolved to select two or more additional missionaries for South America	carried
That amendment to deed of settlement in Discipline striking "United States of America" be taken up	debated
Request from Bangs to Bishops for access to records of General Conference to write history of MEC	granted

1840 MOTIONS	ACTIONS
That the Book Agent, Thomas Mason, be requested to sit in the meetings and give his opinions regarding the Book Concern	carried
That the conference employ a reporter to record the proceedings for publication in the Christian Advocate and Journal expense paid by MEC	tabled
"Dr. Bangs" motioned that above be amended that expense be paid by Book Agents	carried
Read memorial from Liberian Conference "praying" for the appointment of a bishop	tabled
That a committee of five be appointed to refer all matters relating to Sabbath Schools	carried
That change in the Discipline relating to the responsibility of retired preachers be referred to Committee on Revisals	carried
That bishops be empowered to carry cases to General Conference	tabled
That unemployed preachers who refuse work are guilty of "contumacy" and not allowed to preach or function in office	tabled
The secretaries furnish Editor of Christian Advocate and Journal with proceedings of conference up to that time	carried
That "likeness" of Rev. Robert Newton, guest preacher from Wesleyan Methodist Connection, be taken at conference or in New York with expenses paid by Book Agent	carried
That a committee of three be appointed to whom to refer the address of the Wesleyan Methodist Connection	carried
That receiving ministers from another conference be referred to a committee of three	carried

1840 MOTION	ACTION
That address of Rev. John Stinson, President of Methodist Canada be referred to a committee for Wesleyan Methodist Connection relations and publish his address	carried
That the Committee on the Book Concern be instructed to inquire more equitable method of distributing funds from the Book Concern and Chartered Fund to annual conferences	carried
That the conference decline to accept the $74 refund offered by the Book Steward for his expenses	adopted
That the question of Liberia's request for a bishop be tabled	carried
Resolution to appoint a committee to revise the Discipline, harmonize index, remove obscurities, and present specimen to next General Conference	carried
Amendment to above resolution to prepare Discipline in large print for "old people"	withdrawn
Request that Committee on Episcopacy discern why a Bishop has not visited Africa as requested at the 1836 conference	granted
As Chair of Committee on Slavery, referred matters of slavery and abolition and preachers to Committee on Itinerancy	granted
Request to be excused from commenting on Bishop Hedding's address against an annual conference	granted
That the case of James V. Potts be referred back to Philadelphia Conference	carried
That order of the day be suspended to receive protests signed by 11,000 people led by Orange Scott against slavery	granted
That a committee of three superintend and publish Discipline as revised and amended	carried

1844 MOTIONS	ACTIONS
That the address of the Wesleyan Methodist Connection be referred to a committee of three	carried
That Laban Clark be recognized as an alternate delegate replacing Stephen Olin	carried
That report of Board of Managers of the Mission Society regarding revisions to the constitution be printed	carried
That conference take up the request of the Mission Committee to form a German Conference	carried
That William Nast be sent as an emissary for MEC to Germany	carried

That Bishop Soule be allowed to give an account of his trip to the Wesleyan Methodist Conference and Europe	granted
That amendment be approved encouraging belief in MEC doctrines in baptisms, unless an infant	lost
That the New York Conference be divided with approval of the Bishop	lost
That books be sold at 25% discount for cash and 20% discount for credit	tabled
That the Corresponding Secretary meet with the Board of Managers and submit alterations to the constitution recommended by the conference	carried

1848 MOTIONS	ACTIONS
Did not attend, not sent as a delegate. However, a resolution was drafted making him a delegate to the Canada Conference.	n/a

1852 MOTIONS	ACTIONS
That the remains of Bishop Asbury and Bishop Emory be removed to Mount Olivet Cemetery in Baltimore	carried
That the journals of the NY East Conference be offered to the committees dealing with Temporal Economy, Boundaries, and Revisals	accepted
That a committee of seven be formed to study lay delegation	tabled
That D. P. Kidd's report from the 1848 General Conference on the rituals of the Lord's Supper and baptism be considered to revise the catechisms "to promote greater uniformity among us"	carried
That a committee be formed to commemorate the introduction of Methodism into New England by Jesse Lee	tabled
That the action of Troy Conference expelling Ezra Sprague be affirmed	carried
That the Committee on Revisals be instructed to find equitable methods for accusing and bringing to trial delinquent preachers before annual conferences	carried
That the decision of Ohio Conference in the case of J. S. Inskip, found guilty of violating his pledge, be reversed	ruled out of order
That editors and correspondents should avoid controversies in publications	tabled
That previous vote to give depositories to Auburn and Buffalo be reconsidered	lost

(This is Nathan Bangs' last General Conference before retiring in 1852. He was given the honor of presenting Levi Scott to be consecrated as Bishop.)	

APPENDIX B

TIMELINE OF NATHAN BANGS' CAREER[1]

1778	Born May 2 in Stratford, Connecticut, to Lemuel and Mary Keeler Bangs
1799	Moved to Canada to survey and to teach
1800	Converted to Methodism; commenced circuit in upstate New York and Canada
1801	Appointed supply on Niagara circuit with Joseph Sawyer and Seth Crowell
1802	New York Conference, Bay of Quinte and Home district with Joseph Sawyer and Peter Vannest
1803	Same circuit as above with Joseph Sawyer and Thomas Madden
1804	Ordained by Bishop Asbury as a Deacon, then as an Elder; River Le Trench circuit
1805	Oswegatchie circuit with S. Keeler
1806	Quebec circuit; married Mary Bolton
1807	Niagara circuit, with T. Whitehead and N. Holmes
1808	Delaware circuit, New York, with Robert Dillon
1809	Albany circuit, with I. B. Smith; wrote tract contra "Christianism" heresy
1810	New York, with Eben Smith, J. Robertson, James M. Smith, and P. P. Sandford
1810–11	Appointed pastor at John Street Church, New York City

1. Career and biographical material derived chiefly from Stevens, *The Life and Times of Nathan Bangs*; Warriner, *Old Sands Street Methodist Episcopal Church*, 211–15.

1811	Same appointment, with William Phoebus, Laban Clark, William Blaghorne, James M. Smith, and P. P. Sandford
1812	Appointed to Montreal, Canada, but prevented by War with Great Britain
1813–16	Presiding Elder of Rhinebeck District
1815	Wrote *Errors of Hopkinsianism Detected and Refuted* (3000 sold in six months)
1816	Wrote *The Reformer Reformed* as a reply to his critics; proposed Course of Study 1817 New York City, with David Ostrander, S. Crowell, and S. Howe; wrote *Examination of the Doctrine of Predestination*
1817–18	Appointed pastor at John Street Church, New York City
1818	Same circuit as above, with Laban Clark, S. Crowell, S. Howe, and T. Thorp; published sermon *On Opening the Methodist Church in John Street*
1819	Presiding Elder of New York district; founded the Missionary Society of the MEC **1820** General Book Steward of the Methodist Book Concern; wrote *Vindication of the Methodist Episcopacy*
1820–23	Senior Book agent with Thomas Mason
1820–28	Editor of *Methodist Magazine*, monthly publication of MEC
1823	Published Martindale's *Dictionary of the Bible*, with commentary by Nathan Bangs 1824–27 Senior Book agent with John Emory
1824	Revised and published *Doctrines and Discipline of the MEC*
1826	Published *Letters to Young Ministers of the Gospel*, compiled from his articles
1828–31	Editor of *Christian Advocate and Journal*, weekly publication of MEC
1829	Edited and published *The Life of Freeborn Garrettson*
1830	Wrote *The Reviewer Answered, or The Discipline . . . of the MEC Defended*
183?	Wrote *Rites, Ceremonies, and Usages of the Protestant Episcopal Church*

1832–35	Editor of the *Methodist Quarterly Review* and books of the General Catalogue
1832	Wrote *Authentic History of Missions of the Missionary Society of the MEC*
1836	Revised first official *Methodist Hymn Book*
1836–40	Resident Corresponding Secretary of the Missionary Society
1837	Wrote *An Original Church of Christ*
1838–40	Wrote *History of the MEC*, in four volumes
1840	Wrote *A Centenary Sermon*
1841–42	President of Wesleyan University, resigned after one year
1843	New York City, Second Street MEC; wrote *The Life of James Arminius*; published a revised edition of the *Methodist Hymn Book*
1844–45	New York City, Greene Street MEC
1844	Organized the Course of Study training for ministerial candidates
1846	Brooklyn, Sands-Street MEC, with J. C. Tackaberry
1847	Same appointment as above with J. B. Merwin
1848–51	Presiding Elder of New York district, New York East Conference
1848–49	Wrote *Emancipation, Its Necessity and Means of Accomplishment*
1849	Published Watson's *Biblical and Theological Dictionary*, with Bangs' commentary
1850	Wrote *The Present State, Prospects, and Responsibility of the MEC*
1851	Wrote *The Necessity, Nature, and Fruits of Sanctification*
1852–62	Retired; wrote *A Semi-Centennial Sermon . . . before the New York-East Conference*
1858	Published Strickland's *The Life of Francis Asbury* with comments by Nathan Bangs
1862	Died May 4 in New York City, funeral at St. Paul's Church, buried in Greenwood Cemetery, New York

APPENDIX C

SUMMARY OF NATHAN BANGS' CAREER[1]

NATHAN BANGS (1778–1862) WAS a native of Connecticut. He was converted in 1800, and in 1802 admitted on trial in the New York Conference and appointed as missionary to Upper Canada. We cannot agree with J. M. Reid that Nathan Bangs "deserves to be considered the father of the missionary work of the Methodist Episcopal Church." Missions were indigenous to Methodism. It is more accurate to say with Frank Mason North that "as in no other, American Methodism found in Nathan Bangs the inspiring and molding forces which gave [organizational] form to her missionary purpose." To him the Missionary Society owed much for its maintenance during its early years. It is a tribute to his diligence and indefatigable industry that this service was rendered while he was carrying other heavy responsibilities: 1819–20, presiding elder, New York District; 1820–28, book agent (chief executive officer of the Methodist Book Concern); 1827–29, corresponding secretary of the American Bible Society; 1828–32, editor of the *Christian Advocate and Journal*; 1832–36, "Editor of the *Quarterly Review*, and of our books generally." During these same years he was engaged in writing the first two volumes of his *History of the Methodist Episcopal Church*. In 1833, following the resignation of John P. Durbin as editor of the *Christian Advocate*, Dr. Bangs again became its editor, in addition to editing the *Quarterly Review*. Dr. Bangs was president of Wesleyan University only eighteen months, retiring from the presidency in August, 1842, to make possible the reelection of Stephen Olin, whose health had sufficiently recovered

1. Barclay, *History of Methodist Missions*, 1:312–13n.

to enable him to take up the position he had earlier relinquished. He died on May 3, 1862, one day after his eighty-fourth birthday.

APPENDIX D

"SEMI-CENTENNIAL MARRIAGE HYMN"

BY PHOEBE PALMER[1]

To Our Honoured Father in Christ, Rev. Dr. Bangs, and his Esteemed Lady, who for fifty years, has been the sharer of his toils and triumphs, these lines are affectionately inscribed, by one who, from infancy, has known and loved them.
The smile of Heaven our pathway cheers

On this our happy marriage day;
A wedded life of fifty years Demands a joyous festive lay.
Life is not all a wilderness,
O'er hung with clouds, surcharged with tears;
Oh! life hath many things to bless, When holy Faith the spirit cheers.
This world hath clouds; yet blissful rays Of sunshine, from the throne of Love, Have lighted up life's varied ways, While passing to our home above.

In journeying to our home of rest, Full half a century has past;
Each year with still new mercies blest, And yet more favored than the last.
Zion beloved, our chiefest care - Now thousands strong throughout the land-
When first we joined her weal to share, How few in number was her band!

By Zion's Lord to conquest led, We in her bloodless battles fought;
Behold! from hence it shall be said, What hath the God of Israel wrought!

1. Palmer, "Semi-Centennial Marriage Hymn," 22–23.

And now let highest praise abound, Let worship, honor, might, be given;
Angels and men the strain resound, Of glory to the God of Heaven.

Our sons and daughters round us press,
Our children's children too arise;
And all unite our names to bless,
And light our passage to the skies.

Shepherdess [tune].

APPENDIX E

"A CENTENNIAL RHYME"

BY GEORGE LANSING TAYLOR[1]

I.
One hundred years ago, - and now!
How vast the change!
—O God, we bow
In dust before Thy awful throne;
—Thine all the glory,
—Thine alone!

II.
One hundred years ago a band
Of pilgrims trod Manhattan's strand,
Who owned ov'er watery wastes afar
A faith that led them like a star.

III.
An humble handful, feeble, few,
'Mid customs strange, and splendors new,
With barbarous tongue, and bashful fears,
They dwelt in silence five long years.

IV.
Then bright burst forth the heavenly flame
O'er doubt and hate and scorn and shame,
And BARBARA HECK like Deborah rose
When Israel bowed beneath her foes.
V.

1. Taylor, "A Centennial Rhyme," 113–17.

To EMBURY in tears she flew,
God's trembling prophet, meek but true,
And straight with power he spake the word
To five yet faithful souls that heard.

VI.
Then fell God's spirit as of old,
And scores flocked weeping to the fold,
The house o'er flowed, the sail-loft too,
And straight a temple rose to view!

VII.
Hail JOHN STREET's venerable shrine!
Hallowed and crowned with joys divine!
At thought of thee what memories rise,
What praise, like incense, fills the skies!

VIII.
Here EMBURY God's message broke,
Here martial WEBB in thunder spoke;
Here WILLIAMS, BOARDMAN, PILMOOR, told
The tale that woke the world of old.

IX.
Swift o'er the land the influence ran;
STRAWBRIDGE in Maryland began;
KING, OWEN, WATERS, SHADFORD wrought,
And RANKIN ruled them while he taught.

X.
On rolled the tide of heavenly light
O'er wrath and strife and war's long night,
Till, bent with Liberty's first ray,
It dawned in broad celestial day!

XI.
From North to South its beams were spread,
It robed with fire the mountain's head,
And down o'er all the west it rolled,
As sunrise pours its waves of gold!

XII.
Then rose great ASBURY, whose name
Shall grow, and gild millennial fame
And bright evangels round him shone
Where, peerless still, he reigns alone.

XIII.
WHATCOAT, McKENDREE, ABBOTT, LEE,
COOK, COOPER, GARRETSON, LOSEE,
HEDDING and EMORY, BANGS, and BOND,
And hosts that crowd heaven's shore beyond.

XIV.
Where are the Fathers?
Where the Seers?
The patriarchs of immortal years?
But lo, e're scarce their shades are flown,
A grander era beams unknown!

XV.
Ho, year of glory!
Year of God!
Thou break'st th' Oppressor's blood stained rod!
Thou bid'st the down-trod rise and sing,
While bells of peace through the nations ring!

XVI.
The fire-scathed track of war and blood
Thou crown'st with countless, sumless good,
And priceless blessings, hoards on hoards,
Thou pour'st in bounty like the Lords!

XVII.
Ho, church of God, what speechless dower
Of wonders crowns thy triumph-hour!
What treasures, wasteless as the sea!
What love, as shoreless and as free!

XVIII.
Thy children rise and call thee blest
From North to South, from East to West,
From zone to zone, from shore to shore,
With infant's song and organ's roar!

XIX.
They pour their gifts, a golden shower,
The orphan's pence, the rich man's dower,
And mites and millions swell the tide
Of glad thank-offerings sanctified.

XX.
Bring, bring your gains ye sons of toil!
Ye merchants count your princely spoil!
Oceans and climes your stores combine!
Art, learning, commerce, field and mine!

XXI.
Pile high the holocaust of praise!
Let love's adoring incense blaze!
And Pentecost baptize us all!

XXII.
Great God of Israel, Lord of hosts,
Flash thou thy glory 'round our coasts,
Till awe and joy in transport rise,
And shouts of victory fill the skies!

XXII.
Descend in glory on thy throne!
Claim thou earth's kingdoms as thy own!
Subdue new empires for thy Son!
Reign thou, till earth and time are done!

XXIV.
Light on thy church from clime to clime!
Guide, guard her down through farthest time!
Till, when earth's latest century's flown,
Her white-robed hosts sing round thy throne!

APPENDIX F

NEW YORK EAST CONFERENCE

OBITUARY OF NATHAN BANGS[1]

Rev. Nathan Bangs was born in the town of Stratford, CT, May 2, 1778. When about thirteen years old he accompanied an elder brother a hundred and fifty miles on foot, "the vanguard" of his family, emigrating to Stamford, Delaware Co., New York, which was then on the western frontier of the settlements of the state. There he became a school-teacher and surveyor, and in the grand solitudes of the native wilderness formed studious and meditative habits which richly contributed to the development of his intellect and character. The pioneer itinerants of Methodism early penetrated that remote region, and under their occasional ministrations his mind was profoundly awakened to the importance of religion. He sought relief to his troubled spirit in travel, and in 1799 emigrated to Upper Canada, where, after years of mental struggle, he was again met by the Methodist itinerants; and in the twenty second year of his age passed from death unto life, under the ministrations of Rev. Joseph Sawyer, whose name is still precious in Canada and in this conference, and whose remains rest within our territorial boundaries. He suffered severe persecution for his new faith; his school was broken up, and he was threatened with personal violence and with expulsion from the settlement. Providentially these trials confirmed his good resolutions and led him at last into the itinerant ministry. In the month of August, 1801, about one year after he joined the Church, and three months after he had received license to exhort, "I sold," he writes, "my surveyors' instruments to a friend

1. New York East Conference, *Minutes*, 64–65.

whom I had taught the art, purchased a horse, and rode forth to sound the alarm in the wilderness; taking no further thought what I should eat or drink, or wherewithal I should be clothed."

During about seven years he braved the hardships of the itinerancy in those boreal regions; traveling long circuits, sleeping on the floors of log-cabins or in the woods, fording streams, sometimes at the peril of his life, carrying with him food for himself and his horse, and eating his humble meals beneath the trees which sheltered him by night, preaching almost daily, facing wintry storms through unsettled tracts of land forty or fifty miles in extent, and suffering attacks of the epidemic diseases of the country, which sometimes brought him to the verge of the grave. He seldom received fifty dollars a year during these extreme labors and sufferings. He was sometimes assailed by mobs; his life was imperiled by the conspiracy of persecutors to waylay him in the woods by night; but he never faltered. He founded several new circuits and many societies; he preached from the westernmost settlement on the Thames River, opposite Detroit, to Quebec, and on leaving the country records, that he had proclaimed his message in every city, town, village, and nearly every settlement of Upper Canada.

The events of this period of his history, of which he has left ample records, present some of the most interesting illustrations of the primitive Methodist itinerancy, and of the early frontier life of the country, that our Church biography has afforded; but they cannot be cited here. It has been deemed proper that his eminent services to the Church should have a fuller record in another form, and we content ourselves with a rapid glance at the remainder of his remarkable career.

In 1802 he was admitted to the New York Conference, which then included most of the state of New York, all the state of Connecticut west of the Connecticut river, Western Massachusetts and Vermont, and stretched over the Canadas from Quebec to the settlements opposite Detroit. In 1804 he was ordained by Bishop Asbury to both deacons' and elders' orders, and sent, through incredible hardships, a missionary to the Thames River. In 1808 he returned to the states, and was appointed to Delaware Circuit,

N.Y. In 1809 he was sent to Albany Circuit; in 1812 he was reappointed to Montreal, Canada, but the war with Great Britain rendered it impossible for him to reach that city. In 1813 he was appointed presiding elder of Rhinebeck District, which then extended from Rhinebeck through Duchess County and Massachusetts to Pittsfield, and thence through Connecticut to Long Island Sound. It is now covered by some six districts; it then had but three chapels, and not one parsonage: he lived to see it studded with commodious churches and comfortable homes for its preachers. In 1817, he was reappointed to New York District. The General Conference of 1820 elected him Book Agent. In 1824 it appointed him Agent and Editor; in 1828 Editor of the *Methodist Quarterly Review*. His services in these various appointments at the Book Concern were of inestimable value. He may indeed be pronounced the founder of that great institution in its present effective organization. At the time of his appointment to its agency, it was sinking under debt; it was comprised in a small book-store on John-street; it had no premises of its own, no printing-press, no bindery, no newspaper; under his administration it was provided with them all. His co-officers in the establishment, especially Dr. Emory, contributed greatly to these improvements, but without impairing the historical precedence and pre-eminence of his services.

In 1836 he was elected by the General Conference Missionary Secretary. It would be impossible within the restricted limits of our minutes obituary, to even glance at his many services in this great interest of the denomination. His name is forever identified with it, on the brightest page of the Church's history.

It 1841 he was elected President of the Wesleyan University. In 1842 he was appointed to Second-street Church, New York; in 1844 to Greene-street Church; in 1846 to Sands-street Church, Brooklyn: from 1848 to 1851 he had charge of the New York District; in 1852 he took his place in the venerable ranks of the superannuated veterans. He had served the Church publicly fifty-one years, receiving from its official authorities fifty consecutive appointments. He spent twenty-nine years in the pastoral work, eight in the book agency, eight in Church editorship, four in the Missionary secretaryship, and two in the presidency of the Wesleyan University.

Such is a rapid glance at the career of this great and good man - a representative man of not only the Methodism, but of the general Protestantism of the New World. By his talents, or by accidental or providential circumstances, he had a primary or initial agency in the great interests and advancements of American Methodism, beyond, perhaps, any other man whose name appears in its history. He was the founder of the

Church, as has been observed, in several parts of Canada, including the city of Quebec; he assisted in the organization of the Delegated General Conference; he was the founder of our periodical literature, by procuring through the General Conference—the revival of the *Methodist Magazine*; he was the founder of the Conference Course of Study, by originating the act of the General Conference of 1816, which ordained it; also, in a sense, of the modified course of four years, to a motion for which in the session of 1832 his name is attached, though it was not adopted till 1844. He was one of the founders of our present system of educational institutions, by the establishment of the Wesleyan Seminary on Crosby-street, New York; which, with that of Newmarket, NH, now at Wilbraham, MA, began our modern system of literary institutions, years after the abandonment of the educational plans of Coke and Asbury.

He was the first man to open the columns of our General Conference periodicals for the advocacy of institutions for the theological education of our ministry. He was our first resident missionary secretary, the first clerical editor of our General Conference newspaper, the first editor of our *Quarterly Review*, and for many year the chief editor of our *Monthly Magazine* and book publications. He may be pronounced the founder of the American literature of Methodism, and he wrote more volumes in illustration or defense of the Church than any other man. He became its recognized historian. He was one of the founders of our Missionary Society; he wrote its Constitution, its first circular to the conferences, is first appeal to the Churches, presided at its first public meeting, and during more than twenty years wrote all its annual reports. While its resident secretary he devoted to it all his energies, conducting its correspondence, planning its mission-fields, seeking missionaries for it, preaching for it in the churches, and representing it in the conferences.

It will be monumental of his memory in all lands to which its beneficent agency may extend, and if no other public service could be attributed to him, this alone would render him a principal historic character of American Methodism, if not, indeed, of American Protestantism. It has been justly said that few men, if any, have longer or more successfully labored to promote those great interests of his denomination which have given it consolidation and permanence; that no one has, in our days, embodied in himself more of its history; nor one has linked so much of its past with its present; that he ranks next to Asbury in historical importance in the Church. The facts of such a man's life are the best exponents of his character.

His whole nature was vigorous; he was robust in intellect, in soul, and in body. In his prime he was a weighty preacher, a powerful debater, an energetic and decisive, if not an elegant writer. He was a steadfast friend, a staunchly loyal Methodist, a charitable and truly catholic Christian.

He had his faults, and like everything else in his strong nature, they were strongly marked. But if he was abrupt sometimes in his replies, or emphatic in his rebukes, no man was ever more habitually ready to retract an undeserved severity or acknowledge a mistake. This excellence was as common with him as it is rare with most men.

For about ten years after his superannuation, he went in an out among our metropolitan Churches, venerated and beloved as a chief patriarch of Methodism. As he approached the grave his character seemed to mellow into the richest maturity of Christian experience. His favorite theme of conversation and preaching was "entire sanctification." He at last fell asleep in Christ, with many utterances of peace and assurance, aged eighty-four years and one day.

APPENDIX G

PORTRAIT OF MIDDLE-AGE BANGS

Engraving by E. Mackenzie from a painting by Paradise. Archives and Special Collections, Wesleyan University.

APPENDIX H

PORTRAIT OF MATURE BANGS

Engraving by A. H. Ritchie in Stevens, *Life of Nathan Bangs*, frontispiece.

APPENDIX I

PRESIDENTIAL WINDOWS AT MEMORIAL CHAPEL, WESLEYAN UNIVERSITY

Clockwise from top left: Willbur Fisk, Stephen Olin, Nathan Bangs, and George Smith. Bangs' image was adjusted to compensate for his twisted neck. Archives and Special Collections, Wesleyan University.

APPENDIX J

MODEL PREACHING HOUSE, SECOND JOHN STREET CHURCH, NY, 1818

SECOND JOHN-STREET CHURCH.

Wakeley, *Lost Chapters*, 580.

APPENDIX K

ECLECTIC GREEK REVIVAL, THIRD JOHN STREET CHURCH, NY, 1841

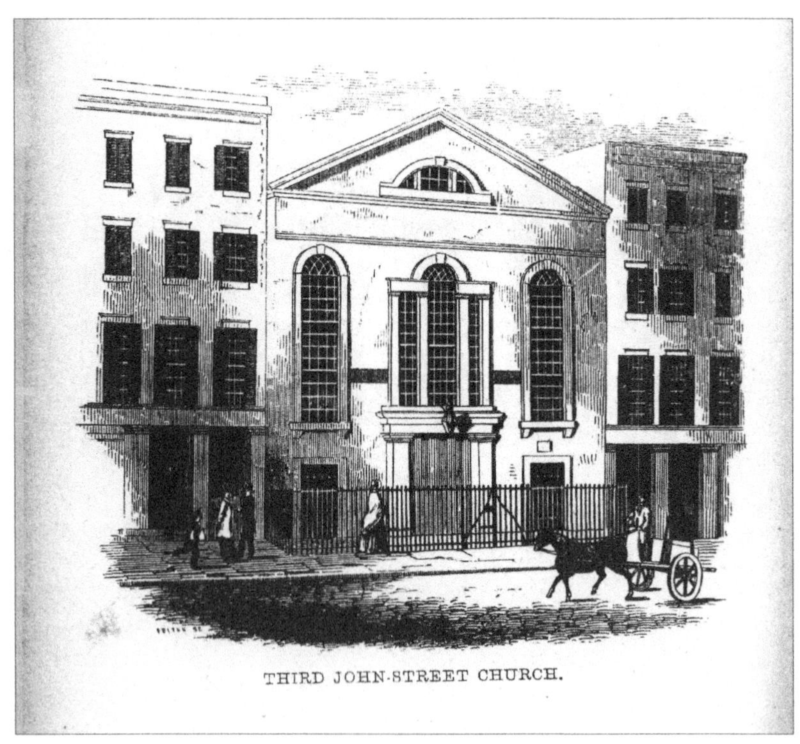
THIRD JOHN-STREET CHURCH.

Wakeley, *Lost Chapters*, 584.

APPENDIX L

AMERICAN GOTHIC REVIVAL, TRINITY METHODIST EPISCOPAL CHURCH, NY, 1856

TRINITY METHODIST EPISCOPAL CHURCH

Wakeley, *Lost Chapters*, 588.

APPENDIX M

POINTED GOTHIC, GRACE METHODIST EPISCOPAL CHURCH, PHILADELPHIA, PA

GRACE METHODIST EPISCOPAL CHURCH, PHILADELPHIA.

The Illustrated Book of All Religions, 310.

APPENDIX N

ROMANESQUE, ST. PAUL'S METHODIST EPISCOPAL CHURCH, NY, 1857

ST PAUL'S M E CHURCH, NEW-YORK.

Wakeley, *Lost Chapters*, 592.

APPENDIX O

ROMANESQUE – AKRON PLAN, BROAD STREET METHODIST EPISCOPAL CHURCH, NEWARK, NJ

BROAD STREET METHODIST EPISCOPAL CHURCH, NEWARK, N. J.

Wakeley, *Lost Chapters*, 595.

APPENDIX P

BANGS WEDDING PORTRAIT

Nathan and Mary Bolton Bangs Wedding portrait, ca. 1806, from private collection. Courtesy of Hoyt V. Bangs family.

APPENDIX Q

BANGS GOLDEN WEDDING ANNIVERSARY PORTRAITS

Nathan and Mary Bolton Bangs Golden Wedding Anniversary portrait, ca. 1856, from private collection. Courtesy of Hoyt V. Bangs family.

APPENDIX R

MARY BOLTON BANGS PORTRAIT

Portrait of Mary Bolton Bangs, ca. 1847, from private collection. Courtesy of Hoyt V. Bangs family.

APPENDIX S

HOYT V. BANGS AT BANGS GRAVE MONUMENT

Photo of Hoyt V. Bangs, great, great, great, great, grandson of Nathan Bangs, at Nathan Bangs grave monument, New York, Kings County, Brooklyn, Green-Wood Cemetery. Courtesy of Hoyt V. Bangs.

BIBLIOGRAPHY

Primary Sources

1. Books, Pamphlets, and Documents by Nathan Bangs

Bangs, Nathan. *An Authentic History of the Missions under the care of the Missionary Society of the Methodist Episcopal Church.* New York: Emory and Waugh, 1832.

———. *A Centenary Sermon, Preached in the Vestry-Street Church, in the City of New York, October 25, 1839, on the one hundredth year of Methodism.* New York: Mason and Lane, 1840.

———. *A Discourse on the Occasion of the death of the Reverend Wilbur Fisk, D.D., president of the Wesleyan University, delivered in the Greene-street Church, New York, on the evening of the 29th of March, 1839.* New York: Mason and Lane, 1839.

———. *Emancipation: Its necessity, and means of accomplishment; Calmly submitted to the Citizens of the United States.* New York: Lane & Scott, n.d.

———. *The Errors of Hopkinsianism Detected and Refuted.* New York: Hitt and Ware, 1815.

———. *An Examination of the Doctrine of Predestination, As Contained in a Sermon, Preached in Burlington, Vermont, By Daniel Haskel, Minister of the Congregation.* New York, 1817.

———. *A History of the Methodist Episcopal Church.* 3rd ed. 4 vols. New York: Mason and Lane, 1839–53.

———. "Inaugural Address." Commencement address, Wesleyan University, August 4, 1841.

———. *Letters to Young Ministers of the Gospel, on the Importance and Method of Study.* New York: Bangs and Emory, 1826.

———. *The Life of James Arminius.* New York: Harper & Brothers, 1843.

———. *The Life of the Rev. Freeborn Garrettson, Compiled from his printed and manuscript journals, and other authentic documents.* New York: Emory and Waugh, 1829.

———. *Memorial of the Golden Wedding of the Rev. Nathan and Mrs. Mary Bangs, April 23, 1856.* New York, 1856.

———. *Methodist episcopacy: vindicated by Scripture and the primitive fathers.* New York, n.d.

———. *The Necessity, Nature, and Fruits, of Sanctification: in a Series of Letters to a Friend.* New York: Lane & Scott, 1851.

———. *An Original Church of Christ, or, A Scriptural Vindication of the orders and powers of the ministry of the Methodist Episcopal Church.* New York: Mason and Lane, 1837.

———. *The Preacher's Manual: Including Clavis Biblica, or A Compendium of Scripture Knowledge by Adam Clarke; and, Letters to Young Ministers of the Gospel on the Importance and Method of Study.* New York: Waugh and Mason, 1834.

———. *The Present State, Prospects, and Responsibilities of the Methodist Episcopal Church.* New York: Lane & Scott, 1850.

———. *The Reformer Reformed: Or a Second Part of the Errors of Hopkinsianism Detected and Refuted: Being an Examination of Mr. Seth Williston's "Vindication of Some of the Most Essential Doctrines of the Reformation."* New York: Totten, 1818.

———. *The Reviewer Answered: or, The Discipline and Usages of The Methodist Episcopal Church defended against the attacks of The Christian Spectator.* New York: Emory and Waugh, 1830.

———. *Rites, Ceremonies, and usages of the Protestant Episcopal Church, tested by Scripture.* New York, n.d.

———. *The Substance of a Sermon preached on opening the Methodist Church in John-Street; in the city of New-York, On the morning of the 4th of January, 1818.* New York: Totten, 1818.

———. *Vindication of the Methodist Episcopacy.* New York: Bangs and Mason, 1820.

2. Eighteenth- and Nineteenth-Century Imprints

Annan, William. *The Difficulties of Arminian Methodism; embracing Strictures on the Writings of Wesley, Dr. Clarke, Fisk, Bangs, and others, in a series of letters addressed to the Rev. ****.* Pittsburgh: Loomis, 1838.

Bakewell, [Mrs.] J. *The Mother's Practical Guide in the Early Training of Her Children: containing the directions for their physical, intellectual, and moral education.* Reprinted from the 2nd London ed. New York: Lane & Sandford, 1843.

Bancroft, George. *History of the United States from the discovery of American continent.* Boston: Little, Brown, 1837.

Bangs, Heman. *The Autobiography and Journal of Rev. Heman Bangs; with an introduction by Rev. Bishop Janes, D.D. Edited by his daughters.* New York: Tibbals & Son, 1872.

Bangs, John. *Autobiography of Rev. John Bangs of the New York Annual Conference.* New York, 1846.

Bart, Sir Edward Bulwer-Lytton. *Pelham, or Adventures of a Gentleman.* New York: Hovendon Company, 1848.

Bledsoe, Albert Taylor. *An Examination of President Edwards' Inquiry into the Freedom of the Will.* Philadelphia: Hooker, 1845.

Carroll, John. *Case and His Contemporaries; or, The Canadian Itinerant's memorial: constituting a biographical history of Methodism in Canada.* Vol. 1. Toronto: Wesleyan Printing Establishment, 1867.

Clarke, Adam, and Thomas Coke. *The Preacher's Manual: Including Clavis Biblica, and, A Letter to a Methodist Preacher I by Adam Clarke; also, Four Discourses on the Duties of a Minister of the Gospel, by Thomas Coke.* New York: Mason and Lane, 1837.

Cook, William. *Ireland and the Centenary of American Methodism*. London: Wesleyan Conference Office, 1866.

Daniels, W. H. *The Illustrated History of Methodism in Great Britain and America, from the days of the Wesleys to the Present Time*. Cincinnati: Walden & Stowe, 1880.

Eaton, H. M. *The Itinerant's Wife: Her Qualifications, Duties, Trials, and Rewards*. New York: Lane & Scott, 1851.

Emory, Robert. *History of The Discipline of The Methodist Episcopal Church*. Revised by W. P. Strickland. New York: Carlton & Porter, 1864.

———. *The Life of the Rev. John Emory, one the Bishops of the Methodist Episcopal Church*. New York: Lane, 1841.

Finley, James B. *Autobiography of Rev. James B. Finley; or, Pioneer Life in the West*. Edited by W. P. Strickland. Cincinnati: Methodist Book Concern, 1853.

Finney, Charles Grandison. *Memoirs of Rev. Charles G. Finney*. New York: Barnes, 1876.

Foster, Randolph S. *A Treatise on the need of the Methodist Episcopal Church with respect to her ministry: embodied in sermon and preached by request before the New York East Conference, May 22, 1855*. New York: Carlton & Phillips, 1855.

Gillies, John. *Memoirs of the Life of the Reverend George Whitefield, MA*. London: Dilly, 1772.

Gregory, Benjamin. *Side Lights on the Conflicts of Methodism during the Second Quarter of the Nineteenth Century, 1827–1852*. London: Cassell and Company, 1899.

Haney, Milton Lorenzo. *The Inheritance Restored or Plain Teaching on Bible Holiness*. 3rd ed. Philadelphia: Gerard, 1897.

Holdich, Joseph. *The Life of Willbur Fisk, D.D.: First President of the Wesleyan University*. New York: Harper & Brothers, 1842.

Holland, John. *Memoirs of the Life and Ministry of Rev. John Summerfield, A.M, seventh edition*. New York: Wellman, 1845.

Holmes, D. *The Methodist Preacher; containing Twenty-eight Sermons, on Doctrinal and Practical Subjects. By Bishop Hedding, Dr. Fisk, Dr. Bangs, Dr. Durbin, and other ministers of The Methodist Episcopal Church*. Buffalo: Derby, Orton, & Mulligan, 1853.

The Illustrated Book of All Religions. Chicago: Hill, 1897.

Isaac, Daniel. *Vocal Melody; or, Singing the only music sanctioned by Divine Authority, in the Public Worship of Christians*. York: Burdekin, 1827.

Jackson, Thomas. *The Life of Rev. Charles Wesley, MA., Some time student of Christ-Church, Oxford: A review of his poetry; sketches of the rise and progress of Methodism; with notices of contemporary events and characters*. New York: Lane & Sandford, 1842.

The Ladies of the Mission. *The Old Brewery, and the New Mission House at The Five Points*. New York: Stringer & Townsend, 1854.

Lee, Jarena. *Religious Experience and Journal of Mrs. Jarena Lee, giving an account of her call to preach the gospel*. Philadelphia: Lee, 1849.

Lyth, John. *Glimpses of Early Methodism in York and the Surrounding District*. London: Hamilton, Adams & Company, 1885.

Maddin, Thomas. *The Apostate Methodist Preacher*. Nashville: Stevenson & Owen, 1857.

Miller, Adam. *Experience of German Methodist Preachers*. Cincinnati: Methodist Book Concern, 1859.

Peck, George. *Early Methodism within the Bounds of the Old Genesee Conference from 1788 to 1828*. New York: Carlton & Porter, 1860.

Perry, James H. *A Defense of the Present Mode of the training for the ministry for the Methodist Episcopal Church: being a review of a sermon entitled A Treatise on the Need of the Methodist Episcopal Church with respect to her ministry: preached by R. S. Foster, D.D., before the New York East Conference, and reprinted by a vote of said conference.* New York: Carlton & Phillips, 1855.

Pilmore, Joseph. *The Journal of Joseph Pilmore.* Edited by Frederick E. Maser and Howard T. Maag. Philadelphia: Message, 1969.

Purviance, David. *The Biography of Elder David Purviance.* Edited by Levi Purviance. Dayton: Ellis & Ellis, 1848.

Redford, Albert Henry. *History of Methodism in Kentucky.* Vol. 3. Nashville: Southern Methodist, 1870.

Reid, J. M. *Missions and Missionary Society of The Methodist Episcopal Church.* Vol. 1. Cincinnati: Walden & Stowe, 1882.

———. *Missions and Missionary Society of The Methodist Episcopal Church.* Vol. 2. Cincinnati: Curtis & Jennings, 1895.

Risely, John E. *Some Experiences of a Methodist Itinerant, in a ministry of half a century.* Boston, 1882.

Rule, William H. *Recollections of My Life and Work at Home and Abroad in connection with the Wesleyan Methodist Conference.* London: Woolmer, 1886.

Scott, Orange. *The Methodist Episcopal Church and Slavery.* Boston: Scott, 1844.

Seaman, Samuel A. *Annals of New York Methodism: being a history of the Methodist Episcopal Church in the City of New York from A.D. 1766 to A.D. 1890.* Cincinnati: Cranston & Stowe, 1892.

Sherman, David. *History of the Revisions of the Discipline of the Methodist Episcopal Church.* 3rd ed. Cincinnati: Cranston & Stowe, 1890.

Simpson, Matthew, ed. *Cyclopaedia of Methodism. Embracing sketches of its Rise, Progress, and Present Condition, with Biographical Notices and Numerous Illustrations.* Philadelphia: Everts & Stewart, 1878.

———. *A Hundred Years of Methodism.* Cincinnati: Cranston & Stowe, 1876.

———. *Lectures on Preaching, Delivered before the Theological Department of Yale College.* Cincinnati: Hitchcock & Walden, 1879.

Stevens, Abel. *The Centenary of American Methodism: A Sketch of its history, theology, practical system, and success.* New York: Carlton & Porter, 1865.

———, ed. *Dr. Cartwright Portrayed, in his visit to Brooklyn, 1861, Speeches and Anecdotes, and Correspondence with the Devil, with Observations on Dr. Cartwright by Dr. Abel Stevens.* New York: Tibbals & Company, 1861.

———. *Essays on the Preaching Required by the Times, and the best methods of obtaining it; with reminiscences and illustrations of Methodist preaching including Rules for Extemporaneous Preaching, and characteristic sketches of Olin, Fisk, Bascom, Cookman, Summerfield, and Other noted extemporaneous preachers.* New York: Carlton and Phillips, 1856.

———. *History of the Methodist Episcopal Church.* Vol. 2. New York: Carlton & Porter, 1864.

———. *History of the Methodist Episcopal Church in the United States of America.* 4 vols. New York: Phillips & Hunt, 1864–84.

———, ed. *The Life and Times of Nathan Bangs, D.D.* New York: Carlton & Porter, 1863.

———. *The Women of Methodism: Its Three Foundresses, Susanna Wesley, The Countess of Huntingdon, and Barbara Heck; With Sketches of Their Female Associates and Successor in the Early History of the Denomination.* New York: Carlton & Porter, 1866.

Stone, Barton W. *The Biography of Elder Barton Warren Stone, written by himself: with Additions and Reflections.* Cincinnati: American Christian Publications Society, 1853.

Stowe, Harriet Beecher. *Uncle Tom's Cabin, or, Life Among the Lowly.* 2 vols. Boston: Jewett & Company, 1852.

Vinet, A. *Homiletics; or, The Theory of Preaching.* Edited and translated by Thomas H. Skinner. 3rd ed. Chicago: Griggs, 1866.

Wakeley, J. B. *Lost Chapters recovered from The Early History of American Methodism.* New York, 1858.

Warriner, Edwin. *Old Sands Street Methodist Episcopal Church, of Brooklyn.* New York: Phillips & Hunt, 1885.

Watson, Richard. *A Biblical and Theological Dictionary: Explanatory of the history, manners, and customs of the Jews, and neighboring nations. With an account of the most remarkable places and persons mentioned in Sacred Scripture; an exposition of the principle doctrines of Christianity: and notices of Jewish and Christian sects and heresies.* Edited by Nathan Bangs. New York: Waugh and Mason, 1833.

Wesley, John. *Thoughts upon Slavery.* 3rd ed. London: Hawes, 1774.

Whedon, Daniel Denison. *The Freedom of the Will as a basis of Human responsibility and a Divine Government Elucidated and Maintained in its Issue with the Necessitarian Theories of Hobbes, Edwards, the Princeton Essayists, and Other Leading Advocates.* New York: Carlton & Porter, 1864.

Wise, Daniel. *The Children's Centenary Memorial.* New York: Tibbals, 1866.

———. *The Convert's Counsellor respecting his church relations: or Popular Objections to Methodism considered and answered: with reasons why Methodist converts should join a Methodist church. An antidote to certain recent publications assailing The Methodist Episcopal Church.* Boston: Magee, 1856.

Wright, John F. *Sketches of the Life and Labors of James Quinn who was nearly half a century a Minister of the Gospel in The Methodist Episcopal Church.* Cincinnati: Methodist Book Concern, 1851.

Youngs, James. *A History of the Most Interesting Events in the Rise and Progress of Methodism, in Europe and America.* New Haven: McLeod, 1831.

3. Collected Works, Anthologies, and Reprints

Allen, Richard. *The Life Experiences and Gospel Labors of the Rt. Rev. Richard Allen.* Bicentennial ed. Nashville: Abingdon, 1983.

Asbury, Francis. *The Journal and Letters of Francis Asbury.* Edited by Elmer T. Clark et al. Vol. 1. Nashville: Abingdon, 1958.

———. *Journal of Rev. Francis Asbury.* 3 vols. New York: Bangs and Mason and Eaton & Mains, 1821.

Baird, Robert. *Religion in America: A Critical Abridgment.* Edited by Henry Warner Bowden. New York: Harper & Row, 1970.

Brown, William Wells. *The Travels of William Wells Brown.* Edited by Paul Jefferson. New York: Wiener, 1991.

Bushnell, Horace. *Christian Nurture.* 1861. Reprint, Yale University Press, 1953.

———. *Sermons on Living Subjects.* 1876. Reprint, New York: Scribner, 1901.

Cartwright, Peter. *Autobiography of Peter Cartwright.* Edited by Charles L. Wallis. Nashville: Abingdon, 1984.

Channing, William E. *The Works of William E. Channing.* Vol. 6. 10th ed. Boston: Channing, 1849.

Douglass, Frederick. *Life and Times of Frederick Douglass.* 1892. Reprint, New York: Collier, 1962.

Edwards, Jonathan. *The Works of Jonathan Edwards.* 2 Vols. Edinburgh: Banner of Truth Trust, 1992.

Finney, Charles Grandison. *Lectures on Revivals of Religion.* New York: Leavitt, Lord, 1835.

Fletcher, John. *The Works of John Fletcher.* Vol. 3. 2nd American ed. New York: Totten, 1809.

Garrettson, Freeborn. *American Methodist Pioneer: The Life and Journals of the Rev. Freeborn Garrettson, 1752–1827.* Edited by Robert Drew Simpson. Rutland: Academy, 1984.

Langford, Thomas A. *Wesleyan Theology: A Sourcebook.* Durham, NC: Labyrinth, 1984.

Machiavelli, Niccolo. *The Prince.* Translated and edited by Daniel Donno. New York: Bantam, 1981.

Norwood, Frederick A. *Sourcebook of American Methodism.* Nashville: Abingdon, 1982.

Noyes, John Humphrey, et al. *Strange Cults & Utopias of 19th Century America.* New York: Dover, 1966.

Olin, Stephen. *The Life and Letters of Stephen Olin Late President of the Wesleyan University.* New York: Harper, 1853.

Palmer, Phoebe. *The Promise of the Father, or A Neglected Speciality of the Last Days.* 1859. Reprint, Salem: Schmul, n.d.

Richey, Russell, et al., eds. *The Methodist Experience in America: A Sourcebook.* Vol. 2. Nashville: Abingdon, 2000.

Sernett, Milton C., ed. *African American Religious History: A Documentary Witness.* 2nd ed. Durham, NC: Duke University Press, 1999.

Tocqueville, Alexis de. *Democracy in America.* Edited by Richard D. Heffner. New York: New American Library, 1956.

Wesley, Charles. *The Journal of The Rev. Charles Wesley, MA.* Edited by Thomas Jackson. 2 vols. 1849. Reprint, Grand Rapids: Baker, 1980.

Wesley, John. *The Bicentennial Edition of the Works of John Wesley.* Edited by Frank Baker and Richard P. Heitzenrater. Nashville: Abingdon, 1976–.

———. *The Works of John Wesley.* 14 Vols. Thomas Jackson edition. Grand Rapids: Zondervan, 1960.

———. *The Works of John Wesley.* Vol. 7, *A Collection of Hymns for the People Called Methodists.* Edited by Franz Hildebrandt and Oliver A. Beckerlegge with the assistance of James Dale. Nashville: Abingdon, 1983.

———. *The Works of John Wesley.* Vol. 23, *Journal and Diaries VI (1776–1786).* Edited by W. Reginald Ward and Richard P. Heitzenrater. Nashville: Abingdon, 1995.

Wesley, Susannah. *The Complete Writings.* Edited by Charles Wallace Jr. Oxford: Oxford University Press, 1997.

Whitefield, George. *George Whitefield's Letters, 1734–1742.* 1771. Reprint, Edinburgh: Banner of Truth Trust, 1976.

———. *Whitefield's Journals.* London: Banner of Truth Trust, 1965.

Wilberforce, William. *A Practical View of the Prevailing Religious System of Professed Christians in the Higher and Middle Classes of This Country Contrasted with Real Christianity.* Edited by Dr. Vincent Edmunds. London: Hodder and Stoughton, 1989.

4. Published Letters

Chevalier, Michael, *Society, Manners, and Politics in the United States: Being a Series of Letters from North America.* Boston, 1839.

Kennerly, Samuel. "Work of God on New-River Circuit." *Methodist Review* 4 (1821) 348.

Ward, W. R., ed. *Early Victorian Methodism: The Correspondence of Jabez Bunting, 1830–1858.* Oxford: Oxford University Press, 1976.

Wesley, John. *The Letters of the Rev. John Wesley, A.M.* Edited by John Telford. 8 vols. Standard ed. London: Epworth, 1931.

Whitefield, George. *Letters of George Whitefield, for the Period 1734 to 1742.* Edinburgh: Banner of Truth Trust, 1976.

5. Published Addresses, Sermons, Speeches

Cartwright, Peter. "Speech in General Conference, 1844." In *Dr. Cartwright Portrayed, in his visit to Brooklyn, 1861, Speeches and Anecdotes, and Correspondence with the Devil, with Observations on Dr. Cartwright by Dr. Abel Stevens,* edited by Abel Stevens, 21–28. New York: Tibbals, 1861.

Clark, D. W. *The Able Minister of the New Testament. An Anniversary Discourse, delivered before the Literary Societies of The Methodist General Biblical Institute, at Concord, New Hampshire, Nov. 7, 1849.* Boston: Rand, 1850.

———. *The Cross of Christ, the one theme of the Christian minister's glorying. A discourse preached before the New-York Annual Conference at its session in Kingston, May 5, 1853.* New York: Carlton & Phillips, 1853.

Clark, Laban. *A Semi-Centennial Sermon delivered before The New York East Conference, and published by their Request.* New York: Lane & Scott, 1851.

Cooper, Ezekiel. *The Substance of a Funeral Discourse, delivered a the request of the Annual Conference, on Tuesday, the 23rd of April, 1816, in St. George's Church, Philadelphia: on the Death of the Rev. Francis Asbury, Superintendent, or Senior Bishop, of the Methodist Episcopal Church, now enlarged.* Philadelphia: Pounder, 1819.

Emerson, Ralph Waldo. "New England Reformers: A Lecture Read before the Society in Amory Hall on Sunday, March 3, 1844." In *Essays and English Traits,* 263–81. Harvard Classics. Danbury: Grolier, 1980.

Janes, Edmund Storer. *Sermon on the Death of Nathan Bangs, D.D.* New York: Carlton & Porter, 1862.

Soule, Joshua. *Object and Nature of Religious Worship: A Discourse delivered at the Dedication of John-Street Church, New York, Jan. 4, 1818*. Nashville: Stevenson & Owen, 1857.

———. *The Substance of a Discourse, delivered in the New Methodist Meeting House in John-Street, New-York: On the Evening of the 4th of January, 1818; being the day on which said house was opened/or Divine Worship*. New York: Totten, 1818.

6. Periodicals

Alvis, William T. "Letter from William T. Alvis." *Methodist Magazine* 4 (1821) 357–58.

"American Colonization Society." Editorial. *Methodist Magazine and Quarterly Review* 16 (1834) 353–59.

Bangs, Nathan. "Letter to a Junior Preacher." *Methodist Review* 7 (1824) 111–15.

———. "Revival of the Work of God in Rhinebeck." *Methodist Review* 4 (1821) 349–51.

———. "Rise and Progress of the Methodist Episcopal Church in New-Haven, Connecticut." *Methodist Review* 10 (1827) 263–66.

D., R. M. Review of *Authentic History of the Missions under the Care of the Missionary Society of the Methodist Episcopal Church*, by Nathan Bangs. *Methodist Review* 14 (1832) 249–54.

Jay, William. "Remarks on Preaching." *Methodist Review* 10 (1827) 208–13.

McNaim, Norman A. "Mission to Canada." *Methodist History* 13 (1975) 46–60.

McTyeire, H. N. "Houses for Worship." Editorial. *Christian Advocate*, February 3, 1859.

Reese, David Meredith. "Brief Strictures on the Rev. Mr. Sunderland's 'Essay on Theological Education.'" *Methodist Magazine and Quarterly Review* (1835) 105–18.

Review of *Lectures on Revivals of Religion*, by Charles G. Finney. *Methodist Review* 30 (1848) 477.

Review of *The Life and Times of Nathan Bangs*, by Abel Stevens. *Methodist Review* 46 (1864) 172–74.

Review of *The Life of Wesley; and the Rise and Progress of Methodism*, by Robert Southey. *Quarterly Review* 24 (1820) 1–55.

"Review on the Economy of Methodism." *Quarterly Christian Spectator* (September 1829) 509–26.

Stone, Barton W. "Revivals of Religion." *Christian Messenger* 5 (1831) 164–67.

Sunderland, La Roy. "Essay on a Theological Education." *Methodist Magazine and Quarterly Review* 16 (1834) 423–37.

"Theological Education." Editorial, *Methodist Magazine and Quarterly Review* 17 (1835) 85–105.

Wesley, John. "Mr. Wesley's Rules for Congregational Singing." *Methodist Magazine* (1824) 189–90.

———. "Thoughts on Preaching the Gospel." *Methodist Review* 11 (1828) 346–48.

"Wesleyan University." *Christian Advocate and Journal* 15 (1841) 127.

7. Proceedings, Reports, Bylaws

A.M.E. Church. *The Doctrine and Discipline of the African Methodist Episcopal Church.* 21st rev. ed. Philadelphia: A.M.E. Book Concern, 1896.

Committee on the Memorial from Washington City. *Journals of the General Conference of the Methodist Episcopal Church.* Vol. 3, *Journal of the General Conference, 1852.* New York: Carlton & Lanahan, 1852.

"General Recapitulation." In *Minutes of the Methodist Conferences, Annually Held in America; From 1773–1813, inclusive.* Vol. 1. New York: Hitt and Ware, 1813.

Genesee Wesleyan Seminary. *Catalogue of the Officers, Faculty, & Students of the Genesee Wesleyan Seminary, Lima, NY.* Rochester: Hamilton, 1845.

Gillett, John S. "Report to the Missionary Board of the West Texas Conference." In *Annual Report of the Board of Missions of the Methodist Episcopal Church,* 35–37. South, 1873.

The Methodist Episcopal Church. *Composing a form of Discipline for the Ministers, Preachers and other Members of the Methodist Episcopal Church in America.* Philadelphia: Cist, 1785.

———. *The Doctrines and Discipline of the Methodist Episcopal Church 1856.* Cincinnati: Swormstedt and Poe, 1856.

———. *The Doctrines and Discipline of the Methodist Episcopal Church the Twenty-Second Edition.* New York: Bangs and Emory, 1824.

———. *A Form of Discipline, for the Ministers, Preachers, and Members of the Methodist Episcopal Church in America.* New York, 1787.

———. *Journals of the General Conference of the Methodist Episcopal Church.* 3 vols. New York: Carlton & Lanahan, 1840–56.

———. *Journal of the General Conference, 1820.* New York: Methodist Episcopal Church, 1820.

———. *Journal of the General Conference, 1824.* New York: Methodist Episcopal Church, 1824.

———. *Minutes of Several Conversations between the Rev. Thomas Coke Ll. D. the Rev. Francis Asbury and Others : At a Conference Begun in Baltimore in the State of Maryland on Monday the 27th. of December in the Year 1784: Composing a Form of Discipline for the Ministers Preachers and Other Members of the Methodist Episcopal Church in America.* Philadelphia: Cist, 1784.

The New York East Conference. *Minutes of the New York East Annual Conference 1863.* New York: New York East Conference, 1863.

Wesley, John. *The Nature, Design, and General Rules, of the United Societies, in London, Bristol, King's-wood, and Newcastle upon Tyne.* Newcastle upon Tyne: Gooding, 1743.

The Wesleyan Methodist Conference. *Minutes of the Wesleyan Conference, 1807.* Collected ed. 1807.

8. Hymnbooks and Poems

Mason, Thomas. *Zion's Songster, or, A Collection of Hymns and Spiritual Songs, usually sung at Camp-Meetings, and also in Revivals of Religion.* 10th ed. New York: Harper, 1835.

Methodist Episcopal Church. *A Collection of Hymns, for the use of the Methodist Episcopal Church, principally from the collection of the Rev. John Wesley, A.M, revised and corrected, with a supplement.* New York: Lane & Sandford, 1843.

Palmer, Phoebe. "Semi-Centennial Marriage Hymn." In *Memorial of the Golden Wedding of the Rev. Nathan and Mrs. Mary Bangs, April 23, 1856*, edited by Nathan Bangs, 22–23. New York: Printed for Private Circulation, 1856.

Taylor, George Lansing. "A Centennial Rhyme." In *The Children's Centenary Memorial*, by Daniel Wise, 113–17. New York: Tibbals, 1866.

9. Engravings, Portraits, and Photographs

"American Gothic Revival, Trinity Methodist Episcopal Church, NY, 1856." In *Lost Chapters Recovered from The Early History of American Methodism*, by J. B. Wakeley, 588. New York: Carlton & Porter, 1858.

"Eclectic Greek Revival, Third John Street Church, NY, 1841." In *Lost Chapters Recovered from The Early History of American Methodism*, by J. B. Wakeley, 584. New York: Carlton & Porter, 1858.

"Model Preaching House, Second John Street Church, NY, 1818." In *Lost Chapters Recovered from The Early History of American Methodism*, by J. B. Wakeley, 580. New York: Carlton & Porter, 1858.

"Pointed Gothic, Grace Methodist Episcopal Church, Philadelphia, PA." In *The Illustrated Book of All Religions*, 310. Chicago: Hill, 1897.

"Portrait of Mature Bangs." Engraving by A. H. Ritchie, frontispiece, in *The Life and Times of Nathan Bangs, D.D.*, edited by Abel Stevens. New York: Carlton & Porter, 1863.

"Portrait of Middle-Age Bangs." Engraving by E. Mackenzie from a painting by Paradise. Archives and Special Collections, Wesleyan University.

"Presidential Windows at Memorial Chapel, Wesleyan University." Special Collections and Archives, Wesleyan University.

"Romanesque—Akron Plan, Broad Street Methodist Episcopal Church, Newark, NJ." In *Lost Chapters Recovered from The Early History of American Methodism*, by J. B. Wakeley, 595. New York: Carlton & Porter, 1858.

"Romanesque, St. Paul's Methodist Episcopal Church, NY, 1857." In *Lost Chapters Recovered from The Early History of American Methodism*, by J. B. Wakeley, 592. New York: Carlton & Porter, 1858.

"Saint Paul's Methodist Episcopal Church, N.Y., 1858." In *Lost Chapters Recovered from The Early History of American Methodism*, by J. B. Wakeley. New York: Carlton & Porter, 1858.

10. Unpublished Letters, Manuscripts, and Speeches

"Acknowledgment of Students respecting the Communication sent by them to by President Bangs, in relation to his official connexion." June 13, 1842. President Nathan Bangs Papers. Wesleyan University, Middletown, CT.

"Addendum to Acknowledgment." July 30, 1842. President Nathan Bangs Papers. Wesleyan University, Middletown, CT.

Bangs, Nathan. "[Chairman's] Address to the Managers of the Missionary and Bible Society of the Methodist Episcopal Church in America." April 21, 1819. Minutes of the Methodist Episcopal Church Board of Missions, Methodist Archives. Drew University, Madison, NJ.

———. Recommendation of Rev. W. Armstrong. November 3, 1845. Folder 18. Thomas Bond Papers. Special Collections. Waidner-Spahr Library, Dickinson College, Carlisle, PA.

———. To James B. Finley. "Wyandott Mission Letter of Invitation for Two Chiefs to attend an 'Anniversary' in New York." February 13, 1824. James B. Finley Papers, Special Collections. Ohio Wesleyan University, Delaware, OH.

———. To Littleton Fowler. San Augustine, TX, January 17, 1840. Box 18-A, Martin Ruter Papers. Archives. Center for Methodist Studies at Bridwell Library, Perkins School of Theology, Southern Methodist University, Dallas.

———. To Stephen Olin, August 20, 1842. President Nathan Bangs Papers. Wesleyan University, Middletown, CT.

Bangs, Nathan, and Thomas Mason. To Martin Ruter. Cincinnati, OH, January 31, 1821. Box 18-A, Martin Ruter Papers. Archives. Center for Methodist Studies at Bridwell Library, Perkins School of Theology, Southern Methodist University, Dallas, TX.

[Bond, Thomas Emerson]. "To the Methodist Conservatives." 1844. Thomas Emerson Bond Papers. Folder 19. Special Collections. Waidner-Spahr Library, Dickinson College, Carlisle, PA.

Edwards, Jonathan. To George Whitefield. February 12, 1740. Methodist Collection. John Rylands University Library, University of Manchester.

Haven, E. Otis. "1842 to Nathaniel C. Lewis." April 4, 1841. N. C. Lewis, Class of 1840 Folder. President Nathan Bangs Collection. Wesleyan University, Middletown, CT.

Martindale, Miles. To Willbur Fisk. December 22, 1834. President Willbur Fisk Papers. Wesleyan University, Middletown, CT.

Pettee, John T. "Apology to the Faculty." N.d. President Nathan Bangs Papers. Wesleyan University, Middletown, CT.

Stockwell, Charles F. To R. B. Hoyt. July 12, 1842. President Nathan Bangs Papers. Wesleyan University, Middletown, CT.

Secondary Sources

Addison, James Thayer. *The Episcopal Church in the United States, 1789–1931*. New York: Scribner, 1951.

Alexander, E. Curtis. *Richard Allen: The First Exemplar of African American Education*. New York: ECA Associates, 1985.

Allsopp, Bruce. *Romanesque Architecture*. New York: Day, 1971.

Anderson, William K., ed. *Methodism*. Nashville: Methodist Church, 1947.

Andersson, Peter K. "The Walking Stick in the Nineteenth-Century: Conflicting Ideals of Urban Walking." *Journal of Transport History* 39 (2018) 275–91.

Andrews, Dee E. *The Methodists and Revolutionary America, 1760–1800*. Princeton: Princeton University Press, 2000.

Andrews, Wayne. *Architecture, Ambition, and Americans: A Social History of American Architecture*. Rev. ed. London: Free, 1978.

Angell, Stephen W., and Anthony B. Pirin. *Social Protest Thought in the African Methodist Episcopal Church, 1862–1939*. Knoxville: University of Tennessee Press, 2000.

Angle, Paul M. *"Here I Have Lived": A History of Lincoln's Springfield, 1821–1865*. Springfield, IL: Abraham Lincoln Association, 1935.

Anson, Peter F. *Fashions in Church Furnishings, 1840–1940*. London: Faith, 1960.

Avery-Quinn, Samuel. *Cities of Zion: The Holiness Movement and Methodist Camp Meeting Towns in America*. Lanham, MD: Lexington, 2019.

Bailey, Albert Edward. *The Gospel in Hymns: Backgrounds and Interpretations*. New York: Scribner, 1950.

Baker, Frank. *From Wesley to Asbury*. Durham, NC: Duke University Press, 1976.

Barclay, William Wade. *History of Methodist Missions*. 6 vols. New York: Board of Missions and Church Extension of The Methodist Church, 1949–57.

Barton, Paul. *Hispanic Methodists, Presbyterians, and Baptists in Texas*. Austin: University of Texas Press, 2006.

———. "Inter-ethnic Relations between Mexican Americans and Anglo American Methodists." In *Protestantes/Protestants: Hispanic Christianity within Mainline Traditions*, edited by David Maldonado Jr., 60–84. Nashville: Abingdon, 1999.

Beckert, Sven. *The Monied Metropolis: New York City and the Consolidation of the American Bourgeoisie, 1850–1896*. Cambridge: Cambridge University Press, 2001.

Behney, J. Bruce, and Paul H. Eller. *The History of the Evangelical United Brethren Church*. Edited by Kenneth W. Krueger. Nashville: Abingdon, 1979.

Bennett, Vicki. *Sacred Space and Structural Style: The Embodiment of Socio-religious Ideology*. Ottawa: University of Ottawa Press, 1997.

Berger, Daniel. *History of the Church of The United Brethren in Christ*. American Church History Series 12. New York: Christian Literature, 1894.

Berkhofer, William, Jr. *The White Man's Indian*. New York: Vintage, 1979.

Bett, Henry. *The Spirit of Methodism*. London: Epworth, 1937.

Bimson, Richard H., and Erna S. Bimson. *Hawaii Mission of the Methodist Church 1855–1955*. s.l.: s.n., 1955.

Body, Alfred H. *John Wesley and Education*. London: Epworth, 1936.

Bond, Francis. *Screens and Galleries in English Churches*. Oxford: Oxford University Press, 1908.

Bonomi, Patricia U. *Under the Cope of Heaven: Religion, Society, and Politics in Colonial America*. Oxford: Oxford University Press, 1986.

Boorstin, Daniel J. *The Americans: The Democratic Experience*. New York: Vintage, 1974.

———. *The Americans: The National Experience*. New York: Vintage, 1991.

Bowden, Henry Warner. *American Indians and Christian Missions: Studies in Cultural Conflict*. Chicago: University of Chicago Press, 1985.

Bready, J. Wesley. *England: Before and After Wesley*. London: Harper Brothers, 1938.

Brekus, Catherine A. *Strangers and Pilgrims: Female Preaching in America, 1740–1845*. Chapel Hill: University of North Carolina Press, 1998.

Brown, Barton. "Quest for the Temple: A Study of the New York Ecclesiological Society, 1848–1855, and Its Effect upon the Architectural Setting of Worship in the Episcopal Church in the United States of America, 1840–1860." STM thesis, General Theological Seminary, 1968.

Brown, Lillian Brooks. *A Living Centennial Commemorating the One Hundredth Anniversary of Metropolitan Memorial United Methodist Church.* Washington, DC: Metropolitan Memorial United Methodist Church, 1969.

Browning, Don S., et al. *From Culture Wars to Common Ground: Religion and the American Family Debate.* Louisville: Westminster John Knox, 1997.

Bruggink, Donald J., and Carl H. Droppers. *Christ and Architecture: Building Presbyterian/Reformed Churches.* Grand Rapids: Eerdmans, 1965.

Burleigh, J. H. S. *A Church History of Scotland.* Oxford: Oxford University Press, 1960.

Burr, Nelson R. *A Critical Bibliography of Religion in America.* Vol. 4. Princeton: Princeton University Press, 1961.

Bushman, Richard L. *Joseph Smith and the Beginnings of Mormonism.* Urbana: University of Illinois Press, 1984.

———. *The Refinement of America: Persons, Houses, Cities.* New York: Knopf, 1992.

Butler, Jon. *Awash in a Sea of Faith: Christianizing the American People.* Cambridge: Harvard University Press, 1989.

Calhoun, Charles W. *The Gilded Age: Essays on the Origins of Modern America.* Wilmington, DE: Scholarly Resources, 2000.

Cameron, Richard M. "The New Church Takes Root." In *The History of American Methodism,* edited by Emory Bucke, 1:251–56. Nashville: Abingdon, 1964.

Carwardine, Richard. *Transatlantic Revivalism.* Westport, CT: Greenwood, 1978.

Case, Riley B. *Faith and Fury: Eli Farmer on the Frontier, 1794–1881.* Indianapolis: Indiana Historical Society, 2018.

Cashdollar, Charles D. *A Spiritual Home: Life in British and American Reformed Congregations, 1830–1915.* University Park: Pennsylvania State University Press, 2000.

Chandler, Douglas A. "Towards the Americanizing of Methodism." *Methodist History* 13 (1974) 3–16.

Cherry, Conrad, ed. *God's New Israel: Religious Interpretations of American Destiny.* Englewood Cliffs, NJ: Prentice-Hall, 1971.

Chilcote, Paul W. *John Wesley and the Women Preachers of Early Methodism.* ATLA Monograph Series 25. Metuchen, NJ: Scarecrow, 1991.

———. *She Offered Them Christ: The Legacy of Women Preachers in Early Methodism.* Nashville: Abingdon, 1993.

Chiles, Robert E. *Theological Transition in American Methodism, 1790–1935.* Nashville: Abingdon, 1965.

Chipman, Donald E. *Spanish Texas, 1519–1821.* Austin: University of Texas Press, 1992.

Clark, S. D. *Church and Sect in Canada.* Toronto: University of Toronto Press, 1971.

Clarke, Basil F. L. *Church Builders of the Nineteenth Century: A Study in the Gothic Revival in England.* London: SPCK, 1938.

Cole, Charles C., Jr. *Lion of the Forest: James B. Finley Frontier Reformer.* Lexington: University Press of Kentucky, 1994.

Conforti, Joseph A. *Jonathan Edwards, Religious Tradition, & American Culture.* Chapel Hill: University of North Carolina Press, 1995.

Conrad, Earl. *Harriet Tubman.* Washington, DC: Associated, 1943.

Cott, Nancy F. *The Bonds of Womanhood: "Woman's Sphere" in New England, 1780–1835.* New Haven: Yale University Press, 1977.

Crouse, Eric R. "Methodist Encounters: Confronting the Western and Urban Frontiers of 19th Century America." *Methodist History* 40 (2002) 157–67.

Danziger, Edmund J., Jr. "Native American Resistance and Accommodation during the Late Nineteenth Century." In *The Gilded Age: Essays on the Origins of Modern America*, edited by Charles W. Calhoun, 163–84. Wilmington, DE: Scholarly Resources, 2000.

Davies, Rupert E. *Methodism*. London: Epworth, 1990.

Davis, David Brion, ed. *Ante-Bellum Reform*. New York: Harper & Row, 1967.

———. "The Emergence of Immediatism." In *Ante-Bellum Reform*, edited by David Brion Davis, 19–34. New York: Harper & Row, 1967.

Davis, Morris L., Jr. "From the Gospel Circuit to the War Circuit: Bishop Matthew Simpson and Upwardly Mobile Methodism." *Methodist History* 38 (2000) 199–209.

Dayton, Donald W. *Discovering an Evangelical Heritage*. New York: Harper & Row, 1976.

———. "Presidential Address: The Wesleyan Option for the Poor." *Wesleyan Theological Journal* 26 (1991) 7–22.

Dieter, Melvin Easterday. *The Holiness Movement of the Nineteenth Century*. 2nd ed. Lanham, MD: Scarecrow, 1996.

Doan, Ruth Alden. "John Wesley Young: Identity and Community among the People Called Methodist." In *The Human Tradition in Antebellum America*, edited by Michael A. Morrison, 19–34. Human Tradition in America 7. Wilmington, DE: Scholarly Resources, 2000.

———. *The Miller Heresy, Millennialism, and American Culture*. Philadelphia: Temple University Press, 1987.

Dolan, Jay P. *Catholic Revivalism: The American Experience, 1830–1900*. Notre Dame: University of Notre Dame Press, 1978.

Donavan, Jane. *Henry Foxall (1758–1823): Methodist, Industrialist, American*. Nashville: New Room, 2017.

Douglass, Paul F. *The Story of German Methodism: Biography of an Immigrant Soul*. New York: Methodist Book Concern, 1939.

Dreff, Ashley Boggan. *Entangled: A History of American Methodism, Politics, and Sexuality*. Nashville: New Room, 2019.

Drummond, Landale. *The Church Architecture of Protestantism: An Historical and Constructive Study*. Edinburgh: T. & T. Clark, 1934.

Drummond, Lewis A. *Charles Grandison Finney and the Birth of Modern Evangelism*. London: Hodder and Stoughton, 1983.

Eayrs, George. *Wesley and Kingswood and Its Free Churches*. Bristol: Arrowsmith, 1911.

Edwards, Maldwyn. "John Wesley." In vol. 1 of *A History of the Methodist Church in Great Britain*, edited by Rupert Davies and Gordon Rupp, 35–79. London: Epworth, 1965.

Elder, Robert. *The Sacred Mirror: Evangelism, Honor, and Identity in the Deep South, 1790–1860*. Chapel Hill: University of North Carolina Press, 2016.

Elsinger, Ellen. *Citizens of Zion*. Knoxville: University of Tennessee Press, 1999.

Embury, Aymar, II. *Early American Churches*. Garden City, NY: Doubleday, Page, 1914.

Ferguson, Charles W. *Organizing to Beat the Devil: Methodists and the Making of America*. Garden City, NY: Doubleday, 1971.

Finke, Roger, and Rodney Stark. *The Churching of America, 1776–1990: Winners and Losers in Our Religious Economy*. New Brunswick, NJ: Rutgers University Press, 2000.

Fishburn, Janet Forsythe. *The Fatherhood of God and the Victorian Family: The Social Gospel in America*. Philadelphia: Fortress, 1981.

Flores, Daniel F. *Nathan Bangs: The Architect of American Methodism*. Fort Worth, TX: CreateSpace, 2015.

———. "Respectable Methodists: Nathan Bangs and the Rise of Respectability in the Methodist Episcopal Church in the Early National Period." PhD diss., Drew University, 2004.

Foner, Eric. *Reconstruction*. New York: Harper & Row, 1988.

Fones-Wolf, Ken. *Trade Union Gospel: Christianity and Labor in Industrial Philadelphia, 1865–1915*. Philadelphia: Temple University Press, 1989.

Foote, Henry Wilder. *Three Centuries of American Hymnody*. Hamden, CT: Archon, 1968.

Ford, Bridget. *Bonds of Union: Religion, Race, and Politics in a Civil War Borderland*. Chapel Hill: University of North Carolina Press, 2016.

Gaustad, Edwin Scott. *A Religious History of America*. New rev. ed. San Francisco: Harper San Francisco, 1990.

Gealy, Fred, et al. *Companion to the Hymnal: A Handbook to the 1964 Methodist Hymnal*. Nashville: Abingdon, 1970.

George, Carol V. R. *One Mississippi, Two Mississippi: Methodists, Murder, and the Struggle for Racial Justice in Neshoba County*. Oxford: Oxford University Press, 2015.

Goldthorpe, John H., et al. *The Affluent Worker in the Class Structure*. Cambridge: Cambridge University Press, 1969.

Graham, J. H. *Black United Methodists: Retrospect and Prospect*. New York: Vantage, 1979.

Greenagel, Frank L. *The New Jersey Churchscape: Encountering Eighteenth and Nineteenth Century Churches*. New Brunswick, NJ: Rutgers University Press, 2001.

Greene, Alison Collis. *No Depression in Heaven: The Great Depression, the New Deal, and the Transformation of Religion in the Delta*. Oxford: Oxford University Press, 2016.

Halevy, Elie. *The Birth of Methodism in England*. Edited and translated by Bernard Semmel. Chicago: University of Chicago Press, 1971.

Handy, Robert T. *A History of Union Theological Seminary in New York*. New York: Columbia University Press, 1987.

Hardt, Philip F. *The Soul of Methodism: The Class Meeting in Early New York City Methodism*. Lanham, MD: University Press of America, 2000.

Harwood, Thomas. *History of New Mexico Spanish and English Missions of The Methodist Episcopal Church from 1850 to 1910*. Vol. 1, 1908. Reprint, First United Methodist Church of Albuquerque, 1983.

Haselby, Sam. *The Origins of American Religious Nationalism*. Oxford: Oxford University Press, 2015.

Hatch, Nathan O. *The Democratization of American Christianity*. New Haven: Yale University Press, 1989.

Hatch, Nathan O., and John H. Wigger, eds. *Methodism and the Shaping of American Culture*. Nashville: Kingswood, 2001.

Hayward, Edward F. *Lyman Beecher*. Boston: Pilgrim, 1904.

Heitzenrater, Richard P. *The Poor and the People Called Methodists, 1729–1999*. Nashville: Kingswood, 2002.

———. *Wesley and the People Called Methodists*. Nashville: Abingdon, 1995.

Hempton, David. *Methodism: Empire of the Spirit*. New Haven: Yale University Press, 2005.

Hendrix, Bishop E. R. "Jonathan Edwards and John Wesley." *Methodist Review Quarterly* 34 (1913) 28–38.

Herrmann, Richard Everett. "Nathan Bangs: Apologist for American Methodism." PhD diss., Emory University, 1973.

Heyrman, Christine Leigh. *Southern Cross: The Beginnings of the Bible Belt*. New York: Knopf, 1997.

Hickman, Hoyt L. *Worshiping with United Methodists: A Guide for Pastors and Church Leaders*. Nashville: Abingdon, 1996.

Hildebrand, Reginald F. *The Times Were Strange and Stirring: Methodist Preachers and the Crisis of Emancipation*. Durham, NC: Duke University Press, 1995.

Hildebrandt, Franz. *Christianity according to the Wesleys*. Grand Rapids: Baker, 1996.

Hobsbawm, E. J. *The Age of Revolution, 1789–1848*. New York: Mentor, 1962.

Holifield, E. Brooks. "Nathan Bangs." In *Makers of Christian Theology in America*, edited by Mark G. Toulouse and James O. Duke, 121–24. Nashville: Abingdon, 1997.

———. *Theology in America: Christian Thought from the Age of the Puritans to the Civil War*. New Haven: Yale University Press, 2003.

Holland, De Witte T. *The Preaching Tradition: A Brief History*. Nashville: Abingdon, 1980.

Holm, April E. *A Kingdom Divided: Evangelicals, Loyalty, and Sectionalism in the Civil War Era*. Baton Rouge: Louisiana State University Press, 2017.

Hornberger, Eric. *The Historical Atlas of New York City: A Visual Celebration of Nearly 400 Years of New York City's History*. New York: Holt, 1994.

Howard, Ivan Cushing. "Controversies in Methodism over Methods of Education of Ministers up to 1865." PhD diss., State University of Iowa, 1965.

Howe, Daniel Walker. *What God Hath Wrought: The Transformation of America, 1815–1848*. Oxford: Oxford University Press, 2007.

Howe, Jeffery. *Houses of Worship: An Identification Guide to the History and Styles of American Religious Architecture*. San Diego: Thunder Bay, 2003.

Hudson, Winthrop S., and John Corrigan. *Religion in America: An Historical Account of the Development of American Religious Life*. 6th ed. Upper Saddle River, NJ: Prentice Hall, 1999.

James, William. *The Varieties of Religious Experience: A Study in Human Nature Being the Gifford Lectures on Natural Religion Delivered at Edinburgh in 1901–1902*. New York: New American Library of World Literature, 1958.

Jeffrey, David Lyle, ed. *English Spirituality in the Age of Wesley*. Grand Rapids: Eerdmans, 1987.

Jennings, Theodore W., Jr. *Good News to the Poor: John Wesley's Evangelical Economics*. Nashville: Abingdon, 1990.

Jervey, Edward D. "La Roy Sunderland: Zion's Watchman." *Methodist History* 6 (1968) 16–32.

Johnson, Charles A. *The Frontier Campmeeting: Religion's Harvest Time*. Dallas: Southern Methodist University Press, 1985.

Johnson, Curtis D. *Redeeming America: Evangelicals and the Road to Civil War*. Chicago: Dee, 1993.

Johnson, Paul E. *A Shopkeeper's Millennium: Society and Revivals in Rochester, New York, 1815–1837*. New York: Hill and Wang, 1978.

Jones, Charles Edwin. *Perfectionist Persuasion: The Holiness Movement and American Methodism, 1867–1936*. ATLA Monograph Series 5. Metuchen, NJ: Scarecrow, 1974.

Kendi, Ibram X. *Stamped from the Beginning: The Definitive History of Racist Ideas in America*. New York: Bold Type, 2016.

Kilde, Jeanne Halgren. *When Church Became Theatre: The Transformation of Evangelical Architecture and Worship in Nineteenth-Century America*. Oxford: Oxford University Press, 2002.

Kimbrough, S T, Jr., ed. *Charles Wesley: Poet and Theologian*. Nashville: Kingswood, 1992.

King, John Owen. *The Iron of Melancholy: Structures of Spiritual Conversion in America from the Puritan Conscience to Victorian Neurosis*. Middletown, CT: Wesleyan University Press, 1983.

Kirby, James E. *The Episcopacy in American Methodism*. Nashville, Kingswood, 2000.

Kirby, James E., et al., eds. *The Methodists*. Westport, CT: Greenwood, 1996.

Lakey, Othal Hawthorne. *The History of the CME Church*. Memphis: CME, 1985.

Langford, Thomas A. "Charles Wesley as Theologian." In *Charles Wesley: Poet and Theologian*, edited by S T Kimbrough Jr., 97–105. Nashville: Kingswood, 1992.

———. *Practical Divinity*. Vol. 1, *Theology in the Wesleyan Theology*. Nashville: Abingdon, 1983.

———. *Practical Divinity*. Vol. 2, *Readings in Wesleyan Theology*. Nashville: Abingdon, 1998.

———. *Wesleyan Theology: A Sourcebook*. Durham, NC: Labyrinth, 1984.

Laqueur, Thomas Walter. *Religion and Respectability: Sunday Schools and Working Class Culture, 1780–1850*. New Haven: Yale University Press, 1976.

Latourette, Kenneth Scott. *A History of the Expansion of Christianity*. 7 vols. New York, 1937–45.

Lazerow, Jama. *Religion and the Working Class in Antebellum America*. Washington, DC: Smithsonian Institution, 1995.

Leclerc, Diane. "Two Women Speaking 'Woman': The Strategic Essentialism of Luce Irigaray and Phoebe Palmer." *Wesleyan Theological Journal* 35 (2000) 182–99.

Lenton, John. "The Education of John Wesley's Preachers." In *Vital Piety and Learning: Methodism and Education: Papers Given at the 2002 Conference of the Wesley Historical Society*, edited by John Lenton, 25–37. Oxford: Applied Theology, 2005.

Lewis, Steven W. "Nathan Bangs and the Impact of Theological Controversy on the Development of Early Nineteenth Century American Methodist Thought." PhD diss., Saint Louis University, 1998.

Lindsley, James Elliott. *A History of Saint James Church in the City of New York, 1810–1960*. New York: St. James Church, 1960.

Lippy, Charles H. "Nathan Bangs." In *The Blackwell Dictionary of Evangelical Biography 1730–1860*, edited by Donald M. Lewis, 53–54. Oxford: Blackwell, 1995.

Loewenberg, Robert J. *Equality on the Oregon Frontier: Jason Lee and the Methodist Mission, 1834–43*. Seattle: University of Washington Press, 1976.

Logan, James C. "After Wesley: The Middle Period (1791–1849)." In *Grace upon Grace: Essays in Honor of Thomas A. Langford*, edited by Robert K. Johnston et al., 111–23. Nashville: Abingdon, 1999.

Long, Kathryn T. "Consecrated Respectability: Phoebe Palmer and the Refinement of American Methodism." In *Methodism and the Shaping of American Culture*, edited by Nathan O. Hatch and John H. Wigger, 281–307. Nashville: Kingswood, 2001.

Lorenz, Ellen Jane. *Glory, Hallelujah! The Story of the Campmeeting Spiritual.* Nashville: Abingdon, 1980.

Loveland, Anne C., and Otis B. Wheeler. *From Meetinghouse to Megachurch: A Material and Cultural History.* Columbia: University of Missouri Press, 2003.

Luccock, Halford Edward. *The Story of Methodism.* New York: Methodist Book Concern, 1926.

Lyerly, Cynthia Lynn. *Methodism and the Southern Mind, 1770–1810.* Oxford: Oxford University Press, 1998.

Macquiban, Timothy. "Practical Piety or Lettered Learning: The Wesley Historical Society Lecture 1995." *Proceedings of the Wesley Historical Society* 50 (1995) 83–107.

Maddox, Jared. "Nathan Bangs and the Methodist Episcopal Church: Bangs's Defense and Adaptation of the Asburian Ethos of Early American Methodism." PhD diss., Southern Methodist University, 2016.

———. *Nathan Bangs and the Methodist Episcopal Church: The Spread of Scriptural Holiness in Nineteenth-Century America.* Nashville: New Room, 2018.

Maddox, Randy L. "A Change of Affections." In *"Heart Religion" in the Methodist Tradition and Related Movements*, edited by Richard B. Steele, 3–31. Lanham, MD: Scarecrow, 2001.

Marcus, Steven. *Engels, Manchester, and the Working Class.* New York: Norton, 1985.

Marti, Donald B. "Rich Methodists: The Rise and Consequences of Lay Philanthropy in the Mid-Nineteenth Century." In *Perspectives on American Methodism: Interpretive Essays*, edited by Russell E. Richey et al., 265–76. Nashville: Abingdon, 1993.

Marx, Karl, and Frederick Engels. *Manifesto of the Communist Party.* Edited and translated by Frederick Engels. New York: International, 2001.

Mathews, Donald G. "Orange Scott: Evangelist-Revolutionary." In *The Antislavery Vanguard: New Essays on the Abolitionists*, edited by Martin Duberman, 71–101. Princeton: Princeton University Press, 1965.

———. "The Second Great Awakening as an Organizing Process, 1780–1830: An Hypothesis." *American Quarterly* (1969) 23–43.

———. *Slavery and Methodism: A Chapter in American Morality, 1780–1845.* Princeton: Princeton University Press, 1965.

Matthews, Jean V. *Toward a New Society: American Thought and Culture, 1800–1830.* Boston: Twayne, 1991.

Matthews, Rex. D. *Ministerial Orders and Sacramental Authority in the United Methodist Church and Its Antecedents, 1784–2016.* Nashville: Wesley's Foundry, 2018.

———, ed. *The Renewal of United Methodism: Mission, Ministry, and Connectionalism: Essays in Honor of Russell E. Richey.* Nashville: General Board of Higher Education and Ministry, 2012.

May, Ernest R. *Imperial Democracy: The Emergence of America as a Great Power.* New York: Harper & Row, 1961.

McCutchan, Robert Guy. *Our Hymnody: A Manual of the Methodist Hymnal.* Nashville: Parthenon, 1937.

McEllhenney, John G., et al., eds. *Proclaiming Grace & Freedom: The Story of United Methodism in America.* Nashville: Abingdon, 1982.

———. *United Methodism in America: A Compact History*. Nashville: Abingdon, 1992.

McLoughlin, William G. "Charles Grandison Finney." In *Ante-Bellum Reform*, edited by David Brion Davis, 97–107. New York: Harper & Row, 1967.

———. *Revivals, Awakenings, and Reform: An Essay on Religion and Social Change in America, 1607–1977*. Chicago: University of Chicago Press, 1978.

Meeks, M. Douglas, ed. *The Portion of the Poor: Good News to the Poor in the Wesleyan Tradition*. Nashville: Kingswood, 1995.

Melton, J. Gordon. *A Will to Choose: The Origins of African American Methodism*. Lanham, MD: Rowan & Littlefield, 2007.

Messenger, Troy. *Holy Leisure: Recreation and Religion in God's Square Mile*. Minneapolis: University of Minnesota Press, 1999.

Miller, Perry. *The Life of the Mind in America: From the Revolution to the Civil War*. New York: Harcourt, Brace, & World, 1965.

Mills, Frederick V. "Mentors of Methodism, 1784–1844." *Methodist History* 12 (1973) 43–57.

Mintz, Steven. *Moralists & Modernizers: America's Pre-Civil War Reformers*. Baltimore: Johns Hopkins University Press, 1995.

Monk, Robert C. *John Wesley: His Puritan Heritage*. London: Epworth, 1966.

Moore, R. Laurence. *Selling God: American Religion in the Marketplace of Culture*. Oxford: Oxford University Press, 1994.

Moorhead, James. H. *World without End: Mainstream American Protestant Visions of the Last Things, 1880–1925*. Bloomington: Indiana University Press, 1999.

Morris, Richard B., ed. *Encyclopedia of American History*. Bicentennial ed. New York: Harper & Row, 1976.

Morrison, Michael A., ed. *The Human Tradition in Antebellum America*. Wilmington, DE: Scholarly Resources, 2000.

Mudge, James. "The Centennial of the Methodist Review." *Methodist Quarterly Review* 67 (1918) 94–105.

———. *History of the New England Conference of the Methodist Episcopal Church, 1796–1910*. Boston: The Conference, 1910.

Muir, Elizabeth Gillan. *Petticoats in the Pulpit: The Story of Early Nineteenth-Century Methodist Women Preachers in Upper Canada*. Toronto: The United Church, 1991.

Murray, Peter C. *Methodists and the Crucible of Race, 1930–1975*. Columbia: University of Missouri Press, 2004.

Nañez, Alfredo. *History of the Rio Grande Conference of the United Methodist Church*. Dallas: Bridwell Library, 1980.

Newman, Richard S. *Freedom's Prophet: Bishop Richard Allen, the AME Church, and the Black Founding Fathers*. New York: New York University Press, 2008.

Niebuhr, H. Richard. *The Social Sources of Denominationalism*. New York: Holt, 1929.

Niebuhr, Reinhold. *The Irony of American History*. New York: Scribner, 1952.

Noll, Mark A. *America's God: From Jonathan Edwards to Abraham Lincoln*. Oxford: Oxford University Press, 2002.

———. "The Contested Legacy of Jonathan Edwards in Antebellum Calvinism." In *Reckoning with the Past: Historical Essays on American Evangelicalism from the Institute for the Study of American Evangelicals*, edited by D. G. Hart, 200–217. Grand Rapids: Baker, 1995.

———. *A History of Christianity in the United States and Canada*. Grand Rapids: Eerdmans, 1992.

North, Douglass C. *The Economic Growth of the United States, 1780–1860*. New York: Norton, 1966.

Norwood, Frederick A. *Sourcebook of American Methodism*. Nashville: Abingdon, 1982.

———. *The Story of American Methodism*. Nashville: Abingdon, 1974.

Oden, Thomas C., ed. *Phoebe Palmer: Selected Writings*. New York: Paulist, 1988.

Oliver, Lon D. *A Guide to the Cane Ridge Revival*. Lexington: Lexington Theological Seminary Library, 1988.

Olleson, Philip. "The Wesleys at Home: Charles Wesley and His Children." *Methodist History* 36 (1998) 139–52.

Outler, Albert C., ed. *John Wesley*. Oxford: Oxford University Press, 1964.

———. *Theology in the Wesleyan Spirit*. Nashville: Tidings, 1975.

Owen, Christopher H. *The Sacred Flame of Love: Methodism and Society in Nineteenth Century Georgia*. Athens: University of Georgia Press, 1998.

Patterson, Louis Dale. "The Ministerial Mind of American Methodism: The Courses of Study for the Ministry of the Methodist Episcopal Church, the Methodist Episcopal Church South, and the Methodist Protestant Church, 1880–1920." PhD diss., Drew University, 1984.

Pearce, Roy Harvey. *Savagism and Civilization: A Study of the Indian and the American Mind*. Berkeley: University of California Press, 1988.

Pope, Liston. *Millhands & Preachers: A Study of Gastonia*. New Haven: Yale University Press, 1942.

Porter, Lee. "'Through the Eye of the Needle': The Religious Culture of Baltimore Methodists in the 1840s." *Methodist History* 36 (1998) 71–85.

Potts, David B. *Wesleyan University, 1831–1910: Collegiate Enterprise in New England*. New Haven: Yale University Press, 1992.

Price, Carl F. "Nathan Bangs, Third President of Wesleyan University: Greatly Misunderstood, He Saved the College." *Wesleyan University Alumnus* 14 (1929) 128–34.

———. *Wesleyan's First Century*. Middletown, CT: Wesleyan University, 1932.

Pudney, John. *John Wesley and His World*. London: Thames and Hudson, 1978.

Pugh, Ben. "The Wesleyan Way of Entire Sanctification and Its Spin-Offs—A Recurring Theme in Evangelical Devotion." *Evangelical Review of Theology* 38 (2014) 4–21.

Raboteau, Albert J. *Slave Religion: The "Invisible Institution" in the Antebellum South*. Oxford: Oxford University Press, 1978.

Rankin, Stephen. "Nathan Bangs and the Methodist Episcopal Church: The Spread of Scriptural Holiness in Nineteenth-Century America." *Wesleyan Theological Journal* 55 (2020) 230–33.

Rattenbury, J. Ernest. *Vital Elements of Public Worship*. 3rd ed. London: Epworth, 1954.

———. *Wesley's Legacy to the World*. Nashville: Cokesbury, 1928.

Redford, Albert Henry. *History of Methodism in Kentucky*. Vol. 3. Nashville: Southern Methodist, 1870.

Reiff, Joseph T. *Born of Conviction: White Methodists and Mississippi's Closed Society*. Oxford: Oxford University Press, 2016.

Reynolds, J. S. *The Birth of Methodism in America*. New York: Reynolds, 1905.

Richey, Russell E. *Early American Methodism*. Bloomington: Indiana University Press, 1991.

———. "Ecclesial Sensibilities in Nineteenth-Century American Methodism." *Quarterly Review* 4 (1984) 31–42.

———. *Formation for Ministry in American Methodism*. Nashville: General Board of Higher Education and Ministry, 2014.

———. *Methodism in the American Forest*. Oxford: Oxford University Press, 2015.

———. *Methodist Connectionalism: Historical Perspectives*. Nashville: General Board of Higher Education and Ministry, 2009.

Richey, Russell E., and Kenneth E. Rowe, eds. *Rethinking Methodist History: A Bicentennial Historical Consultation*. Nashville: Kingswood, 1985.

Richey, Russell E., et al., eds. *Connectionalism: Ecclesiology, Mission, and Identity*. Nashville: Abingdon, 1997.

Richey, Russell E., et al., eds. *American Methodism: A Compact History*. Nashville: Abingdon, 2012.

———, eds. *The Methodist Experience in America*. Vol. 1, *A History*. Nashville: Abingdon, 2010.

———, eds. *The Methodist Experience in America*. Vol. 2, *A Sourcebook*. Nashville: Abingdon, 2000.

———, eds. *Perspectives on American Methodism: Interpretive Essays*. Nashville: Abingdon, 1993.

Rowe, Kenneth E. "Counting the Converts: Progress Reports as Church History." In *Rethinking Methodist History: A Bicentennial Historical Consultation*, edited by Russell E. Richey and Kenneth E. Rowe, 11–17. Nashville: Kingswood, 1985.

———. "New Light on Early Methodist Theological Education." *Methodist History* 10 (1971) 58–62.

———. "Redesigning Methodist Churches: Auditorium-Style Sanctuaries and Akron Plan Sunday Schools in Romanesque Costume, 1875–1925." In *Connectionalism: Ecclesiology, Mission, and Identity*, edited by Russell E. Richey et al., 117–36. Nashville: Abingdon, 1997.

Rudolph, Frederick. *The American College & University: A History*. Athens: University of Georgia Press, 1990.

Ruth, Lester. *A Little Heaven Below: Worship at Early Methodist Quarterly Meetings*. Nashville: Kingswood, 2000.

Salter, Darius L. *"God Cannot Do Without America:" Matthew Simpson and the Apotheosis of Protestant Nationalism*. Wilmore: First Fruits, 2017.

Sanderson, Joseph Edward. *The First Century of Methodism in Canada*. Vol. 1, *1775–1839*. Toronto: Briggs, 1908.

Schaff, Philip, et al., eds. *The American Church History Series*. 13 vols. New York: Christian Literature, 1893–98.

Schantz, Mark S. *Piety in Providence: Class Dimensions of Religious Experience in Antebellum Rhode Island*. Ithaca, NY: Cornell University Press, 2000.

Schmidt, Jean Miller. *Grace Sufficient: A History of Women in American Methodism, 1760–1939*. Nashville: Abingdon, 1999.

———. "Reexamining the Public/Private Split: Reforming the Continent and Spreading Scriptural Holiness." In *Rethinking Methodist History: A Bicentennial Historical Consultation*, edited by Russell E. Richey and Kenneth E. Rowe, 75–90. Nashville: Kingswood, 1985.

Schmidt, Leigh Eric. *Holy Fairs: Scottish Communions and American Revivals in the Early Modern Period*. Princeton: Princeton University Press, 1989.

Schneider, A. Gregory. *The Way of the Cross Leads Home: The Domestication of American Methodism*. Bloomington: Indiana University Press, 1993.

Schneider, Louis, ed. *Religion and Culture & Society: A Reader in the Sociology of Religion*. New York: Wiley, 1964.

Scott, Leland Howard. "Methodist Theology in America in the Nineteenth Century." PhD diss., Graduate School of Emory University, 1973.

Semmel, Bernard. *The Methodist Revolution*. New York: Basic, 1973.

Sernett, Milton C., ed. *African American Religious History: A Documentary Witness*. 2nd ed. Durham, NC: Duke University Press, 1999.

Simmel, Georg. *On Individuality and Social Forms*. Edited by Donald N. Levine. Chicago: University of Chicago Press, 1971.

Singleton, George A. *The Romance of African Methodism: A Study of the African Methodist Episcopal Church*. New York: Exposition, 1952.

Sitterly, Charles Fremont. *The Building of Drew University*. New York: Methodist Book Concern, 1938.

Skinner, Ellouise W. *Sacred Music at Union Theological Seminary, 1836–1953*. New York: Union Theological Seminary, 1953.

Sklar, Kathryn Kish. *Catherine Beecher: A Study in American Domesticity*. New York: Norton, 1976.

Smith, John Abernathy. "How Methodism Became a National Church in the United States." *Methodist History* 20 (1981) 13–28.

Smith, Ryan K. *Gothic Arches, Latin Crosses: Anti-Catholicism and American Church Designs in the Nineteenth Century*. Chapel Hill: University of North Carolina Press, 2006.

Smith, Timothy L. "The Doctrine of the Sanctifying Spirit: Charles G. Finney's Synthesis of Wesleyan and Covenant Theology." *Wesleyan Theological Journal* 9 (1978) 92–113.

Smith-Rosenberg, Carroll. "Women and Religious Revivals: Anti Ritualism, Liminality, and the Emergence of the American Bourgeoisie." In *The Evangelical Tradition in America*, edited by Leonard I. Sweet, 199–231. Macon, GA: Mercer University Press, 1997.

Snyder, Howard A. "Formative Influences on B. T. Roberts: Abolitionism, Revivalism, and Perfection." *Wesleyan Theological Journal* 34 (1999) 177–99.

———. *Populist Saints: B. T. and Ellen Roberts and the First Free Methodists*. Grand Rapids: Eerdmans, 2006.

Spencer, Jon Michael. *Protest & Praise: Sacred Music of Black Religion*. Minneapolis: Fortress, 1990.

Spreng, Samuel P. "History of the Evangelical Association." In vol. 12 of *American Church History Series*, edited by Philip Schaff et al., 383–439. New York: Christian Literature, 1894.

Stanton, Phoebe B. *The Gothic Revival & American Church Architecture: An Episode in Taste, 1840–1856*. Baltimore: Johns Hopkins University Press, 1997.

Stein, Stephen J. *The Shaker Experience in America: A History of the United Society of Believers*. New Haven: Yale University Press, 1992.

Sterling, Dorothy. *Ahead of Her Time: Abby Kelley and the Politics of Antislavery*. New York: Norton, 1994.

Stewart, James Brewer. *Holy Warriors: The Abolitionists and American Slavery*. New York: Hill and Wang, 1976.

Streeter, Lewis R. *Past and Present of the John Street Methodist Episcopal Church, (First Methodist Society in America) New York, Including Earliest and Latest Methodist Edifices in London*. New York, 1913.

Strong, Douglas M. "Exploring Both the Middle and the Margins: Locating Methodism within American Religious History." In *Doctrines and Discipline*, edited by Dennis M. Campbell et al., 233–241. Nashville: Abingdon, 1999.

Stout, Harry S. *The Divine Dramatist: George Whitefield and the Rise of Modern Evangelicalism*. Grand Rapids: Eerdmans, 1991.

Stout, Harry S., and D. G. Hart, eds. *New Directions in American Religious History*. Oxford: Oxford University Press, 1997.

Summerson, John. *Heavenly Mansions and Other Essays on Architecture*. New York: Norton, 1963.

"A Surprise Party—Compliment to the Rev. Dr. Bangs." *New York Times*, January 24, 1859, 1.

Sutherland, Alexander. *Methodism in Canada: Its Work and Its Story, being the Thirty third Fernley Lecture delivered in Penzance, 31 July 1903*. London: Kelley, 1903.

Sutton, William R. *Journeyman for Jesus: Evangelical Artisans Confront Capitalists in Jacksonian Baltimore*. University Park: Pennsylvania State University Press, 1998.

———. "To Extract Poison from the Blessings of God's Providence: Producerist Respectability and Methodist Suspicions of Capitalist Change in the Early Republic." In *Methodism and the Shaping of American Culture*, edited by Nathan O. Hatch and John H. Wigger, 233–35. Nashville: Kingswood, 2001.

Swaney, Charles Baumer. *Episcopal Methodism and Slavery, with Sidelights on Ecclesiastical Politics*. New York: Negro Universities Press, 1969.

Sweet, Leonard I., ed. *The Evangelical Tradition in America*. Macon, GA: Mercer University Press, 1997.

Sweet, Leonard I. "The View of Man Inherent in New Measures Revivalism." *Church History* 45 (1976) 206–21.

Sweet, William Warren. *The Methodist Episcopal Church and the Civil War*. Cincinnati: Methodist Book Concern, 1912.

———. *Our American Churches*. New York: Methodist Book Concern, 1924.

———. *Religion in the Development of American Culture, 1765–1840*. New York: Scribner, 1952.

———. *Religion on the American Frontier, 1783–1840*. Vol. 4, *The Methodists*. Chicago: University of Chicago Press, 1946.

———, ed. *The Rise of Methodism in the West Being the Journal of the Western Conference, 1800–1811*. Nashville: Smith & Lamar, 1920.

———. *The Story of Religion in America*. Rev. ed. New York: Harper & Brothers, 1950.

Sweet, William Warren, and Umphrey Lee. *A Short History of Methodism*. Nashville: Abingdon, 1956.

Swift, David E. "O! This Heartless Prejudice." *Wesleyan Magazine* 67 (1984) 13–17.

Sylvest, Edwin J., Jr. "Hispanic American Protestantism in the United States." In *Fronteras*. Vol. 10, *A History of the Latin American Church in the USA Since 1513*, edited by Moises Sandoval, 279–338. San Antonio, TX: Mexican American Cultural Center, 1983.

Synan, Vinsan. *The Holiness-Pentecostal Tradition: Charismatic Movements in the Twentieth Century*. 2nd ed. Grand Rapids: Eerdmans, 1997.

Tait, Jennifer L. Woodruff. *The Poisoned Chalice: Eucharistic Grape Juice and Common-Sense Realism in Victorian Methodism*. Tuscaloosa: University of Alabama Press, 2011.

Taves, Ann. *Fits, Trances, & Visions: Experiencing Religion and Explaining Experience from Wesley to James*. Princeton: Princeton University Press, 1999.

Tawney, R. H. *Religion and the Rise of Capitalism: A Historical Study*. Holland Memorial Lectures 1922. Gloucester, MA: Smith, 1962.

Taylor, Hubert Vance. "Preaching on Slavery, 1831–1861." In *Preaching in American History: Selected Issues in the American Pulpit, 1630–1967*, edited by De Witte Holland et al., 168–83. Nashville: Abingdon, 1969.

Telford, John. *The Methodist Hymn-Book Illustrated*. 3rd ed. London: Epworth, 1922.

Thompson, David, ed. *Nonconformity in the Nineteenth Century*. London: Routledge & Paul, 1972.

Thompson, E. P. *The Making of the English Working Class*. New York: Vintage, 1966.

Thompson, Ernest Trice. *Changing Emphasis in American Preaching: The Stone Lectures for 1943*. Philadelphia: Westminster, 1943.

Thompson-Allen, Aubrey. "The History of the Organ." *Religion in Life* 24 (1954/55) 127–40.

Thornton, Wallace, Jr. "Behavioral Standards, Embourgeoisement, and the Formation of the Conservative Holiness Movement." *Wesleyan Theological Journal* 33 (1998) 172–97.

Tigert, John. J. *A Constitutional History of American Episcopal Methodism*. 3rd ed. Nashville: Methodist Episcopal Church, 1908.

Tipple, Ezra Squire. *Francis Asbury: The Prophet of the Long Road*. Cincinnati: Methodist Book Concern, 1916.

Touchstone, Blake. "Planters and Slave Religion in the Deep South." In *Masters & Slaves in the House of the Lord: Race and Religion in the American South, 1740–1870*, edited by John B. Boles, 99–126. Lexington: University Press of Kentucky, 1988.

Toulouse, Mark G., and James O. Duke, eds. *Sources of Christian Theology in America*. Nashville: Abingdon, 1999.

Tucker, Karen B. Westerfield. *American Methodist Worship*. Oxford: Oxford University Press, 2001.

———. "Form and Freedom: John Wesley's Legacy for Methodist Worship." In *The Sunday Service of the Methodists: Twentieth-Century Worship in Worldwide Methodism, Studies in Honor of James F. White*, edited by Karen B. Westerfield Tucker, 17–30. Nashville: Kingswood, 1996.

Tuell, Jack M. *The Organization of the United Methodist Church*. Nashville: Abingdon, 1970.

Tuttle, Alexander Harrison. *Nathan Bangs*. Cincinnati: Jennings & Graham, 1909.

Tuttle, Robert G. *John Wesley: His Life and Theology*. Grand Rapids: Zondervan, 1978.

Tyson, John R. *Charles Wesley on Sanctification*. Grand Rapids: Asbury, 1986.

The United Methodist Church. *The Book of Discipline of the United Methodist Church*. Nashville: United Methodist Church, 2000.

———. *The United Methodist Hymnal: Book of United Methodist Worship*. Nashville: United Methodist Church, 1989.

Vernon, Walter N., et al. *The Methodist Excitement in Texas: A History*. Dallas: Texas United Methodist Historical Society, 1984.

Vickers, John. *Thomas Coke: Apostle of Methodism*. London: Epworth, 1969.

Wade, William Nash. "A History of Public Worship in the Methodist Episcopal Church, South, from 1784 to 1905." PhD diss., University of Notre Dame, 1981.

Walls, Andrew F. *The Missionary Movement in Christian History*. Maryknoll, NY: Orbis, 1996.

Wakefield, Gordon S. *The Spiritual Life in the Methodist Tradition, 1791–1945*. London: Epworth, 1966.

Walters, Ronald G. *American Reformers, 1815–1860*. New York: Hill and Wang, 1978.

Warner, Wellman J. *The Wesleyan Movement in the Industrial Revolution*. New York: Russell & Russell, 1967.

Warren, James I. *O For a Thousand Tongues: The History, Nature, and Influence of Music in the Methodist Tradition*. Grand Rapids: Asbury, 1988.

Watson, David Lowes. *The Early Class Meeting: Its Origins and Significance*. Nashville: Discipleship Resources, 1995.

Wason, Kevin M. *Old or New School Methodism? The Fragmentation of a Theological Tradition*. New York: Oxford University Press, 2019.

Wearmouth, Robert F. *Methodism and the Working-Class Movements of England, 1800–1850*. London: Epworth, 1947.

Webber, F. R. *A History of Preaching in Britain and America: Including the Biographies of Many Princes of the Pulpit and the Men Who Influenced Them*. Vol. 3. Milwaukee: Northwestern, 1957.

Weber, Max. *The Protestant Ethic and the Spirit of Capitalism*. Translated by Talcott Parsons. New York: Scribner, 1976.

Weeks, Linton. *St. John's Church in Savannah*. Savannah, GA: St. John's Church, 1985.

Wellings, Martin. "Nathan Bangs and the Methodist Episcopal Church: The Spread of Scriptural Holiness in Nineteenth Century America." *Wesley and Methodist Studies* 12 (2020) 214–15.

Whelchel, Love Henry, Jr. *Hell without Fire: Conversion in Slave Religion*. Nashville: Abingdon, 2002.

Whidden, Woodrow W. "Eschatology, Soteriology, and Social Activism in Four Mid-Nineteenth Century Holiness Methodists." *Wesleyan Theological Journal* 29 (1994) 92–110.

White, Charles Edward. *The Beauty of Holiness: Phoebe Palmer as Theologian, Revivalist, Feminist, and Humanitarian*. Grand Rapids: Asbury, 1986.

White, James F. *The Cambridge Movement: The Ecclesiologists and the Gothic Revival*. Cambridge: Cambridge University Press, 1962.

———. *Introduction to Christian Worship*. 3rd ed. Nashville: Abingdon, 2000.

———. *Protestant Worship: Traditions in Transition*. Louisville: Westminster John Knox, 1989.

———. *Protestant Worship and Church Architecture*. Oxford: Oxford University Press, 1964.

Whitely, W. T. *Congregational Hymn-Singing*. London: Dent, 1933.

Wigger, John H. *American Saint: Francis Asbury and the Methodists*. Oxford: Oxford University Press, 2009.

———. *Taking Heaven by Storm: Methodism and the Rise of Popular Christianity in America*. Oxford: Oxford University Press, 1998.

Williams, D. Newell. *Barton Stone: A Spiritual Biography*. St. Louis: Chalice, 2001.

Williams, Jeffrey. *Religion and Violence in Early American Methodism: Taking the Kingdom by Force*. Bloomington: Indiana University Press, 2010.

Williams, William Henry. *The Garden of American Methodism: The Delmarva Peninsula, 1769–1820*. Peninsula Conference of the United Methodist Church. Wilmington, DE: Scholarly Resources, 1984.

Williamson, Douglas James. "The Ecclesiastical Career of Wilbur Fisk: Methodist Educator, Theologian, Reformer, Controversialist." PhD diss., Boston University Graduate School, 1988.

Willimon, William H. *Word, Water, Wine, and Bread: How Worship Has Changed over the Years*. Valley Forge, PA: Judson, 1980.

Wilson, Christopher. *The Gothic Cathedral: The Architecture of the Great Church, 1130–1530*. London: Thames and Hudson, 1990.

Wright, Elliott. "American Methodism and Public Education: 1784 to 1900." In *Doctrines and Disciplines*, edited by Dennis M. Campbell et al., 181–95. Nashville: Abingdon, 1999.

Wright, Louis B., and Elaine W. Fowler. *Life in the New Nation, 1787–1860*. New York: Capricorn, 1974.

Wuthnow, Robert. *The Restructuring of American Religion: Society and Faith Since World War II*. Princeton: Princeton University Press, 1988.

Yardley, Anne Bagnall. "Choirs in the Methodist Episcopal Church, 1800–1860." *American Music* 17 (1999) 39–64.

———. "What Besides Hymns? The Tune Books of Early Methodism." *Methodist History* 37 (1999) 189–201.

Young, Carlton R. "American Methodist Hymnbooks." In *Companion to the Hymnal: A Handbook to the 1964 Methodist Hymnal*, by Fred Gealy et al., 54–61. Nashville: Abingdon, 1970.

Yrigoyen, Charles, Jr. Review of *Charles G. Finney and the Spirit of American Evangelicalism*, by Charles E. Hambrick-Stowe. *Methodist History* 35 (1997) 199–200.

Yrigoyen, Charles, Jr., and Susan E. Warrick, eds. *Historical Dictionary of Methodism*. Lanham, MD: Scarecrow, 1996.

Made in United States
Orlando, FL
20 June 2024

48082578R00146